Ask Mr. *EasyLanguage*

by

Samuel Knight Tennis

Traders Press, Inc.®

Serving Traders Since 1975

Table Of Contents

Dedication

This book is dedicated to ***Mr. Steven McQuaide Tennis*** and **Ms. Margaret Ros Hudson**. Steve, both my brother and my right hand man, has kept the wolves at bay which enabled me to write this book. Ms. Hudson was assigned as my editor and without her support and skills this book would never have made it to press.

Acknowledgments

Acknowledgment... Appreciation... Thanks... When I start trying to thank all of the people who have helped me get where I am today — well, I just get frustrated. First and foremost, I owe a debt of gratitude to each and every person who has complemented, complained or asked me for help throughout the years. For I am but the sum of my experiences.

I guess the one person to whom I owe the greatest debt is *William R. Cruz*, President of **Omega Research**, for it is he who gave me to this industry. It is from him that I learned most of my business lessons, be they for better or worse.

Charlie Wright and *Larry Williams* were two of my earliest mentors way back in the days of **System Writer Plus**.

I want to thank *Patrick M. Raffalovich* for giving me the spark of confidence to strike out on my own. Pat is the best student I have ever taught. Pat introduced me to *Kent Calhoun, of* **KCI Seminars**, who has taught me so much about what makes and shakes the markets.

Thomas R. DeMark has spent countless hours with me explaining his view of the world. *Tushar S. Chande* has always been willing to share his knowledge. *Neal T. Weintraub* has introduced me to the pits and towers in Chicago.

I would like to thank and acknowledge *Perry J. Kaufman* for making himself available to me day or night. I owe thanks to *Mark Douglas* who has always been willing to share his life with me and who introduced me to my friend *Ted Hearne*. I also take this opportunity to express my appreciation to *Mr. Charlie Drummond* for his tutelage in defining market trends.

To the many people who offered to proof read the manuscript —sorry. It was just not possible because the time from manuscript to the printed page was so short.

You, the reader, should thank *Ed Dobson* of **Traders Press** who believed in me enough to pursue me for three years and my editors *Margaret Ros Hudson* and *Teresa Darty Alligood* without whose sage advice this book would never have reached your hands.

I would like to thank my wife *Ellen*, son *Matthew* and daughter *Rachel* for the sacrifices they have made and endured.

Lastly, I offer my thanks to my brother *Steven McQuaide Tennis* who makes my life possible and my father *Hall Tennis* for lessons in language and living. Both are instrumental in the realization of this dream.

How To Use This Book:

I suggest that you read this book in at least two passes. First, and most important, skim the entire book cover to cover, as fast as you can possibly read. Do not stop for misunderstood words. Do not worry about retention.

What you are doing is taking advantage of your analog brain, building an index, or a matrix, to the information it contains.

Now you are ready to **really** read the book. You can start at the beginning and read through to the end. You can jump around and read the parts that interest you. What you will discover is that you are able to turn right to the part you need when you need it.

The *EasyLanguage* code used in this book will be made available, for a small fee, either electronically or by CD-ROM. Please contact the office of **Vista Research** or **Traders Press** for more information.

Keys to this Book:

ISBN: 0-934380-51-1
Published April, 1999

TRADERS PRESS, INC.®
PO BOX 6206
GREENVILLE, SC 29606

Serving traders since 1975

Foreword

There has long been a need for this book. Traders who own and use **TradeStation Software** for their marketing analysis and system development needs represent the most dedicated and serious traders in the world. It is to them that this book is dedicated.

Sam Tennis, the originator and developer of *EasyLanguage*, the "guts" of **TradeStation**, is the perfect person to write this book. He is so closely associated with *EasyLanguage* that he has become known as "*Mr. Easy Language.*"

It is an honor and a privilege for myself and my publishing staff, ***Margaret Ros Hudson*** and ***Teresa Darty Alligood***, to have collaborated with Sam on the book.

It is our hope that it will prove to be a valuable resource to **TradeStation** owners.

Edward Dobson, President

TRADERS PRESS

Preface

The phrase "*Ask Mr. EasyLanguage*" was first coined back in the Product Support Pit at **Omega Research**. I believe I owe the honor to Mr. Reuben Triana and Ms. Darla Tuttle. In any case, the name has stuck with me ever since.

I have tried to present for your enjoyment all the insight gained from heading up the development team and after years of providing custom solutions for real-world scenarios.

I have tried to demystify *EasyLanguage* by first breaking it down into it's discreet components; explaining their purpose, use and characteristics; demonstrating how (and why) the pieces combine to form logical structures; giving real fully functional examples of *EasyLanguage* at work (and play).

The book is roughly divided into two sections. The first is the language manual and the second is questions and answers. I have not tried to provide a tutorial. This is not a "for dummies" or a "master in 21 days" approach. I have never been able to learn a language using the conversational method. I prefer the grammatical / syntactic approach, conjugating verbs and declining nouns. It is my belief that anyone can learn *EasyLanguage*. You may not become a top-notch programmer but you can learn to speak and read *EasyLanguage* code. At the very least, you can commune with your consultant in the language he understands, saving you both time and money.

Section 1:
EasyLanguage Basics

Overview

What is *EasyLanguage*™?

The **Omega Research** product that you own or use includes a built-in programming language unique in many ways. First, it is available only in **Omega Research** products. Second, it is the only programming language, that I know of, created specifically for use by traders and technical analysts. By learning to use *EasyLanguage*, you will discover the additional depth and versatility that will allow you to use these products to their fullest potential.

EasyLanguage was developed in 1987 by **Omega Research**. Its purpose is to provide a simple, logical, "plain English" programming language that requires little programming background from its users. It was designed to allow traders to describe and test their trading strategies, to program signals based on those strategies, to historically back-test those strategies for profitability, and to generate trading orders and alerts when market conditions meet the specific criteria.

The beauty of *EasyLanguage* is its simplicity. Instead of obscure computer terminology and arcane symbology, *EasyLanguage* uses many of the same terms that you use every trading day (buy, sell, limit, market, etc.). *EasyLanguage* comes with a large built-in collection of functions called a **Library**. This library contains programs for many of the most widely used stock and commodity analysis techniques.

You can extend this built-in versatility by creating your own **User Functions**. *EasyLanguage* is the language used by both the *PowerEditor* and the *QuickEditor*. These are the editors you will use to write Studies, Systems and User Functions.

Using *EasyLanguage*, you can develop your ideas and trading strategies into program modules we call **Analysis Techniques**. *EasyLanguage* checks your program code for you. This process is called ***Verifying the Code***. It locates errors it finds making the development process simple and painless. Once a Study or System has been written and verified, it can be run again and again on new data, pointing out directions or trends in the market.

EasyLanguage is a compiled language, meaning that when you verify (validate for syntactic accuracy) your code it creates a **TOKEN FILE** (with a TOK extension) containing your instructions converted to machine language.

Some statements are evaluated on each bar of data, while others are evaluated only during **LINK TIME**. You can think of LINK TIME as the verification process, when the module is initially loaded into a chart or immediately prior to processing the first bar of data. All are essentially the same.

What is Programming?

A **computer program** is a sequence of instructions designed to be executed, or run, by a computer in order to obtain a specific result. Programs are written in many languages. A **computer language** is a subset of the English language that allows the programmer to give specific commands to the computer.

Most programming languages use combinations of different types of information. All have a list of reserved words. **RESERVED WORDS** are the symbols and words to which the computer language has assigned very specific, and unambiguous meanings. They may only be used as they are defined. Using a RESERVED WORD in a program for a purpose other than it was intended will cause the program to fail or not work properly.

Often, when running a program, you will need to temporarily store values. You may store a price for use in a comparison, or the result of a calculation that you wish to reference multiple times. Instead of having to state that value repeatedly throughout the program, or having to write the same calculation over and over again, programming languages allow for variables. **VARIABLES** are storage locations for information, such as NUMERIC VALUES, BOOLEAN (TRUE/FALSE) CONDITIONS and CHARACTER STRINGS. Each variable is identified by a name or label of your choice. Examples of the variables MYPRICE and BUYOK are:

```
MyPrice = High + 2 points ; { numeric value }
BuyOK = Close > Open ; { Boolean condition }
```

Variables have names. Certain naming conventions, or rules, apply when creating variables. You may not, for instance, use RESERVED WORDS to name variables although a variable name may contain a RESERVED WORD. Also, different programming languages have various rules concerning the length of, and the characters allowed to be used in, variable names. Naming conventions for variables in *EasyLanguage* will be discussed later in this section.

A variable also has a **DATA TYPE (NUMERIC, BOOLEAN, STRING)**, that refers to the type of data the variable may store. For instance, a NUMERIC VARIABLE would be used to store numbers for use in calculations, as in the **MYPRICE** variables above. A BOOLEAN VARIABLE (TRUE/FALSE) would be used to store a condition. In the **BUYOK** example, the condition is evaluated each time and a value of true or false is assigned.

Assignments may also be made to logical variables conditionally. In the following example, you are saying, "If this bar's open is higher than the close of one bar ago then store a value of 'true' to the variable OpenAbove." In *EasyLanguage* this would be stated as:

```
if  Open > Close[1]  then OpenAbove  =  TRUE ;
```

Programming languages also allow for remarks or comments to be inserted into programs to make them easier to read and understand. As you will see later in this section, *EasyLanguage* uses curly brackets "{ }" (also called French Braces) to allow you to make comments. Unlike some other languages, *EasyLanguage* allows one comment to be nested, or included, within another set of comment brackets. The computer will ignore anything inside these curly brackets.

EasyLanguage also allows for the use of **SkipWords** such as **a, an, the,** and **does.** These words are inserted into a program for clarity but are not necessary for the program to run.

Programming languages insist that you use a defined structure, called **Syntax**, for your commands or programs to execute appropriately. **Syntax** refers to the correct order or sequence you arrange the operators, expressions, commands and statements to construct your analysis technique.

English sentences have a certain syntax, the order in which the parts of the sentence occur. In a simple sentence there is: a subject, the person or thing you are talking about; a predicate, the action that is being performed by the subject; and, an object, the receiver of the action. If you change the order of the parts, you may drastically alter the meaning of the sentence. "*Man bites dog*" has a much different meaning than "*dog bites man.*"

Just as in English, programming languages depend on your using the correct syntax in your programs to convey the precise meaning you intend.

Programming languages generally use symbols called **Operators**. These may be **Mathematical Operators** such as the symbols for addition (+), subtraction (-), multiplication (*) and division (/), they may be **Relational Operators** such as greater than (>), less than (<), equal to (=), or not equal to (<>). Relational Operators are used to compare two values.

Finally, the order in which a programming language performs calculations is defined by its **Precedence of Operators**, the order in which the computer will evaluate the operators used in an expression. For example, most computer languages will perform multiplication before addition and perform calculations inside parentheses before others. So, 2 + 3 * 4 will not give you the same result as (2 + 3) * 4. In the first case, the computer would multiply 3 times 4 and add it to 2 giving you 14. In the second case, it would perform the calculation inside the parentheses (2 + 3) before doing the multiplication and you would get 5 times 4 or 20. The Precedence of Operators for *EasyLanguage* will be discussed in depth later in this section.

As you can see, a programming language is just that, a language. As in any language, there are rules that make the language consistent and understandable. *EasyLanguage* is a particularly simple language to learn and uses many words and rules with which you are already familiar. Nothing mysterious, nothing menacing, just old fashioned hard work.

Introduction to *EasyLanguage*

EasyLanguage is the programming language used to write ANALYSIS TECHNIQUES such as STUDIES, SYSTEMS and USER FUNCTIONS for use in **TradeStation** and other **Omega** products. *EasyLanguage* is not, however, a complicated programming language that takes years to learn. In fact, if you diligently apply yourself to the study of this book, and practice in the editor, you will be able to write and test your own USER FUNCTIONS, STUDIES and SYSTEMS using *EasyLanguage*.

- **Studies** are instructions to your **Omega** charting program to plot or draw a mathematical formula in a specified manner. A STUDY creates a visual plot on the chart or in a subgraph of your chart window. What is plotted is determined by your formula and the study properties. Studies do not have to plot what would traditionally be called a formula or indicator. They can be used to plot a dot on a certain calendar day, color the close of every bar a different color than the open, or color every Monday blue.

  Plot statements are commands that tell *EasyLanguage* to present a graphical representation at a specific point on the time price grid. The results of your studies are plotted on the screen as part of your chart. The command to plot can be any numeric expression. *EasyLanguage* allows up to four plots per study. All studies must contain at least one plot statement to be applied to a chart. Using the RESERVED WORD "PLOT" directs the program to create a visual display on your chart. What is plotted is determined by your formula. The format of the plot, such as line, series of points, crosses or histograms, is also determined by you. This can be done in the *PowerEditor* when you write, or edit, the study or in the *QuickEditor* by choosing the STYLE button. When you apply your technique in the charting program this can be done by setting the style in the properties dialog box.

  Indicator is a term **Omega** uses very loosely to refer to all generic studies. That is all studies that are NOT specifically *PAINTBAR* or *SHOWME* studies (see below).

  PaintBar™ is a proprietary kind of technical study created by **Omega Research**. It is used to visually identify your trading patterns by altering the color of the bar upon which your criteria is met.

  ShowMe™ is a proprietary kind of technical study created by **Omega Research.** It is used to visually identify your trading patterns by placing some type of mark on or about the bar upon which your criteria is met. Almost any function can be incorporated as the input of a *ShowMe*™ study.

- **Systems** are analysis techniques that generate buy and/or sell orders. When applied to a chart they generate *Performance Summary* and *Trade by Trade* reports. If applied

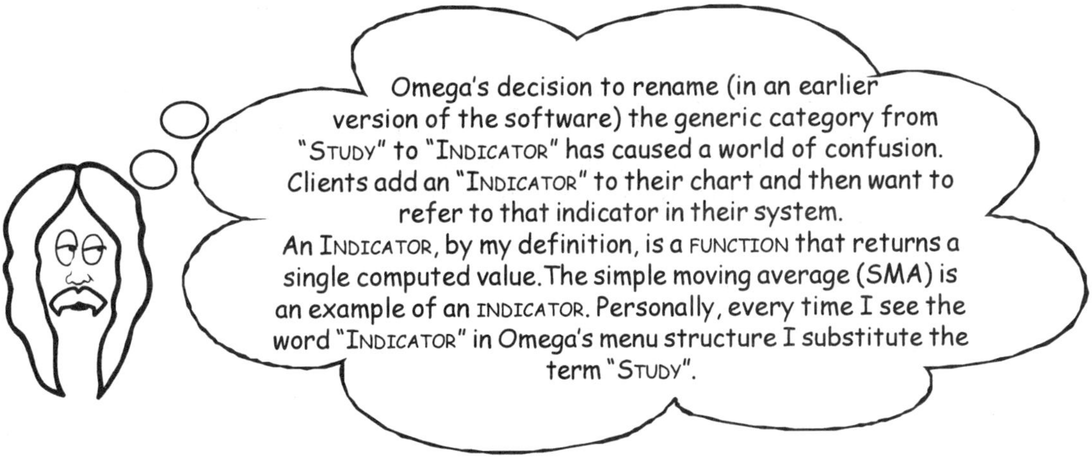

Omega's decision to rename (in an earlier version of the software) the generic category from "Study" to "Indicator" has caused a world of confusion. Clients add an "Indicator" to their chart and then want to refer to that indicator in their system.
An Indicator, by my definition, is a function that returns a single computed value. The simple moving average (SMA) is an example of an indicator. Personally, every time I see the word "Indicator" in Omega's menu structure I substitute the term "Study".

to a chart of current data, systems also generate real-time buy and sell orders with audible and visual alerts.

- A **Signal** is any single discreet entry or exit order. One or more signals make up a trading system.
- **Alerts (TradeStation 3.01** and earlier) are predefined conditions that are monitored on a real-time basis by **TradeStation**. When the condition occurs, **TradeStation** alerts you with an audible alarm and places a bell symbol on your chart window indicating the location at which the alert condition occurred.
- **Alerts (TradeStation 3.5** and later) are predefined conditions that are either contained within the *EasyLanguage* code of a study (*Indicator, PaintBar* or *ShowMe*) or are an intrinsic feature of a 'Drawing Tool' that are monitored on a real-time basis. When the alert condition occurs **TradeStation** informs you with an audible alarm and displays a message box offering you several options.
- **Alerts (TradeStation 5.00** and later) allows you to specify a string constant to be displayed as part of the alert message. You may also cause a .WAV file to be played if the appropriate hardware is available.
- A **function**, whether Built-In or User-Defined, is an analysis technique that returns a single numeric value. Functions are used to perform a specific purpose and return a discreet value. That value may be used in other functions, studies and systems.

An **Indicator**, as defined by *Mr. EasyLanguage*, is a function that is not bound by finite minimum and maximum values. Indicators are graphical representations (generally displayed as lines and histograms) drawn in a chart window. The simple moving average is an example of a commonly used indicator.

An **Oscillator**, as defined by *Mr. EasyLanguage*, is a function with a return value bound within a distinct minimum and maximum range. The RSI (Relative

Strength Index), scaled 0...100, is an example of an Oscillator.

- An **Input** is a parameter of an analysis technique that can be assigned when applied to a chart or used within a larger body of code. Inputs can be any mathematical formula or logical construct.

The basic component of *EasyLanguage* is the STATEMENT. Virtually every valid statement can be verified and saved as a complete, stand alone, (though probably useless) *EasyLanguage* program.

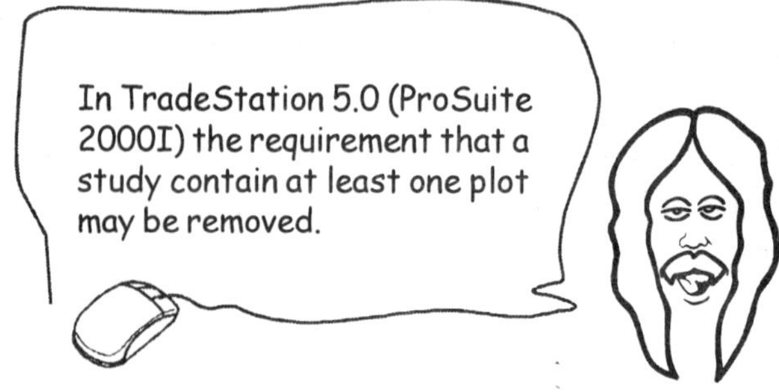

A **STATEMENT** is a single command or instruction to the computer. A statement must, except in very specific circumstances, defined in the syntax of the language, always be followed by a semicolon, the statement terminator. A statement may be used to define a variable or condition, compare two values, plot something on a graph, set off an alarm or generate a trading signal.

STATEMENTS may be made up of combinations of **EXPRESSIONS** and **OPERATORS**. EXPRESSIONS are like the phrases in a sentence. By themselves, they do not offer enough information to form a complete thought. But, if you put expressions together properly, a statement is born. *EasyLanguage* recognizes three types of expressions: NUMERIC and BOOLEAN (LOGICAL OR TRUE/FALSE) and STRING (CHARACTER).

A **NUMERIC EXPRESSION** combines numbers, prices, mathematical operators and/or numeric variables to produce another number. A simple example is "5 + 5". Examples of numeric expressions are shown below.

```
High - 8 points
Close[1] * 0.95
Open * 1.05
```

For what it is worth, internally the computer treats FALSE as a value of zero and TRUE as any non-zero value.

NUMERIC EXPRESSIONS always produce numeric values.

BOOLEAN EXPRESSIONS, often called LOGICAL or "TRUEFALSE," are either, you guessed it, true or false. They are most often used in conditional statements where an action can occur only if some preceding condition is either true or false. Examples of logical expressions are:

```
Close > Open
@DayOfWeek (Date) = 5
Volume < @Average (Volume, 5)
```

Notice that the BOOLEAN EXPRESSIONS above cause no action to happen. They merely resolve to a logical condition.

By combining logical expressions with Reserved Words, Boolean Operators and other Boolean Expressions we create a conditional statement that may cause an action to occur. An example of a conditional statement is :

```
if  (Close  > Open) and (@Average (Volume, 5))
  then  Buy  ("le.MainEntry") at market ;
```

A **String Expression**, often called a Character String, refers to character, rather than Numeric or Boolean Values. You can perform assignments and comparisons with String values.

```
Vars   : MyName ("George") ;
MyName = "George" ;
if  Close > Open then MyName = "Samuel" ;
If  MyName = "Samuel" then ...

Vars   : MyString ("") ;
MyString = "" ;
if  High  > High[01] and Low  > Low[01] then begin
  MyString = "Bullish" ;
  If  Close  > (High + Low) * 0.50 and Close  > Close [01]
    then MyString  = MyString + " confirmed"
    else MyString  = MyString + " divergent" ;
  MyString  = MyString + " bar." ;
end ;
```

Expressions are built with combinations of the following elements:

- Reserved Words
- Numbers
- Prices
- Variables
- Mathematical Operators
- Logical Conditions
- Relational Operators
- Boolean Operators

And may contain:

- Parentheses

- Square Brackets
- Comment Braces
- SkipWords

> In *EasyLanguage*, statements may be written on one or more lines, however, each statement must be followed by a semicolon (;).

In addition, *EasyLanguage* must have reference to the scope, or time period, of the data you will be using in your analysis, and to which point in that stream of data you are referring. These are essential and are known as:

- MaxBarsBack,
- Study Bar and
- Bar Number or Current Bar

> The preceding elements and operators of *EasyLanguage* are used in a specified manner to form statements. Below are examples of statements:

```
Value1 = Open * 1.01 ;
Condition1 = High <  High[01] ;
if Value1  > Close and Condition1
  then Buy  ("le.Entry#1") 100 Shares at Market ;
```

Notice how easily you understood these statements. Programming studies and systems in *EasyLanguage* is a matter of writing multiple statements in a logical sequence to generate the desired result(s).

In the simple example above we used several elements of *EasyLanguage* including VARIABLES, RESERVED WORDS, BOOLEAN CONDITIONS, MATHEMATICAL and BOOLEAN OPERATORS. Let's take some time to define these terms more clearly.

RESERVED WORDS & KEYWORDS

The **RESERVED WORD** list is made up of SYMBOLS, OPERATORS, KEYWORDS and SKIPWORDS.

KEYWORDS are words to which *EasyLanguage* has assigned a very specific meaning. They may only be used as *EasyLanguage* has defined them.

Here are the Reserved Words that actually have some impact upon your life, what we call the **KeyWords** of the language. The only reason the other reserved words (SkipWords) are important is that you cannot create inputs, variables or user functions by those names.

The following is a list of the Reserved Words used most frequently in *EasyLanguage* programming:

Notes	Reserved Word	Abbr.	Keys	PowerEditor
	Above			
	Ago			
	Alert		I	P
	And			
	Array(s)			P
	Bar(s)			
	Begin			P
	Below			
	Buy		S	P
	CheckAlert		I	P
	CheckCommentary			P
	Close	C		
	Condition(0...99)			P
	Contract(s)		S	P
	Cross(es)			
	Data(1...50)			
	Date	D		
	Day(s)			
	DownTicks			
	DownTo			P
	Else			P
	End			P
	ExitLong		S	P
	ExitShort		S	P
	False			
	For			P
	High	H		
	If			P
	IncludeSystem		S	P
	Input(s)			P
	Limit		S	P
	Low	L		

Notes	Reserved Word	Abbr.	Keys	PowerEditor
	Market		S	P
	Next			
	Numeric		F	P
	NumericSeries		F	P
	NumericSimple		F	P
	Open	O		
	OpenInt	I		
	Or			
	Plot(1...4)		I	P
	Point(s)			
	Print			P
	Sell		S	P
	Share(s)		S	P
	Stop		S	P
****	Text			P
	Then			P
	Ticks			
	Time	T		
	To			P
	Today			
	Tomorrow			
	True			
	TrueFalse		F	P
	TrueFalseSeries	F	F	P
	TrueFalseSimple	F	F	P
	Under			
	UpTicks			
	Value(0...99)			P
	Var(s)			P
	Variable(s)			P
	Volume	V		
	While			P
	Yesterday			

ABBREVIATIONS

EasyLanguage affords a certain degree of flexibility, allowing you to develop a style of programming that is comfortable for you. Just as the language provides for COMMENTS and SKIP-WORDS to make your code more readable, at the same time allowing abbreviations to make your programs less cluttered.

For the following elements of price, *EasyLanguage* accepts their corresponding first letter to be used instead of spelling out the whole word each time it is used.

Price Element	Abbreviation
Date	D
Time	T
Open	O *1
High	H
Low	L
Close	C
Volume	V
OpenInt	I *2

*[1] *Note that the letter "O" (Oh) is radically different from the numeral "0" (zero).*

*[2] *Note that for the element OpenInt, EasyLanguage uses the abbreviation "I" since "O" was already used for Open.*

There are no abbreviations for UpTicks, DownTicks and Ticks.

SkipWords

EasyLanguage can be a very terse language. In other words, you may convey your instructions to the computer using a minimum of words.

In general, the fewer the words, the less the computer has to evaluate and the faster your program will verify...*but we are dealing in nanoseconds here*. The downside of writing tersely is that reading, modifying or debugging your program becomes immensely harder. You may want to modify a program weeks, months, or even years after it was last edited. If your program is extremely terse, it will be very hard for you to read and you may waste time attempting to decipher your original train of thought. This can also be a problem when trying to read a program written by another.

To facilitate readability, *EasyLanguage* has included a group of words, called **SkipWords**,

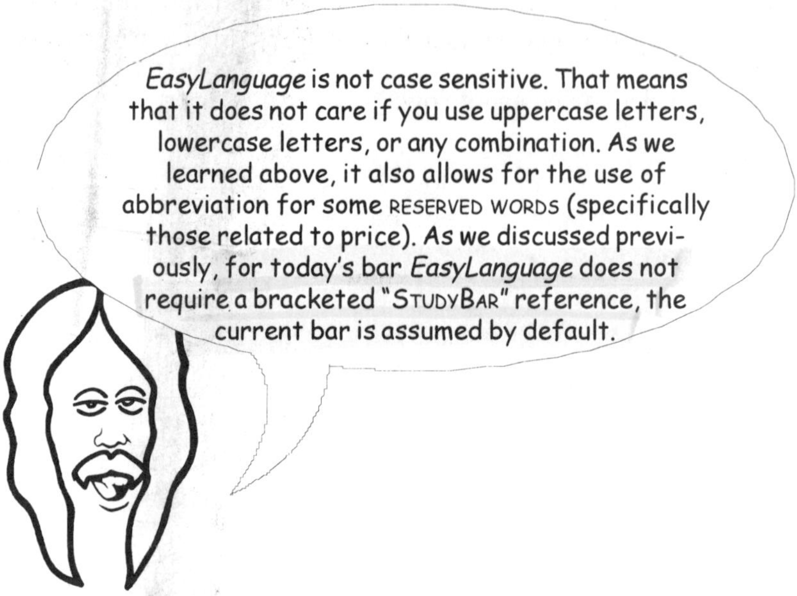

EasyLanguage is not case sensitive. That means that it does not care if you use uppercase letters, lowercase letters, or any combination. As we learned above, it also allows for the use of abbreviation for some RESERVED WORDS (specifically those related to price). As we discussed previously, for today's bar *EasyLanguage* does not require a bracketed "StudyBar" reference, the current bar is assumed by default.

that are automatically ignored by *EasyLanguage*, however, using them makes reading your programs much easier. SkipWords do not cause the program to take any action, but merely "fill in the blanks" in a statement making it more easily understood. The following is the list of SkipWords included in *EasyLanguage*:

A	Is
An	Of
At	On
Based	Place
By	Than
Does	The
From	Was

Whether or not you use SkipWords is a matter of style. The time it takes the computer to evaluate and ignore these words, however, is negligible when compared to the frustration you may experience trying to read a program that is written tersely.

SkipWords are Reserved Words to which *EasyLanguage* has assigned no specific meaning. They may be used any place, in any manner, the user decides. A SkipWord may be thought of as a place holder, sort of like the silent 'e' or a leading zero. The use of SkipWords can make *EasyLanguage* code more readable without altering its interpretation by the compiler.

as a place holder, sort of like the silent 'e' or a leading zero. The use of SKIPWORDS can make *EasyLanguage* code more readable without altering its interpretation by the compiler.

Consider the two equivalent statements below:

```
Buy Market ;
Buy  ("le.Entry#1") 01 Contract
                    on the next bar at the Market ;
```

Try this statement to test all the SKIPWORDS I know:

```
if  @BarNumber <= 01
  then  A AN AT BASED BY DOES FROM IS OF ON PLACE THAN THE WAS ;
```

The above statement, though completely valid, is syntactically equivalent to:

```
if  @BarNumber <= 01  then ;
```

SYMBOLS and OPERATORS

Included in the list of RESERVED WORDS, the following symbols and operators are also reserved in *EasyLanguage* and may be used only for the explicit purpose that *EasyLanguage* has assigned to them. Several of the operators listed (<=, >=, <>) consist of more than a single character. In each case the order is specific and may not be reversed.

;	(	)	[	]
{	}	<	>	<=
>=	=	<>	+	-
*	/	:	&	@

The @ OPERATOR is a remnant of *System Writer* Version 1.0. Originally, the @ SYMBOL was required before every function in *EasyLanguage* code. In this book, I use that @ SYMBOL to help the reader differentiate FUNCTION CALLS from VARIABLES and KEYWORDS.

MATHEMATICAL OPERATORS

MATHEMATICAL OPERATORS, mentioned previously in this section, refer to the common operations performed in mathematics. *EasyLanguage* recognizes the following mathematical operators.

Operator	Description
()	Parenthesis
*	Multiplication
/	Division
+	Addition
-	Subtraction

The ASCII character representing each of these operators is a reserved symbol and may NOT be used in any other fashion within *EasyLanguage*.

PRECEDENCE OF OPERATORS

The order in which a programming language performs calculations is defined by its **PRECEDENCE OF OPERATORS**, the hierarchy in which *EasyLanguage* will evaluate the operations in an expression or statement.

The ORDER OF PRECEDENCE employed by *EasyLanguage* is:

1. Parentheses
2. Multiplication or division
3. Addition and subtraction
4. <, >, =, <=, >=, <>
5. AND
6. OR

> Operators are always referred to in *EasyLanguage* by their symbols rather than by their English labels. *EasyLanguage* will not recognize the words "add," "subtract," "divide" or "multiply." It also will not recognize the letter "x" to signify multiplication. If you can type the '÷' symbol faster than I can then I will (try to) teach *EasyLanguage* to interpret it correctly.

Let's look at the following expression:

3 * 4 / 2

EasyLanguage evaluates this first as:

3 * 4 = 12

then the division is evaluated:

12 / 2 = 6

The operations are performed from left to right because multiplication and division have the same order of precedence. Multiplication is commutative so the order of precedence has no effect here.

If you are using operators from different levels in the order of precedence, however, it becomes more complicated.

Let's try another example:

2 + 2 * 5

At first inspection you might think the answer is:

2 + 2 = 4

and

4 * 5 = 20

But, because multiplication is done first according to the order of precedence, the answer is actually:

2 + (2 * 5), so:

2 * 5 = 10

and

2 +10 = 12

Let's try a tougher one:

4 + 5 * 3 / 3 + 2 * 2 - 1

Evaluated strictly left to right this would be:

4 + 5 = 9

9 * 3 = 27

27 / 3 = 9

9 + 2 = 11

11 * 2 = 22

22 - 1 = 21

Another way of looking at this is:

4 + 5 * 3 / 3 + 2 * 2 - 1

(9 * 3) / 3 + 2 * 2 -1

(27 / 3) + 2 * 2 -1

(9 + 2) * 2 - 1

(11 * 2) - 1

22-1

21

However, because of the PRECEDENCE OF OPERATORS, you have:

4 + 5 * 3 / 3 + 2 * 2 - 1

or

4 + ((5 * 3) /3) + (2 * 2) - 1

or

4 + (15/3) + (2 * 2) - 1

Which evaluates as:

4 + 5 + 4 - 1 = 12

Notice that in this case you do not need the parentheses because the PRECEDENCE OF OPERATORS does multiplication before addition. However, using parentheses makes your meaning more easily understood.

How about a market example? How would *EasyLanguage* evaluate the following expression if close of today = 450 and open of today = 445?

```
Close of Today - Open of Today * 1.1
```

That's right! *EasyLanguage* multiplies the open of today times 1.1 and then subtracts that from the close of today and returns a value of

450 - (445 * 1.1)

or

450 - 489.5 = -39.5

EasyLanguage resolves the expression inside the parentheses first. In this case multiplication supersedes subtraction, so it multiplies the open of today times 1.1 and subtracts that value from the close of today.

If the value that you actually wanted was Open of Today - Close of Today, and that value multiplied by 1.1, you would use parentheses in the expression as follows:

```
(Open of Today - Close of Today) * 1.1
```

EasyLanguage would then interpret this as:

(450 - 445) * 1.1

or

5 * 1.1 = 5.5

That's a radically different value. It's obvious that knowing the PRECEDENCE OF OPERATORS in *EasyLanguage* is essential to using the language properly.

Consider the following situation:

A or B and C

The precedence of operators would evaluate this expression as:

A or (B and C)

When, possibly you wanted:

(A or B) and C

Any time you use both "and" and "or" in an *EasyLanguage* statement, you should use parentheses to control the PRECEDENCE OF OPERATORS.

Making it a practice to use parentheses in cases like this eliminates the danger of the Precedence of Operators causing a result other than intended.

> Always double check your expressions and statements with an eye to the precedence of operators. You could be getting an incorrectvalue and not know it. Anytime you run an *EasyLanguage* program and get a result that completely baffles you, go through your program and recheck your expressions. Insert parentheses wherever it will make your statements less ambiguous. *EasyLanguage* ignores unneeded parentheses, however, sometimes their use does make your program easier to read. They can also help you to force the order of precedence to evaluate expressions as you intend them.

Relational Operators

Relational Operators compare two numeric values or expressions. They are typically used to determine the relationship between prices. A relational operator describes the comparison made between the values to its left and right. *EasyLanguage* recognizes the following relational operators:

Operator/Symbol	Description
=	Equal to
<>	Not Equal to
<	Less than
>	Greater than
<=	Less than or equal to
>=	Greater than or equal to

There need not be space(s) before or after these Relational Operators. They are reserved symbols, and therefore delimiters in their own right. The expressions 'Value1<>0' and 'High[0]*0.95>Low[1]*1.105' are both syntactically correct. The reserved word 'AND', on the other hand, (which is made up of the three alpha characters 'A', 'N' and 'D') does require spaces as delimiters. If you had two Boolean Variables, 's' and 'y' then the expression 'sANDy' would NOT be in any way similar to the expression 's AND y'.

The operators 'not equal to', 'Less than or equal to' and 'Greater than or equal to ' require two characters each ('<>', '<=' and '>=' respectively). The order of the two characters is specific. There may not be any intervening spaces.

In addition to the above common RELATIONAL OPERATORS, *EasyLanguage* recognizes two RELATIONAL OPERATORS that are important to the markets. They are:

Operator/Symbol	Description
Crosses over / above	Greater than current bar but less than or equal to previous bar
Crosses under / below	Less than current bar but greater than or equal to previous bar

CROSSES OVER/ABOVE and CROSSES UNDER/BELOW are abbreviations that were introduced in Version 3.0 of *EasyLanguage*. They can in some cases reduce the repetitive nature of writing code.

Crosses above means on the current bar of data the value on the left has crossed from below to above the value on the right. Conversely, CROSSES BELOW means that on the current bar of data the value on the left has crossed from above to below the value on the right.

The following examples use FASTMA and SLOWMA as labels for the fast and slow moving averages respectfully:

```
FastMA Crosses above SlowMA =      FASTMA[0]   > SLOWMA[0] and
                                   FASTMA[1]  <= SLOWMA[1] ;

FastMA Crosses below SlowMA =      FASTMA[0]  <  SLOWMA[0] and
                                   FASTMA[1]  >= SLOWMA[1] ;
```

BOOLEAN OPERATORS—AND, OR & NOT

The **BOOLEAN OPERATORS AND** & **OR** are used to achieve logical conjunctions between two BOOLEAN EXPRESSIONS. If your study involves multiple conditions you might wish to say, 'If **this** happens **AND that** happens then do such and such.' On the other hand, you might wish to say, 'If **this** happens **OR that** happens then do such and such.' Using AND to connect expressions requires that both conditions be true before an action is taken. Using "or" to connect expressions only requires that one or the other of the conditions be true before an action is taken.

In the following table the "Result column" represents the conjunction of the the two expressions.

Using AND as a logical conjunction

Condition 1	Boolean Operator	Condition 2	Result
True	and	True	Action
True	and	False	No action
False	and	True	No Action
False	and	False	No Action

If, in the above table, you were requiring that both Condition 1 **And** Condition 2 be true, as in the top row of the table above, Condition 1 **And** Condition 2 both proved to be true, then action should be taken.

In the following table the "Result column" represents the conjunction of the the two expressions. If in the table below, you are requiring that either Condtion 1 or Condition 2 be TRUE as in rows one and three, then action should be taken.

Using OR as a logical conjunction

Condition 1	Boolean Operator	Condition 2	Result
True	or	True	Action
True	or	False	No action
False	or	True	Action
False	or	False	No Action

Boolean Operators allow your expressions to be very specific. The rules governing their use will be discussed in greater detail in subsequent sections.

String Operators

The only **String Operator** recognized by *EasyLanguage* is the plus sign (+) used to catenate two string expressions. There is a group of String Functions that provide additional manueverability. These will be covered in greater detail in later sections.

Numbers in *EasyLanguage*

EasyLanguage recognizes **Numeric Constants** in addition to words. Numbers must always be in numeric form, not spelled out. That is, you must always use the numerals 1, 2 or 3 instead of the words one, two or three. Numbers may contain a leading sign (+ **or** -). They may not, however, contain commas, dollar signs or spaces. Neither may they contain spaces after the leading signs.

Examples of correct numbers are:

7	+43	-4598
57988	75654.8	0.4352

Examples of incorrect numbers followed by the same number stated correctly:

Incorrect	Correct
154-	-154
$176.53	176.53
450+	+450
- 323	-323
3,432	3432
+ 212	+212
55,133	55133

Dates

All **DATES** are stored by *EasyLanguage* in 'YYMMDD' format. An example would be the date January 31, 1994 stored and displayed as 940131. In **Tradestation 5.0** this format will change to 'YYYMMDD' for Y2K compatibility. An example would be the date January 31, 2001 stored and displayed as 1010131. To repeat the first example, the date January 31, 1994 stored and displayed as 940131. Another useful method of dealing with dates is in 'JULIAN' form. That is the number of days since some finite point in time. This is explained in full detail in the section on '**DATE AND TIME FUNCTIONS**.'

The "Year 2000 Bug" has been a major thorn in the side for **Omega** owners. **TradeStation 5.0** will be fully Y2K compliant (no surprise there). There are a number of methods that can be used. **Omega** chose a method of displaying dates for Y2K compatibility that maintained backward compatibility. However, the new date format, at first, will not be intuitive. The date December 31, 1999 will be displayed as 991231. No problem there, right? One year in the future, December 31, 2000 will be 1001231. Makes sense? Duhhh?!?! Ok, let me go over that again. You add one to the year 99 and get 100, months and days stay the same. Now you get it? The year 2000 will be represented in "YYY" format as 100 (year 99 in old format + 1), year 2001 as 101, etc...

Omega did not speak to me first, they did not ask my advise. OK, I admit they are not required to get my permission. *Not anymore anyway!* I had a number of ideas on how to handle the Y2K issue, and the solution they chose was NOT one of them, but my ideas would have required more intervention, by both **Omega** and the end user, than the technique they chose. No matter how we purists may complain, their method does have its benefits. It is simple, straightforward, requires no code conversions and is completely backward compatible.

Times

All Times in *EasyLanguage* are stored using a 24 hour clock (Military Time) in 'HHMM' format. For example 10:30am would be represented as 1030 and 4:15pm would be 1615. Another important method of viewing time, critical for manipulating its value, is 'Minutes since Midnight.' Using the same times as above, 10:30am would be represented as 630 ((60 minutes * 10 hours) + 30 minutes) and 4:15pm would be 975 ((60 minutes * 16 hours) + 15 minutes).

Prices

Price is a generic term used to refer to any of a suite of fields for each bar of data. The primary price fields are:

Open	The first tick of the bar
High	The highest tick of the bar
Low	The lowest tick of the bar
Close	The last tick of the bar

In addition to "price" information above, the term price also encompasses the following related information for each bar of data:

Date	Date of the bar
Time	Ending time of the bar
Volume	Only used when testing daily (or greater) data, volume refers to the number of shares/contracts traded during the daily bar
OpenInt	Only used when testing daily (or greater) data, OpenInt refers to the number of shares/ contracts outstanding at the close of a daily bar
UpTicks	Only used when testing intra-day data, refers to the number or ticks whose value was greater than or equal to the previous tick
DownTicks	Only used when testing intra-day data, DownTicks refers to the number of ticks whose value was less than or equal to the previous tick
Ticks	Number of trades (transactions) during a bar

As you can see "price," as used in *EasyLanguage*, refers not only to the four main prices of a security on any given bar, but also to essential, related information to put those prices into context.

StudyBar

All references to '**StudyBar**,' or bars ago, in *EasyLanguage* must obey simple rules. The past is referenced with positive values, *i.e.*: one bar ago can be Close of 1 bar ago or Close[1]. Except for two **very specific** exceptions (TLValue and LinRegValue), negative bar references (into the future) are never allowed.

The bar on which the imaginary (internal) pointer is currently operative is referred to as the Study Bar. *EasyLanguage* begins calculations at the first bar after the MaxBarsBack buffer. For a very brief moment of time this is 'today'. This 'today' bar is known as the Study Bar or the Current Bar. The next moment, 'today' will be the next bar in the series, and so on.

In *EasyLanguage*, if you wish to refer to the price of a bar other than the Current Bar, you can actually offset the Study Bar from the Current Bar ('today') and you specify the offset in the following manner:

```
High[3]     or    High of 3 bars ago

Low [5]     or    Low of 5 bars ago
```

The number inside the square brackets (following the price) refers to the number of bars back in time for that price. In the above examples, the study is referring to the High of three bars ago and the Low of five bars ago. Since the data you are analyzing is always today or in the past, *i.e.*, days (bars) ago, *EasyLanguage* does not require that you put a negative sign in front of the numbers to indicate bars ago. A number within square brackets after a price always refers to 'bars ago'.

A bar counter, **@CurrentBar**, is provided to allow the *EasyLanguage* programmer to track where the 'today' pointer is within the data series.

Another function, **@BarNumber**, is provided for use primarily within User Functions. @BarNumber can be offset by a StudyBar reference where @CurrentBar has no 'history' available. To prove this try the following:

```
Print (@CurrentBar, @BarNumber, @CurrentBar[1], @BarNumber[1]) ;
```

You will get the message:

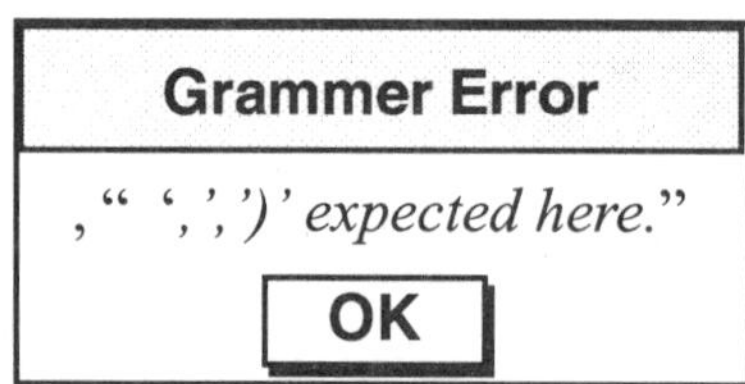

EasyLanguage highlights the left square bracket of "@CurrentBar[01]," which translates to "Rather than a left square bracket, *EasyLanguage* expects either a comma or a close parentheses in this position."

No 'STUDYBAR' reference may be made that exceeds the value of 'MAXBARSBACK.'

One important situation to note is referring to prices of today. In this case you can make reference to "zero days ago," *i.e.*, High[00]. However, if no days ago reference is made, *EasyLanguage* assumes today. Because of this, today's prices can be referred to simply as Open, High, Low and Close. This is a very good practice. Each time *EasyLanguage* encounters a bracketed days-ago reference, it runs a comparison of that value against the MAXBARSBACK value to make sure there is no violation. This uses memory resources that can be better applied elsewhere.

If the study bar is today ([0]), then tomorrow would be referred to as "next bar" and yesterday would be referred to as "1 bar ago" or [1].

Because of the flexibility of *EasyLanguage*, all of the following are acceptable examples of price for a study bar:

```
    Open of today, OPEN[0], OPEN, open[0], Open, or 0 of today.
    High of 1 bar ago, HIGH[1], high[1], High[01], or H[1].
    Close of 3 bars ago, CLOSE[3],
close[03], Close[3], or C[03].
```

VARIABLES

A **VARIABLE** is a name, or label, that designates a temporary storage location for information within the computer memory, or RAM. Variables are frequently used in the comparison of values or conditions, to build expressions, and are identified by descriptive names of your choosing. When you wish to use the information stored in the memory address designated by the variable name, you refer to it by its name, not by its content or address. The content of a memory variable can change during the course of the program, but its name remains the same.

You identify a variable by its name, which in *EasyLanguage* can be up to 20 characters in length. A variable name must begin with a letter (it may NOT begin with a number but some symbols are acceptable) and can contain letters, digits and the special characters '.', '_', '@', '#' and '$'. It may not contain the characters '!', '?', '%', '^', '&', '~', ":", ";", apostrophe, single quote, double quote or comma. The name may not contain any of the mathematical or relational operators.

VARIABLES are usually defined near the top of a program. This is called declaring, or initializing, the VARIABLE. *EasyLanguage* recognizes three types of VARIABLES, NUMERIC, BOOLEAN (TRUE/FALSE) and STRING (CHARACTER). NUMERIC VARIABLES are generally initialized with a value of 0 (zero) unless programming logic dictates another initial value. LOGICAL VARIABLES are generally initialized with a value of false. STRING VARIABLES are usually initialized to null ("" or double quotes).

NUMERIC VARIABLES

A **NUMERIC VARIABLE** is used to store numeric values such as prices, numbers of days or bars, and mathematical calculations.

For instance, you may want to buy 300 shares of a certain stock when its price hits a 30-day high. In *EasyLanguage* you would define a numeric variable, which we might call 'LE.PRICE', to store your target price. The statement for this would be:

```
le.Price = @Highest (High, 30) ;
```

You can then refer to this price by its variable name LE.PRICE and use that variable to compare against your price data to produce a SIGNAL or ALERT when the market price reaches your buy price. To do this you would include a statement that said:

```
Buy  ("le.Main") 300 Shares at le.Price stop ;
```

In the above example you might ask, "Why not just enter the price instead of using a variable?" Good question. Variables are used for values that change, and are especially helpful when a value is employed multiple times during a program. By using a variable, you can change the value in one easy-to-locate place in your program instead of having to search for each usage individually.

EasyLanguage includes the NUMERIC VARIABLES VALUE0 through VALUE99. Each of these variables has already been initialized to 0 prior to the first bar of data. This is an important concept to understand. Before executing your code on the first bar of data, *EasyLanguage* will initialize all variables. This is done **only** once. After that it is the programmer's (your) responsibility to ensure that the appropriate value is in place.

How, I hear you ask, can I accomplish this monumental feat?!? Have no fear. Before I am through with you, this question will be the least of your worries!

You may use these predefined VARIABLES, or you may choose to create your own variables with more descriptive names that make more sense to you and are easier to remember. This process will be covered in detail shortly.

Boolean Variables

Boolean Variables are used for conditions that may be true or false. Let's say you want to define a logical variable named Bingo. You would initialize the variable near the top of your program in the variable declaration area (which will be discussed in a subsequent section) by saying:

```
Vars: Bingo (False) ;
```

Later, in your program you could change the value of Bingo based on a condition.

```
If Close >= Open * 1.07
  Then Bingo =  TRUE ;
```

Throughout this text the use of 'day' shall be synonymous with 'bar'.

Still later in your program you could use the logical value of Bingo to make a decision. You could say, for example:

```
If Bingo = TRUE and @DayOfWeek (Date) = 1
  Then Buy  ("le.Main") 100 Shares at Market ;
```

In the above example, "DayOfWeek (Date) = 1" indicates Monday. The @DayOfWeek will be discussed more thoroughly in Section Three (Functions).

EasyLanguage includes the Boolean Variables Condition0 through Condition99. Each of these variables is automatically initialized to false before the first bar of data. As with numeric variables, you may use the predefined variables names, or you may choose to give your Boolean Variables more descriptive names that will make more sense to you and are easier to remember.

You may abbreviate expressions when using logical variables after they have been initialized. You need not say "= True" after a logical variable name. When the variable name is mentioned by itself, *EasyLanguage* will assume that you mean that the condition is true. So, you can say:

```
If  Condition1  =  True  Then .... ;
```

or you can abbreviate the expression by saying:

```
If  Condition1  Then  ... ;
```

Following are a few more examples of commonly used logical variables:

```
InsideBar  = High <= High[1] and Low >= Low[1] ;
OutsideBar = High  > High[1] and Low <  Low[1] ;
```

String Variables

String Variables have the same naming conventions as Numeric and Boolean Variables. A String is a series of zero or more characters that can thought of as text. One string may be appended to another by using the Catenation Operator (+). A String Variable is normally intilialized to a NULL STRING, two quotation marks containing zero characters (""). *EasyLangauge* uses the "double quote" rather than the 'single quote' (apostrophe) for delimiting STRING CONSTANTS.

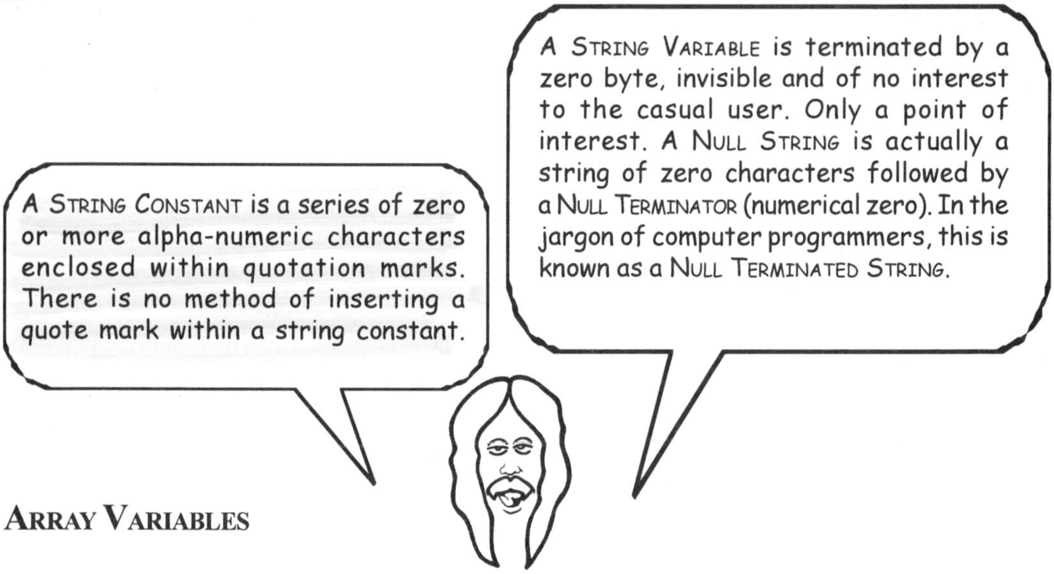

ARRAY VARIABLES

An ARRAY contains a group or list of items, all of the same type, that are referenced by a single name. The individual elements are directly accessed through the use of an ARRAY INDEX.

EasyLanguage ARRAYS were not multidimensional prior to **TradeStation 4.0**. A good analogy for an ARRAY is a spreadsheet. With *EasyLanguage*, think of a single dimensional array as either one column or one row of a spreadsheet. How you imagine it is dependent upon your application. A two dimensional array represents the entire matrix of the spreadsheet, rows and columns combined.

According to the documentation supplied by **Omega Research** each ARRAY in *EasyLanguage* can have up to 16,000 elements. Each individual element of an ARRAY is accessed by specifying its INDEX, or SUBSCRIPT. The INDEX is a NUMERICAL VALUE between 0 and the size value specified in the ARRAY DECLARATION STATEMENT.

ARRAYS are created by an ARRAY DECLARATION STATEMENT. The format for an ARRAY DECLARATION is:

```
Arrays: ArrayName [N] (X) ;
```

Where N refers to the number of elements (0...N) in the array and X initializes all elements with either a NUMERIC, BOOLEAN or STRING value.

ARRAYS can also be tied to a specific data series. For example:

```
Arrays: ArrayName [20] (0, Data2) ;
```

When referencing an ARRAY you specify the ARRAY NAME then the subscript inside square brackets.

For example:

```
Value1 = MyArray [1] ;
```

You would read this in English as "Value one equals MyArray sub one" or "Value one is equal to MyArray sub one." Here is a more practical example of an ARRAY in use:

```
Arrays: MidBar [20] (0, Data1) ;
MidBar [2] = MidBar [1] ;
MidBar [1] = MidBar [0] ;
MidBar [0] = (High of Data1 + Low of Data1) * 0.5 ;
```

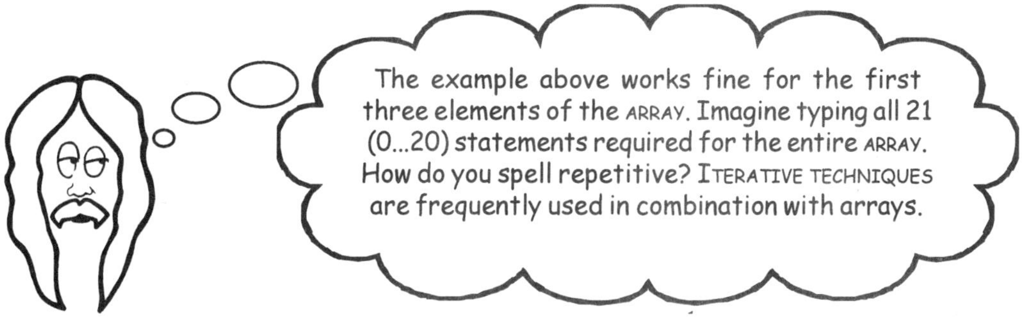

The example above works fine for the first three elements of the ARRAY. Imagine typing all 21 (0...20) statements required for the entire ARRAY. How do you spell repetitive? ITERATIVE TECHNIQUES are frequently used in combination with arrays.

ARRAYS are the simplest and most common type of structured data. In some languages, like *EasyLanguage*, ARRAYS are the only type of structured data. The following notes were generated by a technical writer while doing our background research. I have left them in this document on the rare chance that one of the explanations included may strike some '*nerve of understanding*' (related to the legendary '*glimmer of hope*' and the proverbial '*shred of decency*') in someone still struggling for that '*leap of faith*' that will allow them to *truly believe*.

You access an ARRAY's components by supplying the IDENTIFIER with one or more indexes in square brackets (often called a subscript, say 'MYARRAY[3]' as 'MY ARRAY sub Three').

Tips:

Make sure that all array indexes are within the bounds of the ARRAY. In one way or another, all problems with ARRAYS are caused by the fact that ARRAY elements can be accessed randomly. The most common problem arises when a program tries to access an ARRAY element that's out of bounds. In some languages this produces an error; in others, it simply produces bizarre and unexpected results.

You can think of ARRAYS as sequential structures. The price fields in *EasyLangauge* are actually examples of ARRAYS. CLOSE[01] is no different than MYARRAY[01].

A STRING VARIABLE is actually an ARRAY of characters. However, *EasyLangauge* does not allow you to directly access the individual characters by subscript. STRING FUNCTIONS are provided to allow you to manipulate STRINGS.

Check the end-points of ARRAYS. Just as it's helpful to think through the endpoints in a loop structure, you can catch many errors by checking the endpoints of ARRAYS. Ask yourself whether the code correctly accesses the first element of the ARRAY or mistakenly accesses the element before or after the first element. What about the last element? Will the code make an off-by-one error? Finally, ask yourself whether the code correctly accesses the middle elements of the ARRAY.

Watch out for **INDEX CROSS-TALK**. If you're using nested loops, it's easy to write ARRAY (x) instead of ARRAY (y). Switching loop indexes is called **INDEX CROSS-TALK**. Check for this problem. In order to help you avoid CROSS-TALK mistakes, use meaningful subscript names. For example, instead of:

```
{ Bubble Sort - order all elements in sequence }

for X = 0 to MaxSize - 01 begin
  for Y = X + 01 to MaxSize begin
    if MyArray [X] <  MyArray [Y] then begin
      Scrap       = MyArray [X] ;
      MyArray [X] = MyArray [Y] ;
      MyArray [Y] = Scrap ;
    end ;  { swap elements }
  end ; { Inner loop }
end ; { Outer loop }
```

using 'x' or 'y,' use descriptive variables:

```
{ Bubble Sort - order all elements in sequence }

for Outer = 0 to MaxSize - 01 begin
  for Inner = Outer + 01 to MaxSize begin
    if MyArray [Outer] <  MyArray [Inner] then begin
      Scrap           = MyArray [Outer] ;
      MyArray [Outer] = MyArray [Inner] ;
      MyArray [Inner] = Scrap ;
    end ;  { swap elements }
  end ; { Inner loop }
end ; { Outer loop }
```

Throw in an extra element at the end of an ARRAY. Off-by-one errors are common with ARRAYS. If your ARRAY access is off-by-one and you write beyond the end of an ARRAY, you can cause a serious error. When you declare the ARRAY to be one bigger than the size you think you'll need, you give yourself a cushion and soften the consequences of an off-by-one error.

Types of Bars—@Data Compression

Prices are always evaluated in the context of date/time or sequence. This is done by referencing a specific bar in relationship to the current bar. A bar denotes a specific chronological point in the data stream being studied. DATA COMPRESSION refers to the time interval (unless TICK BARS or POINT & FIGURE) of the bars on the chart.

TradeStation allows you to select the desired data compression within the Chart Setup Dialog Box. Then you are presented with a list of options that allow you to apply a context to or define "BARS" as they apply to your study. The options are:

0. **Tick bar # Ticks**
1. **Intraday # Minutes**
2. **Daily**
3. **Weekly**
4. **Monthly**
5. **Point & Figure**

The first DATA COMPRESSION option, **TICK BAR [#] TICKS**, allows you to enter a number indicating the number of ticks you wish a bar to represent. This choice will be available to you only if you have loaded intraday data.

Intraday bar charts are based on time, in minute intervals. After choosing **Intraday [#] Min** as your DATA COMPRESSION option, type the number of minutes you want to be contained in a single bar. Intraday bars must be created using tick-by-tick data.

The **Daily, Weekly** and **Monthly** options in the DATA COMPRESSION settings will construct bars with one open, high, low, and close for each calendar day, week or month, respectively.

Weekly charts are built using the opening price of Monday and the closing price of Friday or their closest approximation.

Monthly charts use the opening tick of the first calendar day of the month and the closing price of the last day of the calendar month.

Point & Figure Charts

Point & Figure charts are used to show changes in price independent of time. They are used to identify trends and support and resistance levels in the market. In contrast to the ambiguity of the bar chart, the point-and figure method defines the support and resistance levels more precisely. They help establish logical places to buy and sell and they help designate the placement

866.0	X													
865.0	X	O	X											
864.0	X	O	X	O										
863.0		O	X	O	X									
862.0		O		O	X	O								
861.0				O	X	O								
860.0				O	X	O								
859.0				O										
858.0														

In a **Point & Figure chart** the y-axis is made up of prices. The x-axis is made up of columns, into which are entered Xs or Os. A column of Xs represents a rallying market, while a column of Os represents a declining market.

Typically used as a tool for the speculator without access to intraday prices, **Point & Figure** charts tell the trader exactly what penetration of a resistance or support level is necessary to generate a buy or sell signal and exactly where the stop-loss order should be placed to limit risk. **TradeStation** allows us to generate intraday **Point & Figure** charts to perform this same type of analysis on shorter time frames.

The **POINT & FIGURE [BOXSIZE] BY [REVERSALSIZE]** data compression option in the CHART SETUP DIALOG BOX requires you to provide two inputs, BOX SIZE (in points) and reversal amount in terms of boxes. The choice of BOX SIZE determines the sensitivity, or frequency, of signals making the chart more or less sensitive to changes in price direction. This allows the identification of trends and trading ranges of various duration. BOX SIZES are often related to the current volatility of the markets. Choice of BOX SIZE corresponds to whether you are looking for longer or shorter trends or major and minor trends. The smaller the price increment (BOX SIZE), the more changes in direction will be noted. Traders looking for long-term price movement would use a larger box size.

The other required input for the **Point & Figure** data compression choice is the reversal amount (in boxes). The traditional POINT & FIGURE method calls for the use of a 3-box reversal. That means the price must reverse direction by an amount equal to 3 boxes in order to register as a reversal. For example, a $4 box for gold (which trades in dollars) with a three-box reversal means that gold prices must reverse by $12 to indicate a trend change.

In **Point & Figure** charts, NET REVERSAL is the critical value. NET REVERSAL is equal to the box size times the number of boxes in the reversal.

In a **Point & Figure** chart, an X is entered when the price rises by the box size. An O is entered when the price falls by the box size. Each column may contain an X or an O but never both.

To change from an X to an O or vice versa, prices must reverse by the box size multiplied by the reversal amount. For example, if the box size is 2 points and the reversal amount is 2 boxes, the price must reverse direction by 4 points in order to change an X to an O or vice versa.

Point & Figure charting differs from ordinary charting in two important ways:

- It filters out price reversals that are below a minimum value.
- It has no time factor. As long as prices fail to change direction by the reversal value, the trend is intact.

To edit or preview the type, color or size of the bars that will be drawn on your chart, click on the Chart Type Command Button from within the Chart Setup Dialog Box. You will be presented with the Bar Chart Style Box.

MaxBarsBack

In all analyses of markets, whether study or system, you will need a reference to scope and time. **MaxBarsBack** is a setting needed by *EasyLanguage* to define the scope, or number of bars, to be included in your analysis. When **TradeStation** runs a study or system, it moves an imaginary pointer through the data file. At any given time, **TradeStation** has the prices of the current bar ('today'), as well as the prices for the number of bars back to the MaxBarsBack value available for use by *EasyLanguage*.

If the study you are performing requires the evaluation of 30 days of historical data, you would set MaxBarsBack to 30. If you were to set MaxBarsBack to 20 and then run your study, an error would occur advising you to increase the MaxBarsBack setting.

You can set the MaxBarsBack value higher than the number that you actually need. However, **TradeStation** will collect the data for the number of bars specified in the MaxBarsBack value before it will begin your calculation. For example, if you wanted to calculate a moving average of 40 days, beginning 5 bars ago, but set the MaxBarsBack to 65, **TradeStation** would have to collect 65 bars of data before your calculation would begin to run, even though you only require 45 days to perform the calculation you described. This wastes processing time and resources but allowing for extra 'room' in the MaxBarsBack buffer may prevent complications later on, as explained in the note below.

TradeStation defaults to a MaxBarsBack value of 50. It will remain at this value until you change it in your program. The default value of 50 is enough for most common calculations.

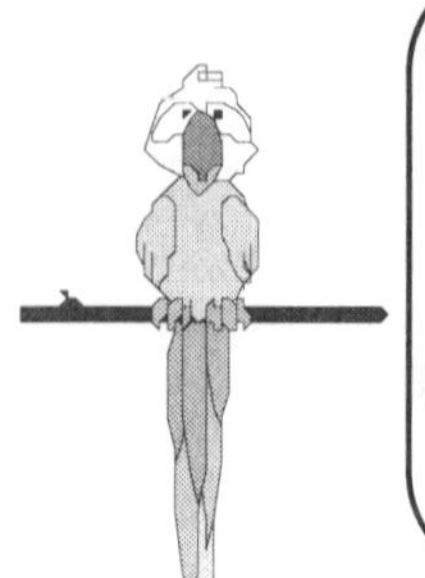

When performing profitability testing during system development it is critical that MaxBarsBack remains set to a constant value. Otherwise, it is a very real possibility that your testing will be tainted by a single trade (either a winner or a loser) being dropped out of the sample period when MaxBarsBack changes the range of dates for calculations and therefore not including that particular trade(s).

A Summary

A **computer program** is a finite sequence of instructions, designed to obtain a specific result, to be executed (or "run") by a computer.

A **computer language** is some subset of the English language that allows the programmer to give specific commands to the computer. Computer languages are ranked from **high level** (very English-like) to **low level** (very cryptic).

Syntax refers to the correct order in which you arrange the parts of an expression or statement. It is the defined structure that causes your commands or programs to execute correctly. Inherent in a discussion of syntax are elements such as rules, structure, sequence and order.

Reserved Words are the words and symbols which a computer language reserves for its internal use. **SkipWords** are included in this list.

SkipWords, which are rather unique to *EasyLanguage*, are used to make your programs easier to read. They do not cause the program to take any action, but merely "fill in the blanks" in a statement to make it more easily understood. SkipWords are reserved words. *EasyLanguage* allows the following SkipWords: A, An, At, Based, By, Does, From, Is, From, On, Place, Than, The and Was.

KeyWords are words to which a computer language has assigned very specific, unambiguous, meanings, *e.g.*, in *EasyLanguage*, High, Low, Market, Buy, Value0...99, Condition0...99, Mathematical, Relational, and Boolean operators (and, or).

Variables are temporary, user defined, locations for the storage of information. They may be used to make comparisons of values or conditions. Variables are identified by descriptive names of our choosing. When we wish to use the information stored in the variable we refer to it by name, not by its contents. The contents of a variable can change during the course of the program, but its name remains the same.

- A **Numeric variable** is used to store numeric values, such as prices, numbers of days or bars, oscillators, indicators or the result of other mathematical calculations.

- A **Boolean Variable** is used to store logical conditions that may be either False (zero) or True (non-zero).

An **Array Variable** is the simplest (and only) form of data structure supported by *EasyLanguage*. An array is a set of contiguous memory locations all referenced by the same name identifier and indexed by a subscript.

- **Array Variables** are an advanced programming topic that will be covered in much greater detail later in this book and in the course material itself. Please do not allow yourself to get overly concerned about understanding the usefulness of Arrays. Let is suffice to understand the basic syntax of declaring and referencing an array. Practical application can, and will, develop in the fullness of time.

Mathematical Operators are the symbols for addition (+), subtraction (-), multiplication (*) and division (/).

Relational Operators are used to compare two values. Relational Operators are typically used to describe relationships between prices. *EasyLanguage* recognizes the following relational operators: = (equal to) ; <> (not equal to) ; < (less than) ; > (greater than) ; <= (less than or equal to) ; and >= (greater than or equal to).

The **Boolean Operators AND** and **OR** are used to achieve logical conjunctions between two expressions; *i.e.*: to require that 'this' AND 'that' happen or that 'this' happens OR 'that' happens before an action is taken.

EasyLanguage also recognizes two special relational operators unique to the markets. They are **Crosses Over/Above** (greater than current bar but less than or equal to previous bar) and **Crosses Under/Below** (less than current bar but greater than or equal to the previous bar).

Parentheses may be used to clarify order of execution of your expressions and statements.

Precedence of Operators defines the order that calculations are performed with in an expression or statement. The order of precedence employed by *EasyLanguage* is defined earlier in this section.

A **Statement** is a single command or instruction to the computer. The statement is the smallest stand alone unit of the language. A statement may be used to define a variable or condition, to compare values, to plot something on a graph, or to trigger an alarm or signal. Statements are the basic component of *EasyLanguage*.

Statements are made up of combinations of Expressions. **Expressions** are like phrases in a sentence. By themselves, they do not offer enough information to form a complete thought. But, if you put expressions together properly, a statement is formed. *EasyLanguage* recognizes three types of expressions, Numeric, Boolean and String.

A **Numeric Expression** is arithmetic and combines numbers, prices, operators and/or variables to produce a new number, *e.g.*, 5 + 5, High - 8 points, Close[1] * 1.003, Open * 1.005.

Logical Expressions are either true or false. They are most often used in conditional statements where an action can occur only if some preceding condition is either true or false, *e.g.*, High >= Close[1], Open > Close, RSI > 20.

Price is a generic term used to refer to any of the information available for a single trading day or bar. The complete list of available fields is: Date, Time, Open, High, Low, Close, Volume, OpenInt, UpTicks, DownTicks and Ticks.

OpenInt (the number of total contracts outstanding at the close of a daily bar).

Volume (the number of shares/contracts that changed hands during this trading period).

The term **Price** is frequently used as an input to a study, system or function. In many cases it will have a default value of **Close** but that can be replaced with <u>any</u> series price field, input or function.

Prices are always used in the context of date/time or sequence. This is done by referencing specific bars. A **Bar** denotes a specific point in the data stream being studied.

Data Compression refers to the time interval of the bars on the chart.

MaxBarsBack is a variable needed by *EasyLanguage* to define the number of bars, or scope, to be included in your analysis. When *EasyLanguage* runs a study, it moves an imaginary pointer through the data file. At any given time, *EasyLanguage* has the prices of the current bar, as well as the prices for the number of bars up to the *MaxBarsBack* value.

The **Study Bar,** by default, is the price bar currently being analyzed. It also is used to refer to a previous bar to the current bar being the study bar. To reference past bars, place the number of bars back (ago) within square brackets. *e.g.*, High[2] means the high two bars ago.

Commenting your code means {including helpful information and notes to yourself} within curly brackets. This information is not needed by the program to run, but allows you to easily refresh your memory about different parts of the program, long after it was written. Anything within comment braces ({}) is ignored by *EasyLanguage*.

EasyLanguage allows the following **abbreviations** of price:

D (Date), T (Time),O(Open), H (High), L (Low), C (Close), V (Volume), I (OpenInt).

Technical Notes:

Internally, the Price information is stored in a data structure for each bar of data loaded into your chart. For intraday bars, the daily open, high, low, and close are stored in a header for the structure. This is why I have always maintained that the user should **<u>not</u>** be forced to load daily data into Data2 of a MultiData Chart in order to reference daily information. I feel that if the user asks for the high of yesterday on a fifteen minute chart he should get yesterday's high, **<u>not</u>** the high of one fifteen minute bar ago!

Due to my knowledge of the development processes used to add intraday capabilities to *EasyLanguage*, I know that the VOLUME field is identical to UPTICKS and that the OPENINT field is the same as DOWNTICKS. I believe that the TICKS field is not actually stored in the structure itself, but is the sum of the UPTICKS and DOWNTICKS fields.

Your *EasyLanguage* code can only access the price information that is currently within the MAXBARSBACK buffer.

TIME (the moment of time immediately following close of the bar). In other words, if the S&P 500 closes at 4:15pm then the last tick possible for the day would be time stamped 4:14.59, if seconds were stored. There can never be a tick with the same time as the time stamp of the bar. On a one minute S&P chart, the 9:31am bar is the first bar of the day and it is composed of all the ticks that were stored between 9:30.00am and 9:30.59am (one sixty second bar).

Here's a helpful hierarchy chart.

EasyLanguage

STATEMENT

EXPRESSIONS

RESERVED WORDS

VARIABLES

NUMBERS

LOGICAL CONDITIONS

PRICES

MATHEMATICAL OPERATORS

RELATIONAL OPERATORS

BOOLEAN OPERATORS

(All the above may contain:)

PARENTHESES

SQUARE BRACKETS

COMMENT BRACES

SKIPWORDS

Section 2:
Writing Statements

OVERVIEW / OBJECTIVES

After completing this section you should be comfortable with the following concepts:

- Writing:
- **DECLARATION STATEMENTS**

  INPUTS, VARIABLES, ARRAYS, INCLUDESYSTEM, DEFINEDLLFUNC
- **ASSIGNMENT STATEMENTS**

  SIMPLE, ACCUMULATOR, COUNTER, SWITCH or FLAG
- Block BEGIN...END Statements
- **DECISION (CONDITIONAL) STATEMENTS**
  - Simple IF...THEN statements
  - Complex IF...THEN...ELSE statements
  - Block IF...THEN statements using "BEGIN...END"
  - Block IF...THEN...ELSE statements using "BEGIN...END"
  - Nested IF statements
  - PLOT statements
  - BUY and SELL statements
- **ITERATIVE (LOOPING) STATEMENTS**
  - *For loop = start To stop Begin* statement *End;*
  - *For loop = start DownTo stop Begin* statement *End;*

- *While expression Begin* statement *End;*
- **Trading Systems & Signals**
  - *Entry (Buy and Sell) Orders*
  - *Exit (ExitLong and ExitShort) Orders*
- **Output Statements**
  - *Alerts, Plot, Print, Commentary*
- **Review of Points as used in Trading**

Review of Expressions...

As we learned in Section 1 an Expression is a term or phrase that can be resolved down to a single value. An expressions may also be thought of as a 'clause' or a 'sentence fragment.'

Every expression will be of a recognized Data Type (Numeric, Boolean or String). Examples of Expressions follow:

```
12 + 5 * 2 = 12 + 10 = 22 = Numeric
Close * 1.02 = 102% of the Close = Numeric
Open > Close = Boolean
3 > 2 = TRUE = Boolean
"Samuel " + "K." + " Tennis" = "Samuel K. Tennis" = String
```

An Expression may be substituted any place a value (of the correct Data Type) is expected.

Review of Statements....

As we learned in the previous section, the basic building block of *EasyLanguage* is the statement. A Statement is a single command or instruction to the computer. A Statement is equivalent to a sentence in English. Statements may be used to define variables, solve equations, compare values, plot graphs, trigger alarms, generate trading signals and more. Every statement is terminated with a semicolon.

Statements may contain Expressions made up of various elements and operators each serving particular purposes and must be used in a specified manner. These rules are the Syntax of the language.

EasyLanguage recognizes many kinds of statements including, but not limited to, Declaration, Assignment, Block, Decision, Iterative, Procedure, Output and Comment. Each of these is described in greater detail below.

WHAT'S A STATEMENT?

Types of Statements

The DECLARATION STATEMENT

There are five distinct types of DECLARATION STATEMENTS in *EasyLangauge*: INPUT, VARIABLE, ARRAY, INCLUDESYSTEM and DEFINEDLLFUNC (DYNAMIC LINK LIBRARY) STATEMENTS.

The INPUT, VARIABLE and/or ARRAY you declare must have a DATA TYPE (NUMERIC, BOOLEAN or STRING) specified. The default value that you supply serves two purposes. First, it tells *EasyLanguage* the DATA TYPE of the declared item. Second, it instructs *EasyLanguage* to initialize the item (INPUT, VARIABLE or ARRAY) to this default value. This initialization occurs immediately prior to the execution of the first bar of data.

The INPUT STATEMENT

The first and most commonly used DECLARATION STATEMENT is the INPUT DECLARATION STATEMENT. Many beginning programmers find the INPUT STATEMENT to be confusing, even intimidating, yet they are often familiar with the concept in a different environment. For instance, many users are comfortable using a function, such as AVERAGE or SUM, within Microsoft Excel or a similar spreadsheet application. The AVERAGE function in Excel requires that you supply a range of cells. The INPUT in *EasyLanguage* is essentially identical to this user-specified range value.

Let me give you an example. **Omega Research** provides us with the generic function @AVERAGE. You must specify what you want to average and over what time period.

The syntax for the INPUT STATEMENT is the KEYWORD INPUT or INPUTS followed by a colon (:), the name of the INPUT followed by the default value in parenthesis. The default value will also serve to define the type of this input (NUMERIC, BOOLEAN, STRING). Additional inputs may be appended by using a comma as a list separator. The input statement is terminated by a semicolon.

```
Inputs: Price (Close) ;
```

```
Inputs: Length (12), DoReport (FALSE), Sys.Name ("Best Buy") ;
```

The INPUT STATEMENT for a FUNCTION is a special case. You can not specify a default value inside the function. Instead of a DEFAULT VALUE, you are required to use one of the TYPE IDENTIFIER (NUMERIC, NUMERICSIMPLE, NUMERICSERIES, TRUEFALSE, TRUEFALSESIMPLE, TRUEFALSESERIES, STRING, STRINGSIMPLE, STRINGSERIES) KEYWORDS. An example follows:

```
Inputs: Price  (NumericSeries),
        Length (NumericSimple) ;
```

The concept of SIMPLE VS. SERIES will be explained later.

The VARIABLE STATEMENT

The VARIABLE DECLARATION STATEMENT is used to declare working storage variables for use within your code module. *EasyLanguage* provides one hundred predefined NUMERIC VARIABLES termed VALUE0 through VALUE99 and one hundred BOOLEAN VARIABLES, CONDITION0 through CONDITION99. VALUE100 and CONDITION100 are valid variable names but they are not pre-declared. In order to use them you would need to use the VARIABLE DECLARATION STATEMENT. It is perfectly acceptable to use these predefined variables. However, I find it preferable to declare my own variables with meaningful, descriptive names. This habit can improve the readability of *EasyLanguage* code by making it nearly self-documenting.

The VARIABLE STATEMENT consists of the KEYWORD VARIABLE, VARIABLES, VAR or VARS separated by a colon, the name or label of your variable, followed by the default value inside parenthesis. You may append multiple variables in one statement by using the comma as a list separator. Terminate the VARIABLE STATEMENT with a semicolon.

The default value serves two purposes. First, it tells *EasyLanguage* the type of this variable (NUMERIC, BOOLEAN, STRING). Second it instructs *EasyLanguage* to initialize the variable to this default value immediately prior to the execution of the first bar of data.

You may use the singular and plural variants of the VARIABLE KEYWORD interchangeably, either will work regardless of whether you are declaring one variable or multiple variables.

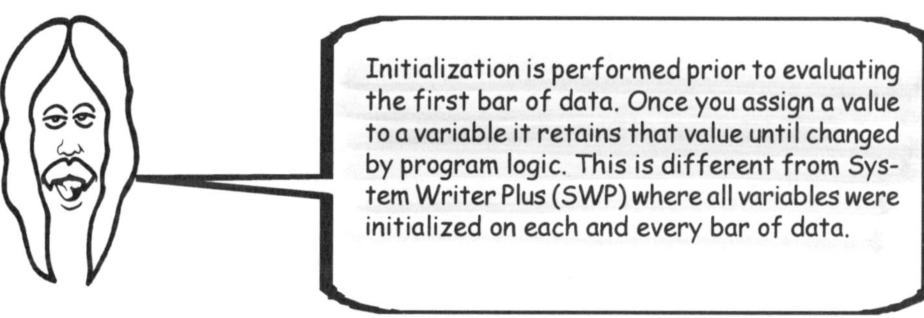


```
Variable: MyPercent (0), MyMultiple (0) ;
Vars: ClosedAbove (False) ;
```

It is not necessary to declare NUMERIC VALUES in a separate DECLARATION STATEMENT from BOOLEAN and STRING values nor are you confined to a single line. Formatting the code is mainly a matter of personal style and may facilitate documentation.

When your programs get more complex you may find it helpful to group variables by function and document their intended purpose. See examples in our supplied code for guidance.

It is possible to use an expression as the default value within the VARIABLE DECLARATION STATEMENT. In the code examples later in this book you will find many cases where I place equations within my DECLARATION STATEMENTS.

```
Vars  : OnePoint (1 Point),
        OneTick  (MinMove * 1 Point),
        IntraDay (DataCompression < 2) ;
Vars  : MyRange (@TrueRange) ;
```

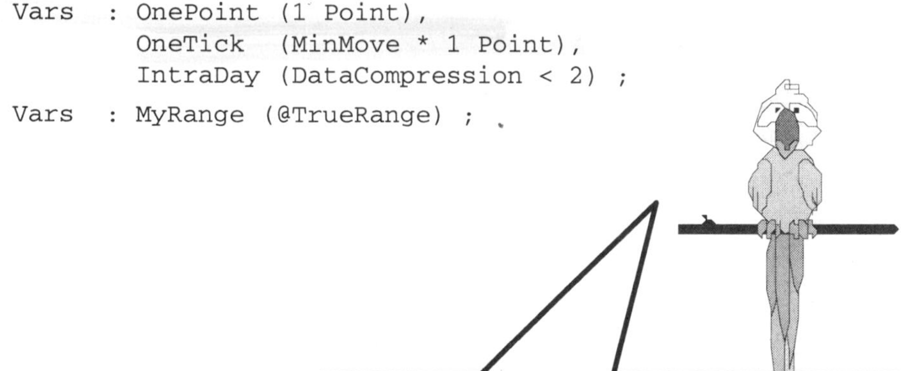

The Array Statement

The Array Declaration Statement is very much like the Variable Declaration Statement with the addition of an 'Array Size' element.

To declare an Array start with the KeyWord Array or Arrays separated by a colon then the name or label. Follow this with the number of elements in this array inside square brackets. Next you specify the default value inside parenthesis. Terminate the statement with a semicolon. You may use the comma as a list separator to declare additional arrays in a single statement.

The default value serves two purposes. First, it tells *EasyLanguage* the type of this array (Numeric, Boolean, String). Second, it instructs *EasyLanguage* to initialize the variable to this default value immediately prior to the execution of the first bar of data.

When you declare the number of elements in your array *EasyLanguage* will always create one more than you specify, the zero element. Let us look at an example.

```
Arrays: Months [12] ("") ;
if BarNumber <= 01 then begin
  Months [00] = "Illegal Month Value" ;
  Months [01] = "January" ;
  Months [02] = "February" ;
  Months [03] = "March" ;
  Months [04] = "April" ;
  Months [05] = "May" ;
  Months [06] = "June" ;
  Months [07] = "July" ;
  Months [08] = "August" ;
  Months [09] = "September" ;
  Months [10] = "October" ;
  Months [11] = "November" ;
  Months [12] = "December" ;
end ;
```

Please see listing #6.22g, Chapter 6.

The first statement in the example above declared a thirteen element (0 through 12 inclusive) array named Months of the type String.

The Decision Statement "If @(BarNumber <= 01) then" tests for the first bar of data. If the condition is TRUE then we execute the series of Assignment Statements that initialize the array with the names of the months. Notice that I am using the zero element to hold an error message.

The Array Statement is generally used in advanced programming and is rarely needed by the average trader.

The INCLUDESYSTEM STATEMENT

The syntax for the INCLUDESYSTEM DECLARATION STATEMENT consists of the KEYWORD INCLUDESYSTEM followed by a colon, the name of the system inside quotation marks followed by the list of inputs, separated by commas, if required. The statement is terminated with a semi-colon.

```
IncludeSystem: "Inputless System" ;
IncludeSystem: "My Best System", Input#1, Input#2 ;
```

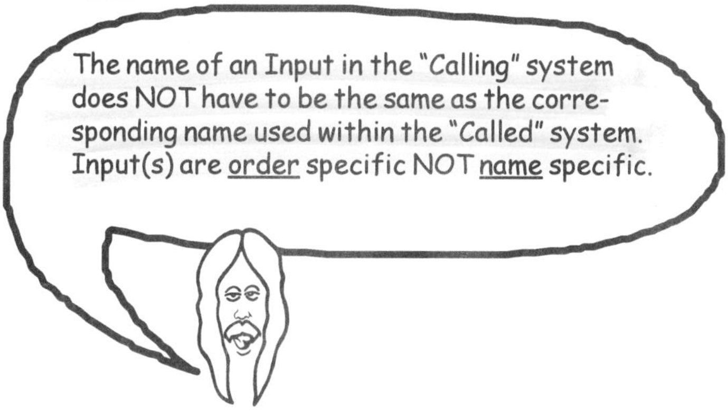

The DEFINEDLLFUNC STATEMENT

The DEFINEDLLFUNC DECLARATION STATEMENT begins with the KEYWORD DEFINEDLLFUNC separated by a colon, the fully qualified file name (drive, path, filename and extension) of the DLL (DYNAMIC LINK LIBRARY) file, the return type of the function, the name of the function and the list of input values separated by commas.

```
DefineDllFunc: "C:\UserDLL\MyFile.DLL", Int,
               "dll_Function", Float, Float ;
```

In the example above we are instructing *EasyLanguage* to find the function "DLL_FUNCTION" in the library "MYFILE" located in the "C:\UserDLL\" directory. The DLL FUNCTION in my example requires two inputs of type FLOAT (a FLOATING POINT NUMBER) and returns an INTEGER (a WHOLE NUMBER) value.

Use of the DEFINEDLLFUNC STATEMENT is not required of the casual investor. Users who purchase FUNCTION LIBRARIES that contain DLL FUNCTIONS have the right to expect proper documentation to accompany the package.

There are a number of reserved words specific to the DEFINEDLLFUNC. See Appendix A for detailed list.

Assignment Statements

Assignment Statements are used to store a value to the variables previously declared within your Analysis Technique.

EasyLanguage comes with the Numeric variables Value0 through Value99, each of which has been initialized to 0. It also includes the Boolean variables Condition0 through Condition99, each having been initialized to False.

Numeric values and expressions may be stored in any of the value variables. This is done using assignment statements in the following manner:

```
Value1 = 12 ;
Value2 = Close[03] ; { close of 3 bars ago }
Value50 = Value2 * 1.001 ;
Value99 = Value50 / Value2 ;
Value10 = Open + 10 Points ;
Value10 = Value10 - Close[01] ;
```

Notice that in the last example we modified the current value of a variable. We subtracted Close[1] from the variable Value10 (that we had previously assigned the value of Open + 10 points) and reassigned the result of that calculation again to the variable Value10. This is an example of a variable's value changing during a study.

We may even use assignment statements to assign values conditionally. If we only want to alter a value in certain cases then we can say:

```
if  Value5  >  24  Then  Value2  =  10 ;
```

In this example the value of the variable Value2 is conditional upon the value of the variable Value5 being greater than 24. If the value of Value5 were to be 24 or less, the value of the variable Value2 would retain its previous value. If no other assignment had been made to that value previously in the program, its value would remain at its initial setting of 0.

As with numeric variables, you may use assignment statements to assign values to logical variables. This is done, as in the following examples, by either assigning a value of True or False, or by making a variable's value conditional on the result of a Boolean Expression.

```
Condition1  =  TRUE ;
Condition2  = FALSE ;
Condition4  = Value5  > Value6 ;
Condition10 = Close  > Close[01] ;
```

In the last example, Condition10 will be true if this bar's close is greater than the close of one bar ago. If the current bar's close is equal to or less than the close one bar ago, Condition10's value will be false.

When an assignment statement is made, only the variable to the left of the equal sign is affected; the value or values to the right remain unchanged.

Note that there are several types of assignment statements.

SIMPLE ASSIGNMENT:

The most common type of assignement statement, we are using the VARIABLE to store the resolved expression for later reference.

```
My.Val = Close - Close [1] ;
```

ACCUMULATOR:

We want to accumulate values. Generating a report of regional sales totals would be an example in the business world. Calculating the ON BALANCE VOLUME would be an example in the trading world.

```
Sum.Val = Sum.Val + This.Val ;
```

COUNTER:

The functions CURRENTBAR and BARNUMBER are examples of invisible counters, that is the incrementing that goes on behind the scenes. Counting INSIDE BARS and OUTSIDE BARS for a report is an example we explore elsewhere in this book.

```
Count = Count + 01 ;
```

FLAG or SWITCH:

The idea of tracking the state of an indicator, toggling a trend variable and "paper trading" a methodology are examples that would use this type of ASSIGNMENT STATEMENT.

```
if RSI (Close, 14) > 75 then OverBought = TRUE
                        else OverBought = FALSE ;
InsideBar = High <= High [01] and Low >= Low [01] ;
```

Remember that the variables VALUE0 through VALUE99 and CONDITION0 through CONDITION99 are pre-declared. They are automatically initialized in *EasyLanguage* with values of zero (00) and FALSE, respectively. You may redefine these variables in the VARIABLE DECLARATION STATEMENT of your own code, if necessary.

Block Statement

Up to this point we have been discussing Simple Statements. Now for something entirely new! There is a special type statement, the Begin…End or Block Statement, that allows you to group multiple statements together into what is called a Compound Statement. The Block Statement starts with the KeyWord Begin and is terminated with the KeyWord End followed by a semicolon. The only exception to this rule is when the End precedes the KeyWord Else. The Block Statement is most commonly used as part of a Decision Statement and always with the Iterative Statements (both described below).

```
begin
  { zero or more statements }
end ; { begin statement }
```

The statements within a Block are said to be "Nested". The act of putting statements there is "Nesting." Sort of… as a matter of style, programmers are in the habit of indenting each level of nesting a couple of spaces. This indenting is cosmetic and has nothing to do with the syntax of the language.

```
begin
  begin
    { zero or more Simple Statements }
  end ; { compound statement - nesting level #2 }
  { One Block and zero or more Simple Statements }
end ; { compound statement - nesting level #1 }
```

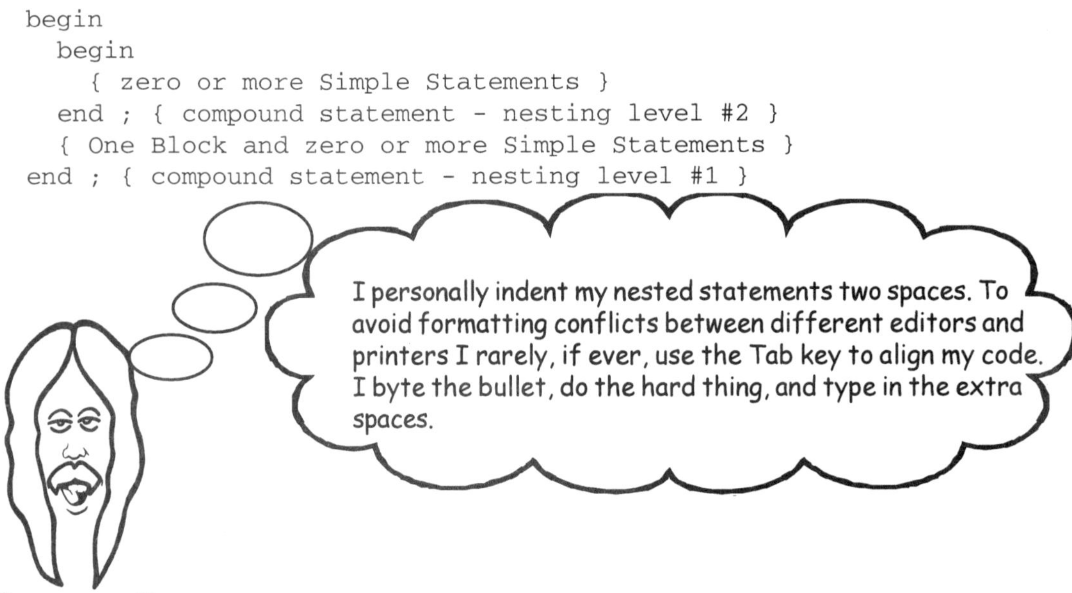

Decision Statements

If Condition1 Then Statement;

Simple If…Then Statement

EasyLanguage programs may contain simple If...Then propositions; if one specific condition occurs, then a specific action is taken. The initial condition is the proposition; the result or action is predicated on the proposition. For example:

```
if  (Close <  Close[01])
  then  Sell ("se.Main") 300 Shares at Market ;
```

In this example, "Close < Close[1]" is the proposition and "Sell at Market" is the resulting action (predicate).

The proposition may also contain multiple criteria with BOOLEAN OPERATORS joining the criteria. For example:

```
if  Close <  Close[01] and High <  High[01]  then  ... ;
```

Another example:

```
if  High <  High[01] and High[01]  > High[02]
  then  Plot1[01] (High[01] + 05 points, "MktTop") ;
```

The KEYWORD IF in an IF...THEN STATEMENT is followed by a BOOLEAN EXPRESSION. This expression frequently contains a comparison between two or more VALUES or CONDITIONS that results in a logical condition of true or false. It is possible that this expression consists of a single BOOLEAN EXPRESSION such as a CONDITION VARIABLE or a USER FUNCTION.

If that condition is true, then the action specified in the THEN clause of the statement occurs. If that condition is false, no action is taken and the program continues on the next line of code.

Complex IF...THEN...ELSE Statement

The complex IF...THEN...ELSE STATEMENT starts with the simple IF...THEN STATEMENT mentioned above and adds a statement to be executed if the condition is False. The basic structure is:

If *Condition* Then *statement#1* Else *statement#2* ;

For example:

```
if  Close  > Open
  then  Buy  ("le.Main") 300 Shares at Market
  else  Sell ("se.Main") 300 Shares at Market ;
```

If the condition is true then execute the statement following the KEYWORD THEN. If the condition is false then execute the statement following the KEYWORD ELSE.

There is never a semicolon immediately before the ELSE KEYWORD. I personally indent my nested statements two spaces. To avoid formatting conflicts between different editors and printers I rarely, if ever, use the Tab key to align my code. I byte the bullet, do the hard thing, and type in the extra spaces.

BLOCK IF STATEMENTS (BEGIN...END)

In programming you may sometimes wish to link multiple instructions to a condition that may or may not be true. That is, your proposition would encompass multiple predicates. Unlike a simple IF...THEN STATEMENT that contains a test for a condition that if true results in a single action, a BLOCK IF STATEMENT tests for a condition that if true, causes multiple actions to occur.

You may want to say, 'If this condition is true, then begin doing this list of actions.' There would be no need to do any of the actions if the original condition were false. The alternative would be to place a simple IF...THEN statement before each statement in the list.

Here's an example of a BLOCK IF STATEMENT (BEGIN...END):

```
Value1   = High [01] ;
Value2   =  Low [01] ;
if  Close > Close[01]
Then Begin
  Value1   = High ;
  Value2   =  Low ;
End ;
```

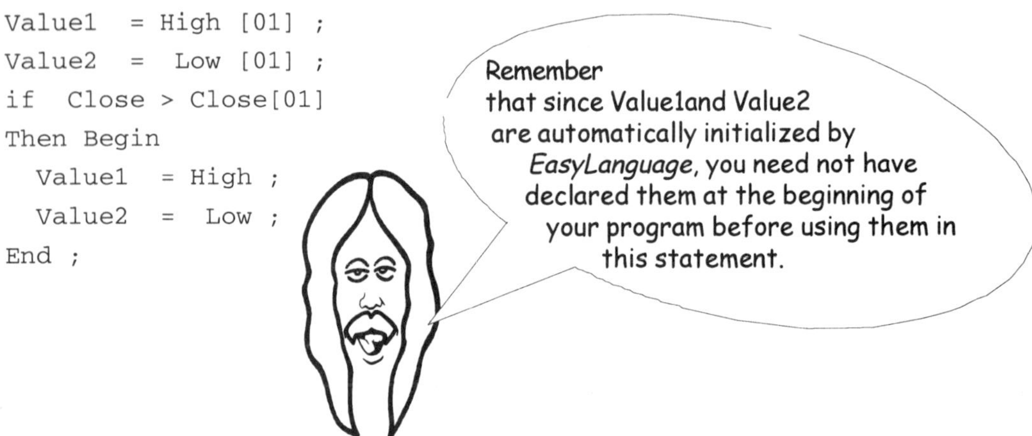

There are three classes of statements, SIMPLE, COMPOUND and COMPLEX, in most programming languages. So far we have only introduced the SIMPLE STATEMENT. Using the BEGIN..END KEYWORDS creates a COMPLEX STATEMENT which starts with the word BEGIN, includes all subsequent statements and is terminated with the END KEYWORD.

Here's an example of a BLOCK IF STATEMENT using custom variables which would have had to be initialized in a variable declaration statement at the top of the program prior to assigning them new values and using them in the following BLOCK IF STATEMENT.

```
PctMove    = Close / Close[01] ;
MoveUp     = FALSE ;
BuySignal = FALSE ;
if  PctMove >=  1.01  Then Begin
  MoveUp      =  TRUE ;
  BuySignal   =  TRUE ;
end ;
```

In a BLOCK IF...THEN STATEMENT, you first write the KEYWORD IF then your conditional expression followed by the KEYWORD THEN followed by the KEYWORD BEGIN. BEGIN alerts *EasyLanguage* that it is about to receive a list of (zero or more) actions to perform if the conditional proposition is true. This is followed by the list of actions (predicates) terminated by the KEYWORD END.

You must tell *EasyLanguage* when your list of actions is complete. This is done by entering an END at the bottom of your list of statements. When *EasyLanguage* executes your END statement it 'ends' consideration of your original conditional expression. That is, it ceases to use the criteria from the BLOCK IF...THEN STATEMENT when running the rest of your program.

Here's a more complicated example:

```
if  High  > High [01]  then begin
  Condition1  =  Low  >  Low[01] and Close  > Close[01] ;
  Condition2  = Open[01] > Open[02] ;
  if  Condition1 and Condition2
    then Buy  ("le#1") 300 Shares at Market ;
end ;
```

> Note in all these examples that each complete statement is always followed by a semicolon, including the END statement. The KEYWORD BEGIN is never followed by a semicolon because it is not a complete statement. The two RESERVED WORDS BEGIN and END act together to define a single compound statement.

Similarly, never follow the KEYWORD THEN with a semicolon since it is not a complete statement. The semicolon would terminate the IF...THEN STATEMENT.

Though we highly recommend indenting any nested statements do not be fooled into believing that the act of indenting itself will force a compound statement.

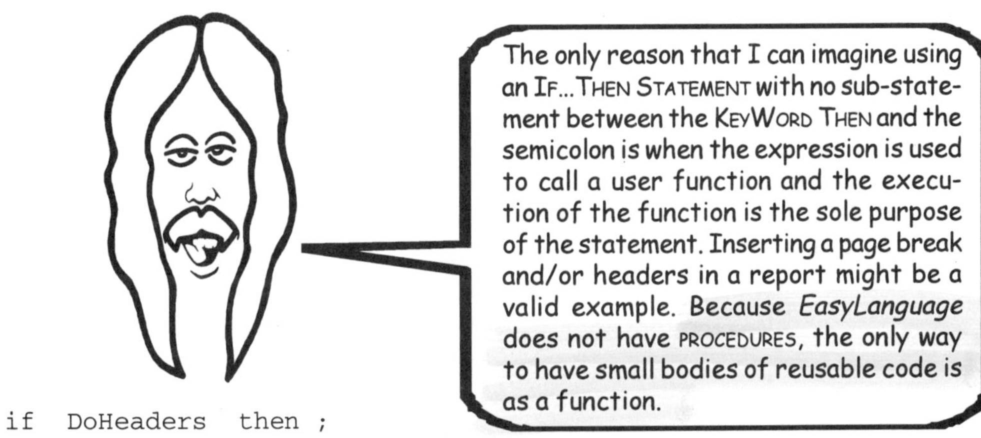


```
if  DoHeaders  then ;
```

In the example above PageBreak is a USER FUNCTION of type BOOLEAN that checks the value of @CURRENTBAR and prints report headers to the Print Log Window every twenty bars. An equivalent statement would be :

```
Condition1 = DoHeaders ;
```

However, the IF STATEMENT is very fast to execute and an ASSIGNMENT STATEMENT generates more code. Unless you need to reference the return value (Condition1) then the first example is marginally more efficient.

If the above explanation has left you 'quaking in you sandals' then test the following statement.

```
if  (Close[00] <  Open[00]) and (High[00]  > High[01])  then ;
  Print (Date:6:0, "Is this a conditional statement?") ;
```

What have we learned? If you tested the code above, then you discovered that it is NOT a conditional statement at all. The PRINT STATEMENT is executed on each and every bar of data. The indenting makes it look like it is part of the IF STATEMENT but the semicolon following the KEYWORD THEN terminated the IF...THEN STATEMENT.

Block IF...THEN...ELSE Statements

In the preceding types of statements we had actions that were only taken if the original condition was true. But, there are times when you want to say, "If a condition is true, then do this. However, if the condition is not true, then do something else." This is accomplished in *EasyLanguage* by using BLOCK IF...THEN...ELSE STATEMENTS. Here's an example:

```
if  High  > High[01]  then begin
  Value1  = Open [00] ;
  Value2  = Close[00] ;
end  { Note that there is no semicolon before the else }
else begin
  Value1 = Open [1] ;
  Value2 = Close[1] ;
end ;
```

Let me reiterate that there is no semicolon after the first END in a block IF...THEN...ELSE STATEMENT because the statement is not complete until you state the action to happen if the original condition is false (ELSE clause).

Here's the outline for a block IF...THEN...ELSE STATEMENT:

```
if  expression  then begin
  {statement#1} ;
  {statement#2} ; { if expression is  TRUE }
  {statement#3} ;
end
else begin
  {statement#4} ;
  {statement#5} ; { if expression is FALSE }
  {statement#6} ;
end ;
```

NESTED IF...THEN STATEMENTS

Just as BLOCK IF...THEN STATEMENTS are used when possible multiple actions are based on one condition, NESTED IF...THEN STATEMENTS are used when multiple propositions must be satisfied before a choice of actions is taken. NESTED IF...THEN STATEMENTS allow you to save calculation time by only executing code when the preceeding expression is true. Here's an example:

```
if  Close  > Close[01]  then begin
{*
 * We only need to test the open
 * if the close is greater than the close of yesterday
 *}
  if  Open  > Open[01]
    then  Buy  ("le.#1") 300 Shares at Market
    else  Sell ("se.#1") 100 Shares at Market ;
end ;
```

In the above example, if the first condition (Close > Close[1]) is false, no further action is taken. If, however, the first condition is true, **TradeStation** obeys the THEN BEGIN command and evaluates the second NESTED IF...THEN STATEMENTS. If that statement is true *EasyLanguage* executes the THEN part of that statement. If the second NESTED IF...THEN STATEMENTS returns a false value, *EasyLanguage* moves on to the ELSE portion of the NESTED STATEMENT and takes that action.

After negotiating the choices within the NESTED IF...THEN STATEMENTS and taking the appropriate action, *EasyLanguage* looks for the END STATEMENT that closes out that block. Here's another example:

```
if  High  > High[01]  then begin
  if  High / High[01]  >  1.02
    then  Buy  ("le.#1") 500 Shares at Market
    else  Buy  ("le.#2") 100 Shares at Market ;
end ;
```

Nesting allows you to imbed an IF...THEN...ELSE statement within another IF...THEN STATEMENT.

Here's the outline for a NESTED IF...THEN STATEMENT:

```
if ... then begin
  if ...
    then ...
    else ... ;
end ;
```

IF Condition1 THEN statement #1 ELSE statement #2 ;

IF Condition1 THEN BEGIN statement #1; statement #2 ; END ELSE BEGIN statement #3; statement #4 ; END ;

ITERATIVE STATEMENTS

EasyLanguage contains two types of ITERATIVE (LOOP) STATEMENTS, the FOR LOOP

```
for  VarName  = StartVal to StopVal  begin
  { body of loop goes here... }
end ;
or
for  VarName  = HiVal DownTo LoVal  begin
  { body of loop goes here... }
end ;
```

and the WHILE LOOP.

```
while  (Loop <= MaxBarsBack) and (Expression  =  TRUE)  begin
  { body of loop goes here... }
end ;
```

The FOR LOOP is used when there is a predetermined number of iterations to be processed. Counting the inside bars within the ten most recent bars is an example of knowing the number of iterations in advance.

```
Inputs: MinVal   (00),         MaxVal  (10),
        Inside   (High[00] <  High[01] and Low [00]  > Low [01]) ;
Vars  : Loop     (00),         Count   (00),        Done (FALSE) ;
{
  Example using the for loop}
Count  = 00 ; { start off with zero inside bars }
for  Loop = MinVal to MaxVal  begin
  Print (Loop:6:0, Inside[Loop]:6) ;
  if  Inside[Loop]
    then  Count  = Count + 01 ; { increment counter }
end ; { for loop }
if  (Count  >  00)
  then  Print ("I found ", Count:1:0,  " Inside Bars.")
  else  Print ("No inside bars found within ",
                MaxVal:1:0,  " bars.") ;
```

The FOR LOOP can increment the LOOP VARIABLE using the KEYWORD TO or decrement the LOOP VARIABLE using the KEYWORD DOWNTO. Always increment/decrement 1(one).

The WHILE LOOP is used when there is a variable, or indeterminate, number of iterations to be processed. If I wanted to know the bar number of the most recent INSIDEBAR then the number of iterations is indeterminate.

```
{
  Example using the while loop
}
Loop  = MinVal ;
Done  =  FALSE ;
while  Loop <= MaxVal and Done  = FALSE  begin
  if  Inside [Loop]
    then  Done  = ' TRUE
    else  loop  = loop + 01 ;
end ; { while loop }
if  Done
  then  Print ("Most recent Inside Bar was ",
               Loop:1:0, " bars ago.")
  else  Print ("No inside bar found within ",
               MaxVal:1:0, " bars.") ;
```

Note that a BLOCK STATEMENT (BEGIN...END) must always follow an ITERATIVE STATEMENT.

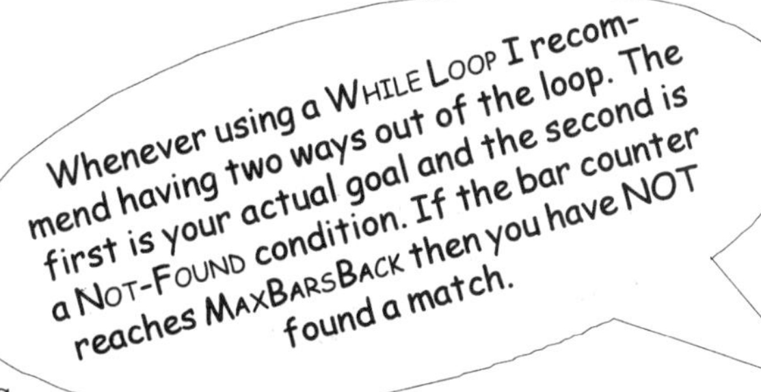

OUTPUT STATEMENTS

Plot Statement

The PLOT STATEMENT is used exclusively in Studies (INDICATOR, PAINTBAR and SHOWME) to graphically display your Analysis Techniques. In the classical application, the PLOT STATEMENT is used for Indicators and Oscillators. **Omega Research** has added additional functionality to include *PaintBar* and *ShowMe* studies. A Study must contain at least one PLOT STATEMENT. Four plots (PLOT1, PLOT2, PLOT3 and PLOT4) are available.

The PLOT STATEMENT consists of the KEYWORD PLOT1 followed by the left parenthesis, the numeric expression to be displayed, a comma, a string literal that labels this plot in the Charting Application, the right parenthesis and a statement terminator. Examples follow:

```
Plot1 ( Open, " Open") ; {  Left Tick }
Plot2 ( High, " High") ; {  Bar  High }
Plot3 (  Low, " Low ") ; {  Bar   Low }
Plot4 (Close, "Close") ; { Right Tick }
```

The BarHigh and BarLow styles must be used in tandem, as a pair, complimentary. The color and weight must be set the same. The order and values of the BarHigh and BarLow plots may be interchanged.

Print Statement

The Print Statement consists of the KeyWord Print followed by a set of parenthesis that surround the list of zero or more field(s) to be displayed. Output is sent to the Print Log Window.

```
if  BarNumber <= 01 then begin
  Print ("") ;
  Print ("Report : '", App.Name, "'  Run Date ",
         CurrentDate:8:0, CurrentTime:5:0) ;
  Print ("——————————————") ;
end ;
Print (Date:8:0, Time:5:0,
       "  V1 = ", Value1:4:4, ",  Cond01 = ", Condition1:6) ;
```

Remember that the Print Log Window fills from the bottom up. You must scroll down to find the most recent information.

Output may be directed to a printer by inserting the KeyWord Printer after the left parenthesis and before the first item in the parameter list. An example follows.

```
Print (Printer, "Output will go to the default print device.") ;
```

Output sent to the printer will be stored in a Print Buffer that may be emptied periodically. It is possible to get strange results, especially if another program uses the printer while your Analysis Technique is active.

Output may be directed to a disk file by inserting the KEYWORD FILE and the fully qualified filename (drive, path, filename and extension) surrounded by quotes and parenthesis after the left parenthesis and before the first item in the parameter list. An example follows.

```
Print (File ("C:\Temp\MyFile.TXT"), "Output Text Goes Here") ;
```

As you can see in the above examples the PRINT STATEMENT may contain NUMERIC, BOOLEAN and STRING values. The values you print can be constants, variables or functions. The PRINT STATEMENT is most commonly used for debugging your *EasyLanguage* code but I frequently use it to generate custom reports. More extensive examples may be found later in this book.

The Print Log Window is not available in any version of **SuperCharts**.

In **TradeStation 5.0** the Print Log has been renamed the Message Log and behaves quite differently than in earlier versions.

TEXT

The @TEXT FUNCTION is a special case similar to the PRINT STATEMENT. Since it is a function you must "use" the return value in some manner. The @TEXT FUNCTION will generally be used in an ASSIGNMENT STATEMENT to a STRING VARIABLE. Another common use will be in the @FILEAPPEND FUNCTION. Examples are given below.

```
Vars   : fName ("C:\Temp\MyFile.TXT"),
         MyStr ("") ;
MyStr = Text (Date:8:0, ", ", Time:5:0, ", ") ;
FileAppend (fName, MyStr) ;
FileAppend (fName, Text (Open, ", ", High, ", ",
                          Low, ", ", Close) + NewLine) ;
```

EXPERTCOMMENTARY

The EXPERTCOMMENTARY STATEMENT consists of the KEYWORD COMMENTARY or COMMENTARYCL followed by a list of zero or more items inside by parenthesis. An example follows. More examples may be found in later sections.

```
Inputs: FastLen (07), SlowLen (14) ;
Vars  : FastMA  (00), SlowMA (00), st ("") ;
FastMA = Average (Close, FastLen) ;
```

```
SlowMA = Average (Close, SlowLen) ;
if  CheckCommentary  then begin
  if  FastMA  > SlowMA  then  st = "above" else st = "below" ;
  CommentaryCL ("") ; { insert a blank line }
  CommentaryCL ("The Fast Moving Average (", FastMA, ") is ", st,
               " the Slow Moving Average (", SlowMA, ").") ;
end ;
```

Plot

The KeyWord Plot(1…4) can also be used as a Function. It returns the numeric value of the plot from the most recent bar on which the plot was executed. Notice that if you test the value before executing the Plot Statement then it will hold the value from the previous bar.

```
Inputs: FastLen (07), SlowLen (14) ;
Vars  : FastMA  (00), SlowMA  (00),
        hi.Bars (00), LowBars (00) ;
FastMA = Average (Close, FastLen) ;
SlowMA = Average (Close, SlowLen) ;
Plot1 (FastMA, "FastMA") ;
Plot2 (SlowMA, "SlowMA") ;
if  FastMA  > SlowMA and Close  > Plot1 then HiBars = HiBars + 01
;
if  FastMA <  SlowMA and Close <  Plot1 then LoBars = LoBars +
01;
```

EasyLanguage is executed from the top down, from the first line of code to the last line of code. The exception to this rule is calling a Series Function. A Series Function will be executed immediately prior to the first line of your Analysis Technique. When the function call is executed in the body of your code the value of the function is substituted for the actual function call. If the Series Function is called several times within the body of your code the calculation is only executed once. This is different from a Simple Function which is executed each and every time you call the function.

Systems and Signals

Omega uses the term **System** to describe a set of trading rules that can generate entry and exit orders. This methodology can vary from simple to very complex. There are many sources of assistance in creating trading systems. My purpose here is to explain the proper syntax and recommend style. I am not pretending that any examples here are profitable trading systems.

A **Signal** is a type of statement available only within a System that generates Entry and/or Exit Orders. Strictly speaking, the Signal itself consists of the KeyWord Buy, Sell, ExitLong or ExitShort followed by an optional Signal Name which would be surrounded by quotation marks and parenthesis. Optionally this may be followed by a numeric value (Constant, Input, Function or Variable) and the KeyWord Contract(s) or Share(s). The Order Type (Close, Market, Stop and Limit) should appear last. Stop and Limit orders require you specify the target price. Newer versions of *EasyLanguage* may allow you to omit the type of order but you will see no examples of that syntax here.

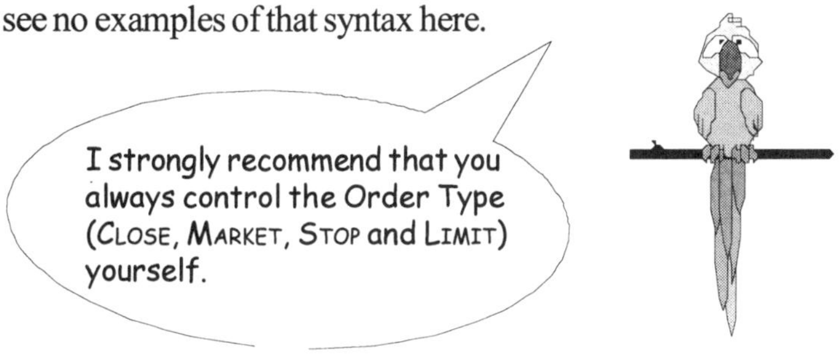

I strongly recommend that you always control the Order Type (Close, Market, Stop and Limit) yourself.

Speaking more generically, we use the term Signal to include the Order statement mentioned above, the logical decision(s) that trigger the order and the calculations that pertain to that order.

The Signal statement itself contains a single order but it may be considered to include the preliminary code that set up the individual signal itself. A signal may consist of a single condition or series of conditions that, when true, instruct *EasyLanguage* to place an order. Signals may be used to enter or exit a market. They may also be used to reverse existing positions.

A System is the group of one or more signals, along with all necessary support code, that creates the entire trading methodology. In *EasyLanguage*, these programs are logical sequences of statements written in the appropriate order and syntax to produce the desired result.

A System can be created that contains absolutely no Signals. I do this frequently to create custom reports in an IncludeSystem. Examples of this can be found in the code listings later in the book. {6.12 and 6.13}

Following are examples of simple signals:

```
Buy  ("le.Main#0") on the close ;
Sell ("se.Main#0") at Market ;
Buy  ("le.Entry#0") 10 contracts at Market ;
```

```
Sell ("se.Entry#0") 300 Shares at Market ;

ExitLong  ("lx.Fail") 10 Contracts Total
  from Entry ("le.Main#0")
  at Lowest (Low, 3) stop ;
```

Following are examples of more complex signals:

```
if  High  > High[01] * 1.001

  then  Buy  ("le.Main#1") on the Close ;

if  Close - Value3  > 0.45  Then  Sell ("se.Main#1") at Market ;

if  Close[1] > Open [1] * 1.005
  then  Buy  ("le.Entry#1") 10 Contracts at Market ;

if  Condition2  then  Sell ("se.Entry#1") 300 Shares at Market ;
```

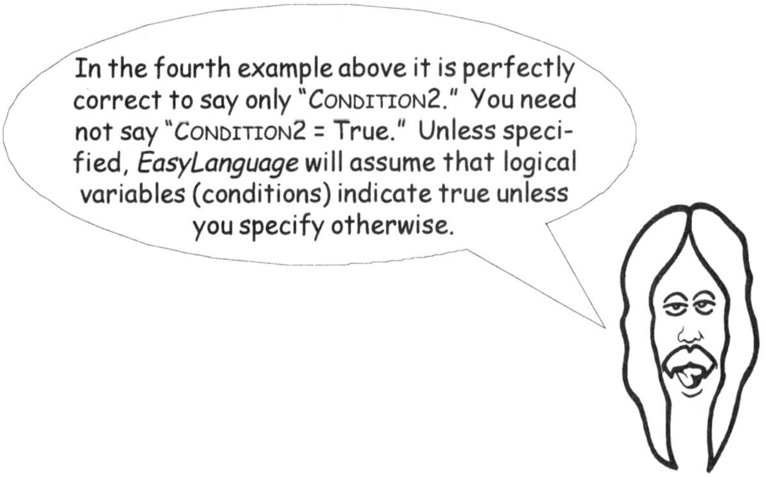

In the fourth example above it is perfectly correct to say only "CONDITION2." You need not say "CONDITION2 = True." Unless specified, *EasyLanguage* will assume that logical variables (conditions) indicate true unless you specify otherwise.

Functions

A **FUNCTION** is a term or word in the language that returns a single value. *EasyLanguage* comes with a great number of FUNCTIONS PRE-DEFINED and also allows the user to create their own CUSTOM FUNCTIONS.

Every FUNCTION has a defined DATA TYPE. A FUNCTION may be used on the right side of an Assignment Statement assuming the expression matches the DATA TYPE of the receiving VARIABLE.

Any FUNCTION in *EasyLanguage* may be preceded by the "at sign" (@). This is a legacy from **System Writer 1.0** and can be very useful. First, you can determine if a term is a function by inserting the at sign before the term and then verifying the code. Second, it can make your code more readable by visually differentiating FUNCTIONS from INPUTS and VARIABLES.

BUILT-IN FUNCTIONS

The term BUILT-IN FUNCTION refers any member of the library of *EasyLanguage* Functions marked READONLY in the *PowerEditor*. Many well known oscillators and indicators used by ers are supplied in this library. The entire list of BUILT-IN FUNCTIONS is found in Section 3.

USER FUNCTIONS

The term USER FUNCTION refers to the library of *EasyLanguage* Functions, exclusive of the BUILT-IN FUNCTIONS. Some of the User Functions that I feel are important are listed in Section 3. I feel they are too numerous to be listed in their entirety.

DRAWING TOOLS

There are two distinct types of DRAWING TOOL FUNCTIONS, TEXT and TRENDLINE. In brief, each category has a set of functions to CREATE, MODIFY, INTERROGATE and ERASE drawing objects.

See the example on SWINGS for examples of using these functions to access the DRAWING TOOLS.

COMMENT STATEMENT

A COMMENT, or remark, consists of the left comment brace with any and all text up top and including the next right comment brace in your code. The COMMENT, including any code it includes, is not a statement according to the **SYNTAX** of *EasyLanguage* since it does NOT require the statement terminator. It causes no action to take place at runtime. It adds no code to the TOKEN FILE (your executable code).

Commenting your program means including comments within the program that explain what is happening at that particular point in the program. This is also referred to as documenting your program. The purpose of commenting your program is to make the source code more understandable and to make it easier to locate the specific statements or commands that control specific actions. Again, remember that you may be reading or modifying a program long after it was written. If the program is well documented, it will be much easier for you to tell what is intended to happen at each juncture in the program.

To facilitate easy, readable comments within your programs, *EasyLanguage* allows you to set aside words, sentences, even paragraphs within comment braces ({ }). These are also called French or Curly Braces and are the uppercase characters on the square bracket keys on your keyboard, immediately to the right of the "P" key. Any verbiage within comment braces is completely ignored by *EasyLanguage* and is used only to make notes to yourself and your descendants.

You begin a comment in *EasyLanguage* by typing an open comment brace, "}" symbol. You end a comment by typing a close comment brace, "}" symbol. The comment itself does not have to be on the same line as the comment brace. Below are several examples of comments:

```
{* this is a comment *}
{*
 *  So is this.
 *}
```

```
{*This is a program to identify buy and sell signals
in order to corner the silver market.*}

{*
 *  Moving Average Analysis
 *  written by Samuel K. Tennis
 *  October 12, 1994.
 *}
```

Comments may also contain other comments. This is referred to as nesting comments. Here is an example of nesting comments:

```
{**Fourscore and seven years ago {* that's 87 years *}
 our forefathers ...**}
```

Points as Used in Trading

EasyLanguage includes functions that allow you to manipulate and convert between prices, points and dollars without the programmer knowing the underlying security. These functions allow you to easily convert Dollars to Points and Points to Dollars.

Summary

We have thoroughly explored the world of DECLARATION STATEMENTS. Use the section of Program Listings for more sophisticated examples.

There are several types of ASSIGNMENT STATEMENTS (COUNTER, ACCUMULATOR, FLAG OR SWITCH).

BLOCK STATEMENTS allow you to group multiple statements together logically and use them in your program logic.

DECISION STATEMENTS allow you to build the decision trees necessary for more complex methodologies.

Many *EasyLanguage* terms and concepts cross boundaries. The PLOT STATEMENT can be used as both a "FUNCTION" and an "OUTPUT" statement. In other cases, *EasyLanguage* may define it as a function but it acts like a constant. @MAXBARSBACK, @SESS1STARTTIME, @COMMODITYNUMBER and @DATACOMPRESSION are examples of this duality.

If, instead of using VALUE0...VALUE99 or CONDITION0...CONDITION99, you decide to use more descriptive variable names of your choosing, such as MYPRICE or BUYNOW, you will need to declare these variables using a VARIABLE DECLARATION STATEMENT near the beginning of your program.

The part of the program, usually near the top, where you group the DECLARATION STATEMENTS becomes known as the VARIABLE DECLARATION AREA.

After declaring your variables and initializing them you may assign your values.

```
MyPercent = 0.15 ;
MyMultiple = Close[1] * 1.002 ;
ClosedAbove = Close[1] > Close ;
ClosedUpSharp = Close[1] >= Open[1] * 1.05 ;
```

Section 3:
Functions, Procedures
and
Programming Tips

OBJECTIVES

After reading this section you will have been briefly exposed to each BUILT-IN FUNCTION available within *EasyLanguage*. I suggest that you read through this list frequently, possibly as often as every day to three. What you will frequently find is that one function in particular will seem to leap off the page at you—start flashing in neon. You were lying in bed last night, trying not to awaken your spouse with the thrashing, your cold sweat of dread, the fear that you would have to write a function from scratch—assuming that you prove up to the (daunting) task. Now you realize that **Omega** has already done the work for you! Oh, what a relief it is!

FUNCTIONS

Data Information

DATA INFORMATION FUNCTIONS allow you access to the specific characteristics of the data to which an analysis technique is applied. For example, you might want your code to use TICKS (UPTICKS + DOWNTICKS) on an intraday chart but VOLUME on a daily or weekly chart. For this you would use the @DATACOMPRESSION FUNCTION.

BARINTERVAL

BIGPOINTVALUE

BOXSIZE

CommodityNumber

CurrentBar

DailyLimit

DataCompression

DataInUnion

DeliveryMonth

DeliveryYear

HistFundExists

LastCalcJDate

LastCalcMMTime

MaxBarsBack

MinMove

PointValue

PriceScale

RevSize

Sess1EndTime

Sess1FirstBarTime

Sess1StartTime

Sess2EndTime

Sess2FirstBarTime

Sess2StartTime

SnapFundExists

UnionSess1EndTime

UnionSess1FirstBar

UnionSess1StartTime

UnionSess2EndTime

UnionSess2FirstBar

UnionSess2StartTime

Date and Time

The DATE & TIME FUNCTIONS are used frequently in STUDIES, SYSTEMS and other FUNCTIONS. It can be important to know the time and date on which an event occurred. It can be equally important to ensure that activities occur only at specific dates and/or times. Seasonality Testing and the First HOUR BREAKOUT SYSTEM are well known examples that take advantage of these functions. Use of the DATE & TIME FUNCTIONS enable you to do this and more!

Unlike other functions, @DAYOFWEEK, @MONTH and @YEAR require that you put a data series modifier inside the parenthesis immediately after the DATE INPUT.BLOCKNUMBER

CurrentDate

CurrentTime

DateToJulian

DayOfMonth

DayOfWeek

JulianToDate

Month

PRODUCT

YEAR

Drawing Objects

The functions in the DRAWING OBJECTS category allow you to create, modify, query and remove TEXT and TRENDLINE objects on the chart. They also enable you to access and manipulate existing TEXT and TRENDLINE objects. These functions are not available from the *QuickEditor.*

The note below comes directly from the **TradeStation 4.0** help file. I guess the point is that if you do not query the return value then why ask for it?

When using TRENDLINE FUNCTIONS (they begin with TL_), keep in mind that some return a value and some do not. You can have all of them return values if you want the *PowerEditor* to return an error code if and when the function is not successful. However, having the function return a value when not necessary will slow down the performance of your function. GETBACKGROUNDCOLOR TEXT_DELETE

TEXT_GETDATE

TEXT_GETCOLOR

TEXT_GETFIRST

TEXT_GETHSTYLE

TEXT_GETNEXT

TEXT_GETSTRING

TEXT_GETTIME

TEXT_GETVALUE

TEXT_GETVSTYLE

TEXT_NEW

TEXT_SETCOLOR

Text_SetLocation

Text_SetString

Text_SetStyle

TL_Delete

TL_GetAlert

TL_GetBeginDate

TL_GetBeginTime

TL_GetBeginVal

TL_GetColor

TL_GetEndDate

TL_GetEndTime

TL_GetEndVal

TL_GetExtLeft

TL_GetExtRight

TL_GetFirst

TL_GetNext

TL_GetSize

TL_GetStyle

TL_GetValue

TL_New

TL_SetAlert

TL_SetBegin

TL_SetColor

TL_SetEnd

TL_SetExtLeft

TL_SetExtRight

TL_SetSize

TL_SetStyle

EasyLanguage Functions

The *EasyLanguage* or Built-In Functions, are written in **Omega Research's** *EasyLanguage* but are Read-Only, meaning you can open them and read the code but you can NOT change them. There is only one list of *EasyLanguage* functions in the *PowerEditor* that combines User and Built-In Functions into a single list. You can identify the Built-In Functions by the capital R (for Read-Only) by the name.

If you want to modify a Built-In Function, you can copy the code into the clipboard, create a new User Function with a similar name and paste the code from the clipboard into the new function. Change the name of the function inside the code (the verifier will point it out to you) and you are ready to make changes.

AccumDist

AccumSwingIndex

ADX

ADXCustom

ADXR

ADXRCustom

Average (Simple and Series)

AvgPrice

AvgTrueRange

BarNumber

BearishDivergence

BollingerBand

BullishDivergence

BullishEngulfing

Call

CCI

ChaikinOsc

CloseD

CloseM

CloseW

Correlation

CSI

Cum

DMI

DMICustom

DMIMinus

DMIMinusCustom

DMIPlus

DMIPlusCustom

EaseOfMovement

FastD

FastDCustom

FastHighestBar (EasyLanguage Internal)

FastK

FastKCustom

FastLowestBar (EasyLanguage Internal)

HighD

Highest (Simple and Series)

HighestBar (Simple and Series)

HighM

HighW

HPI

IFF

LinearRegAngle (Simple and Series)

LinearRegSlope (Simple and Series)

LinearRegValue (Simple and Series)

LowD

Lowest (Simple and Series)

LowestBar (Simple and Series)

LowM

LowW

LWAccDis

MACD

MassIndex

MedianPrice

MidPoint

MinutesToTime

Momentum

MoneyFlow

MRO "Most Recent Occurance"

NthHighest

NthHighestBar

NthLowest

NthLowestBar

OBV

OpenD

OpenM

OpenW

Parabolic

PercentR

PriceVolTrend

Put

Range

RateOfChange

RSI

SlowD

SlowDCustom

SlowK

SlowKCustom

SmoothedAverage

StdDev

Summation (Simple and Series)

SwingHigh

SwingHighBar

SwingIndex

SwingLow

SwingLowBar

TimeSeriesForecast

TimeToMinutes

TLAngle

TLSlope

TLValue

TrueHigh

TrueLow

TrueRange

TrueRangeCustom

TypicalPrice

UltimateOsc

Volatility

VolumeOsc

VolumeROC

WAverage

WeightedClose (Simple and Series)

XAverage

File Writing

The File Writing functions are available only in the **TradeStation** *PowerEditor* and enable you to create and delete text files. I have a set of File Writing tools that provide greater functionality than provided here.

FileAppend

FileDelete

Fundamental (Historical) Data

The 12 functions within the Fundamental (Historical) Data category use three fundamental fields that may be supplied by your daily data vendor, along with the price information. The fields provide not just fundamental data for a specific point in time, but historically over a period of time. Specifically, these functions are computed use the EARNINGS-PER-SHARE (EPS), STOCK SPLIT (SPLITVALUE), and DIVIDEND (DIVIDEND) FIELDS.

Important: These functions calculate their values based on the fundamental data provided by **DialData** that you have downloaded using the **Omega** *Downloader*. Therefore, these functions are for use **only** when you are applying them to a chart containing daily data stored in **Omega** *Downloader* format and downloaded from **DialData**.

Omega provided the paragraph below in their on-line help. I assume it means that fundamental information is available for the primary data series (DATA1) **only**.

> *"The 12 functions give you the ability to perform fundamental analysis in order to determine if your stock is fairly priced, undervalued or overvalued when compared to the market. The values the functions return are true for the current price series, that is, for the data you have plotted in the chart to which you are applying the function."*

DIVIDEND

DIVIDENDCOUNT

DIVIDENDDATE

DIVIDENDTIME

EPS

EPSCOUNT

EPSDATE

EPSTIME

STOCKSPLIT

STOCKSPLITCOUNT

STOCKSPLITDATE

STOCKSPLITTIME

FUNDAMENTAL (SNAPSHOT) DATA

The functions within the FUNDAMENTAL (SNAPSHOT) DATA category use the FUNDAMENTAL DATA that may be supplied by your data vendor along with the price data for a symbol. These functions give you the ability to perform fundamental analysis on the symbol in order to see how your symbol is doing in relation to the rest of the market as a whole. These functions provide you with the FUNDAMENTAL DATA at a specific point in time, as opposed to historically.

The functions are for use only when you are applying them to a chart based on daily data downloaded from **DialData** or **Telescan** in **Omega** *Downloader* format. If you use real-time or delayed data, but want to work with fundamental data, you should consider having an account with **DialData** and downloading nightly using the **Omega** *Downloader.*

These functions return the corresponding value provided by the data vendor.

BETA

BETA_DOWN

BETA_UP

BOOK_VAL_PER_SHARE

CURRENT_RATIO

EPS_PCHNG-Y-AGO

EPS_PCHNG-YTD

FREECSHFLWPERSHARE

GR_RATE_P_EPS

G_RATE_EPS_NY

G_RATE_NT_IN_NY

G_RATE_P_NET_INC

INST_PERCENT_HELD

NET_PROFIT_MARGIN

QUICK_RATIO

RET_ON_AVG_EQUITY

TtlDbt_By_NetAssts

Last_Split_Date

Last_Split_Fact

Dividend_Yield

Price_To_Book

SGA_Exp_By_NetSales

Math and Trig

The functions in the Math & Trig category each perform common yet valuable mathematical and trigonometric calculations. Review this list carefully as they are important building blocks you will use frequently.

AbsValue

ArcTangent

AvgList

Ceiling

Cosine

CoTangent

ExpValue

Floor

FracPortion

IntPortion

Log

MaxList

MaxList2

MinList

MinList2

Mod

Neg

NthMaxList

NthMinList

Pos

Power

Round

Sign

Sine

Square

SquareRoot

SumList

Tangent

Multimedia

The functions in the MULTIMEDIA category are new in **TradeStation 4.0**. They enable you to work with movie (.AVI format) and audio (.WAV format) files.

To use movies in your alerts and commentary, you assign up to 15 movie files to a movie chain. The movie files in the movie chain will be played back seamlessly.

Audio alerts are possible using the PLAYSOUND FUNCTION. An example is provided in the "Ask

Mr. *EasyLanguage*" and "*EasyLanguage* Spoken Here" sections.

MakeNewMovieRef

AddToMovieChain

GetCDROMDrive

PlayMovieChain

PlaySound

Pager

The two functions in the Pager category allow you to send text to an alphanumeric string pager. These functions are only available when you enable **TradeStation's** optional pager notification service.

These functions can only be accessed from the **PowerEditor**.

Pager_DefaultName

Pager_Send

Performance Information

Performance Information functions provide information about the overall performance of a trading system. These functions, like the Position Information functions, are not practical for use in any analysis technique other than trading systems. They return the information that is normally viewed in your charting applications *System Report*. They refer to trades only, not to positions.

A trade is a position that is completely liquidated (closed out). All numbers are based on closed out trades only and are updated after the end of the closed out trade.

The listing of each Performance Information function includes a brief description of the purpose of the function, the correct syntax, and the corresponding formula.

AvgBarsLosTrade

AvgBarsWinTrade

GrossLoss

GrossProfit

LargestLosTrade

LargestWinTrade

MaxConsecLosers

MaxConsecWinners

MaxContractsHeld

MaxIDDrawdown

NetProfit

NumLosTrades

NumWinTrades

PercentProfit

TotalBarsLosTrades

TotalBarsWinTrades

TotalTrades

Position Information

The Position Information Functions provide information about a specific position. A position is defined as one or more entries into a trade. A position can be made up of multiple trades, such as scaling in or out. Your position changes when you go:

Long to Short	(Sell)
Long to Flat	(ExitLong)
Short to Flat	(ExitShort)
Short to Long	(Buy)
Flat to Long	(Buy)

FLAT TO SHORT (SELL)

A position may consist of any number of individual entries and exits. If there is no position, all functions return zero (0). If you pass a 3 as PosNumAgo, but have only had two positions, all of these functions will return zero. All functions are based on and are current as of the Close of the previous bar.

These functions cannot use any data series but Data1. All trades in *EasyLanguage* are executed solely on the primary data series. To trade a spread you MUST run the system on two separate charts.

In the Position Information functions, entry refers to the first entry in a position and exit refers to the exit that closed out your position. You can never have a non-zero value for ExitDate, ExitTime or ExitPrice for the current (PosNumAgo = 0) position. The position number ago (PosNumAgo) logic is the same.

When using these functions, if PosNumAgo is used it must be a number between 0 and 10, and equivalent to the number of positions ago (0 = current Open position; 10 = 10 previous positions ago). The use of PosNumAgo is optional; the default is 0.

The exceptions are @AvgEntryPrice, @CurrentContracts, and @CurrentEntries, which do not have an input because they **always** refer to the current Open Position.

In @ExitDate, @ExitPrice and @ExitTime, PosNumAgo should be a number between 1 and 10. I believe we can all agree that the exit of the current position is undefined.

AvgEntryPrice

BarsSinceEntry

BarsSinceExit

CurrentContracts

CurrentEntries

EntryDate

EntryPrice

EntryTime

MarketPosition

MaxContracts

MaxEntries

MaxPositionLoss

MaxPositionProfit

OpenPositionProfit

PositionProfit

String Related

The String Related (character) functions are new in **TradeStation 4.0** along with the String variable type. The functions below are provided to help you manipulate character based information.

These functions can only be accessed from the *PowerEditor*.

GetSymbolName

InStr

LeftStr

LowerStr

MidStr

NewLine

NumToStr

RightStr

Spaces

StrLen

StrToNum

UpperStr

System Information

Functions within the System Information category give us access to the particular settings defined within your charting application. The functions do not perform any calculations. Their purpose is to return information on such settings as commission, margin (on futures), slippage, etc. If the user has not changed the setting, the value returned will be the default value of the charting application.

One notably missing function is the default number of contracts. Access to this value would make certain money management routines more easily possible.

BreakEvenStopFloor

Commission

Margin

MoneyMgtStopAmt

ProfitTargetStop

Slippage

TrailingStopAmt

TrailingStopFloor

TrailingStopPct

SYSTEM INFORMATION FOR PLOTS

New in **Trade Station Version 4.0**, the SYSTEM INFORMATION FOR PLOTS FUNCTIONS are listed incorrectly ("I_" prefix omitted) in **Omega's** help files. Notice there is no access to "BARSSINCEENTRY", "ENTRYDATE" or many of the more important system related fields.

Prior to Version 4.0, you could not plot the equity information generated by a trading system without first exporting the information to an external file. You could not see a graphical representation of how much money you were losing or making based on your system. Note that this ability was available in **System Writer Plus (SWP), Omega's** earlier DOS product. However, beginning with **TradeStation 4.0, Omega Research** has made available a category of functions that can be called from an indicator and may be used to visibly display system equity information.

I_AVGENTRYPRICE

I_CLOSEDEQUITY

I_CURRENTCONTRACTS

I_MARKETPOSITION

I_OPENEQUITY

SYSTEM TO INCLUDE

The SYSTEM TO INCLUDE category technically does not contain functions. Rather, it is made up of actual trading systems found in your **TradeStation** trading SYSTEM LIBRARY. The fact that you can access them and use them as functions allows you to place them within another system.

These systems can only be accessed by means of the *PowerEditor*; they are not available when using the *QuickEditor*.

SYSTEM: CCIAVGCROSSOVER

SYSTEM: CHANNELBRKINTRABAR

SYSTEM: CHANNELBRKONCLOSE

SYSTEM: CHANNELBRKWEIGHTED

System: ConsecutiveCloses

System: Divergence

System: KeyReversalMajor

System: MACD

System: MovAvg(3)Crossover

System: MovAvgCrossover

System: Parabolic

System: PercentROscillator

System: RSIOscillator

System: StochasticCrossover

System: WeightedAvgCrossover

System: XAverageCrossover

SetPlotSize

New in **TradeStation 5.0**, this function allows the size of the PLOT to be altered under program control.

SetPlotColor

New in **TradeStation 5.0**, this function allows the color of the PLOT to be altered under program control.

Scaling

When you add a study to a chart **Omega** will either place it in the same subgraph as the data or insert it in the next available (unused) subgraph.

If the study is scaled to "Same as Price Data" then **Omega** will place the study in the same subgraph as the data

If the study is scaled to Screen, Entire Data Series or User Defined then **Omega** will either place it in the same subgraph as the data or insert it in the next available (unused) subgraph.

Summary

In this section we have gained an appreciation for the depth and diversity of the functionality available in *EasyLanguage*. There is not room here, nor is it the purpose of this book, to describe each function in detail. Omega's documentation does that in some detail. I hereby request that you go through that documentation at least one time in great detail.

The information in this section is intended to be used exactly as presented. As a list. I suggest that you skim through the functions quite regularly. I feel certain you will find the exercise well worth your while.

Section 4:
Advanced Topics
OVERVIEW

One of my jobs in life is to remove the proverbial blinders from your eyes. To open your awareness of the vast possibilities available to you. This section is designed to show you some of the less obvious applications available using *EasyLanguage.*

Some of the topics we will explore include the use of charts with MULTIPLE DATA SERIES, DRAWING TOOLS and ADVANCED SYSTEM TECHNIQUES.

When you combine the subjects covered in this section with the questions and answers in the following two sections you can gain powerful insights into the 'outer limits' of *EasyLanguage* programming.

Using Multiple Data Series

Price Fields

EasyLanguage allows you to reference up to a maximum of 50 DATA SERIES files (DATA1, DATA2, ... DATA50) within a SIGNAL, STUDY or USER FUNCTION by using a multi-data chart. Using MULTIPLE DATA FILES allows you to make Intramarket (different time frames of same symbol) or Intermarket (two different symbols) comparisons. In commodities, for example, it allows you to track various contract months for a particular commodity, or to track multiple commodities, such as interest rates and currencies.

EasyLanguage can only place BUY and SELL orders for DATA1. Because of this DATA1, the primary data, should always be the DATA for the market you want to actually trade.

If no data modifier is specified, *EasyLanguage* assumes that you refer to DATA1. Let us suppose that you are writing a SIGNAL to BUY LIVE CATTLE contracts based upon the relationship between FEEDER CATTLE (DATA2) and Corn (DATA3) prices, as in the following:

```
If   (Close of DATA3 <  Close[01] of DATA3) and
     (Close of DATA3 <  Average (Close, 20) of DATA3 and
     (Close of DATA2  > Close[01] of DATA2) and
     (Close of DATA2  > Average (Close, 20) of DATA2
  Then  BUY  ("le.Main") at Market ;
```

If the conditions in this example are true, the BUY would go in for LIVE CATTLE (DATA1) although "DATA1" is not specifically mentioned in the BUY statement.

When you are comparing data files of different time periods, your multi-data window should be set up so that the shortest (fastest spinning) time period is DATA1 and the next shortest time period is DATA2, etc. For instance, when using hourly, daily, weekly and monthly data, hourly should be DATA1, daily should be DATA2, weekly should be DATA3, and monthly should be DATA4.

Until you get **TradeStation 5.0**, which will remove most all limitations, you are unable to save a WorkSpace (Page) that contains more than twenty some odd data series. Now, you can create a chart with up to fifty data series in it, you just cannot save it. Makes sense, huh? The actual number that you can save varies based upon the number of charts, the Analysis Techniques and Drawing Tools you have applied to the chart(s).

Using Functions with Multiple Data Series

In general, it is suggested that we place the DATA SERIES MODIFIER (ex: DATA2) after the function name and outside the parenthesis, if any. As mentioned in the section on DATE & TIME FUNCTIONS, the @DAYOFWEEK, @MONTH and @YEAR functions are treated slightly differently.

```
Condition1 = DayOfWeek (Date      of DATA2) <
             DayOfWeek (Date [01] of DATA2) ;

Condition2 = Close of DATA2 > Average (Close, 20) of DATA2 ;
```

Using VARIABLES with Multiple Data Series

When using multiple data series, you can bind the VARIABLES to a specific DATA SERIES. This is done with the VARIABLE DECLARATION STATEMENT in the following manner:

```
VARS: VARIABLE1 (0, DATA1), VARIABLE2 (0, DATA2) ;
```

In the example above, VARIABLE1 and VARIABLE2 could be any variable names that you assign. Within the parentheses following the variable names, 0 (zero) is the initial value of the variable(s) and the Data Modifier (DATA1 or DATA2) binds the variable to its respective data series.

If a data series is not specified, *EasyLanguage* assumes DATA1. This is true of both the pre-defined VARIABLES (VALUE0 ... VALUE99) and any custom VARIABLES you declare.

```
Average (Close of DATA2, 20) ;   {correct but not recommended}
Average (Close, 20) of DATA2 ;   { suggested usage }
```

When referencing SIMPLE FUNCTIONS and prices, the data series (sometimes referred to as DATANUM) that you wish to use can be a Variable or Input, as in the following example:

```
VALUE0 = Average (High, 20) of Data (X) ;
```

In this example we are assigning the value to the NUMERIC variable VALUE0 of the simple moving average of the highs of the last 20 bars for the data series DATAX where X is a variable between 1 and 50 inclusive. This technique may only be used with SIMPLE FUNCTIONS. A series function will result in an error.

Using this technique, I created studies that use MULTIPLE DATA SERIES to compute the ADVANCE DECLINE RATIO with inputs ADV_DNUM (02) and DCL_DNUM (03). Using this technique, the order of the data series within the chart is not as critical because the Inputs can be altered to reflect the chart the STUDY is applied to!

Be forewarned that the ability to use the syntax "CLOSE OF DATA (DNUM)" is not a documented feature of *EasyLangauge* and may not be supported in future versions.

In the example below, the average is computed using DATA2 but Value1[01] (Value1 of one bar ago), assuming you have NOT declared Value1 for DATA2 in a VARIABLE DECLARATION STATEMENT, refers to one bar ago of DATA1.

```
Value1 = Average (Close, 20) of DATA2 ;
if  (Close of DATA1  > Value1 [00]) and
    (Close of DATA1 <  Value1 [01])
  then ...
```

This mistake can lead to unpredictable results. Anytime you are using MULTIPLE DATA SERIES to make Trading Decisions give a long look at which data series is stored where and all STUDYBAR references.

DRAWING TOOL FUNCTIONS

The **DRAWING TOOL FUNCTIONS** were added to *EasyLanguage* as a direct result of my (past tense) contract to provide the Tom DeMark indicators for the **Omega** platform. Mr. DeMark and I managed to convince the powers that be at **Omega** that we could not make the package competitive with the other platforms without additional functionality in the language. To all of you who have found these functions useful, "You are most welcome.".

There are two types of DRAWING TOOL FUNCTIONS: TRENDLINES and ON-SCREEN TEXT. The available functions were listed in Section #2. You can find examples of these functions in Sections #5 and #6.

Note that once the Drawing Tool has been created on the chart it may be treated exactly like any other DRAWING TOOL OBJECT. You can right click on the item, select it with the arrow pointer and drag it to another position on the chart.

DRAWING TOOL CONSTANTS

DRAWING TOOL CONSTANTS are terms defined as NUMERIC CONSTANTS that have been added to *EasyLanguage* for use with the DRAWING TOOL FUNCTIONS. TOOL_WHITE and TOOL_SOLID are examples but do not be fooled —not all these CONSTANTS start with the "TOOL_" prefix! These terms have a predetermined value and can be thought of as CONSTANTS. In other programming languages, a CONSTANT is defined as a data item initialized at runtime and unable to be changed.

The following COLOR VALUES are used or returned by certain functions in the DRAWING OBJECTS CATEGORY:

TOOL_BLACK	**1**
TOOL_BLUE	**2**
TOOL_CYAN	**3**
TOOL_GREEN	**4**
TOOL_MAGENTA	**5**
TOOL_RED	**6**
TOOL_YELLOW	**7**
TOOL_WHITE	**8**
TOOL_DARKBLUE	**9**
TOOL_DARKCYAN	**10**
TOOL_DARKGREEN	**11**
TOOL_DARKMAGENTA	**12**
TOOL_DARKRED	**13**
TOOL_DARKYELLOW	**14**
TOOL_DARKGRAY	**15**
TOOL_LIGHTGRAY	**16**

The following TEXT STYLE CODES are used or returned by certain functions in the DRAWING OBJECTS CATEGORY:

DATE-LINE = HORIZONTAL / X-COORDINATE

HRIGHT	**0**	**DRAWN RIGHT OF THE DATE-LINE**
HLEFT	**1**	**DRAWN LEFT OF THE DATE-LINE**
HCENTER	**2**	**DRAWN CENTERED ON THE DATE-LINE**

PRICE-LINE = VERTICAL / Y-COORDINATE

VBELOW	**0**	**DRAWN BELOW THE PRICE-LINE**
VABOVE	**1**	**DRAWN ABOVE THE PRICE-LINE**
VCENTER	**2**	**DRAWN CENTERED ON THE PRICE-LINE**

The following Style Values are used, or returned, by certain functions in the Drawing Objects Category:

Tool_Solid	**1**
Tool_Dashed	**2**
Tool_Dotted	**3**
Tool_Dashed2	**4**
Tool_Dashed3	**5**

The following Line Thickness Values are used, or returned, by certain functions in the Drawing Objects Category:

Thinnest	**0**
Very Thin	**1**
Thin	**2**
Medium	**3**
Thick	**4**
Very Thick	**5**
Thickest	**6**

See Section #6.02b and #6.17 for examples that demonstrate these terms being used to change the color of a Text Object or the line thickness of a TrendLine Object.

Modifying Prices —Increments and Rounding

Prices are transmitted in Points, or Units of PriceScale. Some markets move in MinMove increments of Points which we call a Tick. As an example, the S&P 500 is transmitted in hundredths (1/100 or 0.01) but MinMove has a value of ten (10).

When *EasyLanguage* places a Buy Stop Order the fill will be rounded up, as necessary, to the next higher Tick. Conversely, a Buy Limit Order will be rounded down, as necessary, to the next lower Tick.

Since a bar has only four price fields (Open, High, Low, Close) *EasyLanguage* can not determine which direction the market moved first. The best they can do is make an educated guess. The assumption is that the market moves from the open (safe so far) to the closest price extreme, on to the farthest price extreme and then on to the close. Statistically, I believe this is a valid assumption statistically but it not be absolutely correct.

Applying ShowMe Studies

A ShowMe Study is most useful when more than one condition can occur on a given bar.

When the Charting application draws your Point or Cross on the chart it uses a virtual brush. This brush is round and the rounding becomes more pronounced when you increase the size of the plot. To avoid obscuring the actual high or low of the bar I move the displayed value away from the price bar by a number of points or Ticks.

```
Inputs: nTicks (01) ;
Vars  : nPoints (MinMove * nTicks Points) ;

If  Close [00]  > Close [01] and Close [01]  > Close [02]
  then Plot1 ( Low - nPoints, "UpClose") ;

If  Close [00] <  Close [01] and Close [01] <  Close [02]
  then Plot2 (High + nPoints, "DnClose") ;
```

Applying PaintBar Studies

A PaintBar Study is most useful when **only** one condition can occur on a given bar. Inside Bars and Outside bars, which are mutually exclusive, are likely candidates for a PaintBar Study.

When the Charting application paints the bar it uses a virtual brush. This brush is round and the rounding becomes more pronounced when you increase the size of the plot(s). To avoid obscuring the actual high or low of the bar I move the displayed value into the price bar by a number of Points or Ticks.

```
Inputs: nTicks (01) ;
Vars  : nPoints (MinMove * nTicks Points) ;

if  High [00]  > High [01] and
     Low [00] <   Low [01]
then begin
  Plot1 ( Low + nPoints, "Outside") ; { Bar High }
  Plot2 (High - nPoints, "Outside") ; { Bar Low }
end ;
```

If you have a case where more than one condition can be true it is possible to paint only half of the bar. The Bullish / Bearish Bar example shown below demonstrates this concept.

```
If  High [00]  > High [01] and Low [00]  > Low [01] then begin
  Plot1 (High,                "Bullish") ;
  Plot2 (High - Range * 0.50, "Bullish") ;
end ; { paint the upper half of the bar }

Buy  ("le.Main#1") at lePrice stop ;

Sell ("se.Main#1") at sePrice stop ;
```

```
if  High [00] <  High [01] and Low [00] <  Low [01] then begin
  Plot2 ( Low + Range * 0.50, "Bearish") ;
  Plot1 ( Low,                "Bearish") ;
end ;
```

Specifying Signal Names

When placing ENTRY and EXIT SIGNALS it is possible, and highly recommended that you name each signal. The SIGNAL NAME is within parenthesis and must be a STRING LITERAL. I have certain standard prefixes which I always use:

le	**Long Entry**
lx	**Long Exit**
se	**Short Entry**
sx	**Short Exit**

Sample naming conventions:

le.Main	**Primary entry order**
le.Entry#2	**Pyramiding order**
le.Scale#1	**Pyramiding order into position**
lx.MMStop	**Money Management or Protective Stop**
sx.Target	**Profit Target**
lx.BEStop	**Break Even Stop**
le.SARStop	**And Reverse**
se.ReEntry	**Reenter in same direction as previous trade.**

```
Buy  ("le.Main#1") at lePrice stop ;

Sell ("se.Main#1") at sePrice stop ;

ExitLong  ("lx.MMStop") at lx.MMStop stop ;

ExitShort ("sx.MMStop") at sx.MMStop stop ;
```

Notice that by using a proportional font (all characters are the same width) such as *Courier New*, and by inserting an extra space occasionally, how neatly my code lines up. It's all a matter of Style.

Controlling number of contracts in Entry and Exit Signals

The SetUp box of the Analysis/System choice includes a <Costs> button which will allow you to control the number of contracts or shares purchased by each Entry of your system. This value can be overridden within your system. Below is an example of this process.

```
INPUTS: Equity (1000000) ;

VARS  : nCntrs      (01) ;

if (Margin  > 00) then begin
  nCntrs = (NetProfit + Equity) / Margin ;
  nCntrs = MaxList (nContracts, 01) ;
end ;

BUY  ("le#1") nContracts contracts at lePrice stop ;

EXITLong  ("lx.PTarget")
    CurrentContracts * 0.50 contracts
    at ENTRYPrice + (2500 * BigPointValue) stop ;

EXITLong  ("lx.PanicStop")
    CurrentContracts * 0.50 contracts
    at$ lowest (Low, 03) stop ;
```

Restricting Exit Orders to Specific Entry Orders

All Exit Orders start out the same—global. An unqualified Exit order will Exit all contracts from all entries. If you specify the number of contracts to Exit then the system will take off that many contracts, if available, from each and every Entry into the position. To limit an Exit to ONLY one Entry Order you use the From Entry KeyWords and specify the name of the Entry Order as a String Literal inside parenthesis.

```
EXITLong  ("lx#1") from ENTRY ("le#1") on the close ;
```

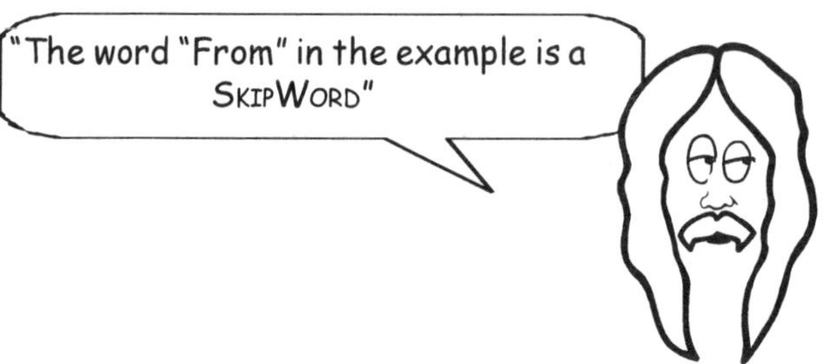

Anchoring Prices of Exit Signals Using AT$

It is possible to anchor the price of an Exit Order at the value it held on the bar of Signal generation. The Syntax of *EasyLanguage* does not allow the use of the AT$ operator in a global Exit. In other words, you must specify the Entry Order by using the From Entry KeyWords.

```
ExitLong ("lx#1") from Entry ("le#1") at$ Lowest (Low, 3) stop ;
```

The Exit Order **must** be executed on the bar of order generation or unexpected results **will** occur. This means that there may not be any if statement that might prevent execution of the Exit Order. Neither of the examples below will function as expected.

```
if  (MarketPosition  = +01)  then begin
  if  (BarsSinceEntry  =  00)  then begin
    lxPrice = Close[0] - MMSpoints ;
  end ;
  ExitLong ("lx.MMStop") from Entry ("lx#1") at$ lxPrice stop ;
end ;
If MarketPosition  = -01  then begin
  ExitShort ("sx.Main") from Entry ("se.Main")
                              At$ Highest (High, 03) stop ;
end ;
```

Performance Enhancements

Some *EasyLanguage* code generates instructions which will be executed repeatedly as your program runs. Your Assignment and Condition Statements are good examples of **'Executable' statements**. These statements take processing time (unless a condition statement prevents execution) on each bar of data.

Other code that you write will only be used at load (or Link) time. Your Inputs:, Vars: and Array: statements are examples of **'Link Time' Statements**. These statements take no pro-

Other code that you write will only be used at LOAD (or LINK) time. Your INPUTS:, VARS: and ARRAY: STATEMENTS are examples of **'LINK TIME' STATEMENTS**. These statements take no processing time on a bar by bar basis. Of course, one should keep in mind that errors of design and/or typing may certainly cause delaying effects upon your research.

Spaces in your code cause no execution cost but will take marginally more disk space and might cause a reduction in verification speed (once again—nanoseconds).

Unnecessary parentheses in your code will cause a slight execution cost and will add to the size of the executable code.

Specifying a bar offset, *i.e.,* [0], when not necessary will cost more because it puts in error checking for MAXBARSBACK violations.

Using division does the same, since *EasyLanguage* will always insert error checking code for the division by zero NoNo. In many cases you can get around this by multiplying instead.

Using an INCLUDESYSTEM to move code to another code segment may be helpful.

LOOPS and ARRAYS

There are many examples of using LOOPS and ARRAYS in Sections 5 and 6. Some of the techniques you will learn include:

Storing DAILY prices on an INTRADAY Chart #6.2

Storing WEEKLY prices on a DAILY Chart #6.3

Store the ten most recent PIVOT POINTS Chart #6.17

EXPERT COMMENTARY

The Basic Structure : When writing code to use the EXPERT COMMENTARY TOOL your first step is to limit execution to the commentary bar itself. There are several ways to do this. I have included examples demonstrating them in Sections 5 and 6.08, 6.11, 6.13b.

```
#BeginCmtry

{*
 *  Any code within the BeginCmtry block structure in only
 *  executed if the commentary tool is selected.
 *}

if  CheckCommentary  then begin

{*
 *  Any code within the CheckCommentary block structure will only
 *  be executed on the commentary bar itself.
 *}
```

Print Log

The PRINT STATEMENT is used to display information to the PRINT LOG WINDOW. This information could be the value or condition of a variable, for instance, or the result of a calculation.

All the examples below will assume the INPUT STATEMENT below:

```
Inputs: Price    (Close),
        Length      (14),
        tDate   (941231),
        Report   (False) ;
```

In TradeStation Version 5.0 the Print Log Window has been renamed the "Message Log" window.

One very handy trick is to display the name of your program and its INPUT VALUES on the first bar of data.

```
if  (@BarNumber <= 01)  then begin
  Print ("") ;     { blank line as separator }
  Print ("System : 'My First System' (",
         Length:1:0, ",", tDate:1:0, ",", Report:1, ")") ;
  Print ("————————————————") ;
end ; { first bar of data only }
```

One improvement I have made in the last year or two to this technique is to store the name of the module in a variable. This way you can change it in one centralized place in your code rather than searching for each place you might be displaying headings. It also allows the use of standard output modules.

```
VARS   : App.Name ("My Second System") ;

if  (@BarNumber <= 01)  then begin
  Print ("") ;     { blank line as separator }
  Print ("System : '", App.Name, "' (",
         Length:1:0, ",", tDate:1:0, ",", Report:1, ")") ;
  Print ("————————————————") ;
end ; { first bar of data only }
```

Another important use of the PRINT STATEMENT is to generate a report on the last bar of data or at some other significant point.

```
Inputs: tDate (vrt.LastCalcDate),
        tTime (vrt.LastCalcTime) ;

Vars   : TotalFound  (00),
         TotalValue  (00) ;

{ … }

if  (Report = True) and (Date = tDate) and (Time = tTime)
then begin
  Print ("————————————————————— ") ;
  Print ("Sample size = ", CurrentBar:5:0,
```

```
          "  Matches = ", TotalFound:4:0,
          "  Total Value = ", TotalValue:6:2) ;
end ; { report on specified (?last?) bar of data }
```

Sometimes it can be useful to display information upon each ENTRY and/or EXIT into a position.

```
if   (Date = EntryDate (0)) and (Time = EntryTime (0))
then begin
  Print (Date:6:0, Time:5:0,
         MarketPosition (0):3:0, EntryPrice) ;
end ;

if   (Date = ExitDate (1)) and (Time = ExitTime (1))
then begin
  Print (Date:6:0, Time:5:0,
    iff (MarketPosition (01) = +01,
         ExitPrice (1) - EntryPrice (1) * BigPointValue,
      iff (MarketPosition (01) = -01,
           EntryPrice (1) - ExitPrice (1) * BigPointValue, 0) ;
end ;
```

SetPlotSize

New in **TradeStation 5.0**, this function allows the size of the PLOT to be altered under program control.

SetPlotColor

New in **TradeStation 5.0**, this function allows the color of the PLOT to be altered under program control.

Plot Style

Your PLOTS have a STYLE attribute that is set under the PROPERTIES DIALOG BOX. You can select from LINE, HISTOGRTAM, POINT, CROSS, BARHIGH, BARLOW, LEFT TICK and RIGHT TICK styles. You can also adjust the thickness, or size, of the PLOT and its color.

Scaling

When you add a STUDY to a chart **Omega** will either place it in the same subgraph as the data or insert it in the next available (unused) subgraph.

If the STUDY is scaled to "SAME AS PRICE DATA" then **Omega** will place the STUDY in the same subgraph as the data

If the STUDY is scaled to SCREEN, ENTIRE DATA SERIES or USER DEFINED then **Omega** will either place it in the next available (unused) subgraph.

Using Pseudo Code

The phrase **Using Pseudo Code** refers to writing your logic in an English-like manner that approaches *EasyLanguage*. You can probably write faster if you do not try for the exact Syntax but instead get close.

Programming Style

Let us assume that I want to do something only when a specific condition is met: I type If Condition Then and I type the word Begin, press the <Enter> key and type the word

```
if  Condition1  then begin
{b}
end ; { Condition1 }
```

End, optionally an Else clause, terminating with a semicolon and optionally a comment.

Then I would go back up to that {b} that you see above and start typing the rest of this. In other words, this procedure is enclosed in the above mentioned If Condition Then Begin...End Statement, OK?

The point I am trying to make here is that whenever I type the word begin I immediately type the matching end. This way I avoid the dreaded "Dangling Block Syndrome."

The "Dangling Block Syndrome." You can not imagine how many times I receive a file with a last line similar to :

```
end ; end ; end ; end ; end ; { OK, one more } end ; { whew! }
```

I refer to this as the "Dangling Block Syndrome." The author began boldly typing his methodology, opening new Block Statements as needed but did not manage to close them at the right time or in the proper sequence. One should be warned that unexpected results and/or flawed data can occur.

The same rule applies to comment braces, parenthesis and to a lesser degree quotation marks (because it is limited to a single line of code, the problem is easier to isolate and correct).

Debugging

Comparing two studies by

1) Loading on the chart and comparing the values in Chart Status.

2) Loading in two sub-graphs and comparing visually

Common Errors

Speaking as a support technician, what is the most common mistake I have seen, you ask? Try the following system. Looks like it should trade frequently, right? Why does it not?

```
If  High  > Highest (High, 10)  then  Buy  ("le.Main") at market ;
If   Low <   Lowest ( Low, 10)  then  Sell ("se.Main") at market ;
```

What is happening here? Have you tried it yet? No? I am waiting. OK, here goes.

The Highest function is inclusive—so today's high can never be higher than itself, right?!? To correct the problem offset the highest function one bar "High > Highest (High, 10)[01]" or test for greater than or equal to "High >= Highest (High, 10)".

Using the letter "O" (Oh) rather than the number "0" (Zero) can easily generate a MaxBarsBack error. It will not on all markets but it sure will on the S&P 500 Index! So, even if it does not cause a MaxBarsBack error, it can easily cause the program to execute unpredictable.

Summary

You have been introduced to multi-data charts and some of the idiosyncrasies when using *EasyLanguage* with multiple data series.

Combined with Sections 5 and 6 you will have new ideas of how the DRAWING TOOL FUNCTIONS can facilitate your research and trading.

After you implement some of the ideas you have been exposed to here, your trading systems will never know what hit them! Standardized naming conventions for your signals. Controlling the number of contracts in your orders. Anchoring prices with the AT$ OPERATOR. All these combine to make *EasyLanguage* a powerful platform for both research and real-time trading.

Debugging your code will never seem easier now that you can use the PRINT STATEMENT and the EXPERT COMMENTARY TOOL.

Section 5:
EasyLanguage Demystified

1 *EasyLanguage* Templates

Question ⇒ When I open a new module in the *PowerEditor* I find typing the first few lines to be most difficult. Is there a proper structure I should follow when creating my *EasyLanguage* module?

Answer ⇒ In a word - NO. There is no right or wrong way to write code. There may be more or less efficient ways but one thing you will learn —there is [effectively] always more than one way to solve the same puzzle.

When I began teaching my *EasyLanguage* workshops, it immediately became apparent that some users are intimidated by the blank white screen of the *PowerEditor*. I have created a series of code modules the can be used as 'fill in the blank' forms. I call these, naturally, Templates (see Chapter 6.)

To use one of these templates, open the appropriate file and use the "File", "Save As" menu choice to avoid overwriting the original file.

6.01a - Study "skt.EZL Template"

Enter the type of this study (Indicator, Oscillator, *PaintBar*, *ShowMe*, Report, etc....), the name and any notes you want or need. You can define the various Plots, their names and their suggested settings. See Listing 6.1a

6.01b - System "skt.EZL Template"

Enter the type of this study (Top Level or Include), the name and any notes you want or need. You can list the signal(s) by type and name. See Listing 6.1b

6.01c - Function "skt.EZL Template"

Enter the Return Type (Numeric, Boolean or String), the Function Name, some note to yourself and the return type. Optionally you can enter a description and/or sample usage.

Be sure to change the ASSIGNMENT STATEMENT at the bottom of the code listing to reflect the new FUNCTION NAME. See Listing 6.1c

2 Building DAILY BARS out of INTRADAY BARS

Question ⇒ I am developing a position trading system. How can I see if the fills I am getting on DAILY BARS are accurate?

Answer ⇒ I am frequently employed to test a position trading system against intraday data in an attempt to validate the test results received after running the system on daily data.

Before we decide the best technique to use to solve your problem we have to answer a couple of questions. We must determine how many daily bars you are referencing. If you are only referencing two or three bars of data then we can get away with storing the daily values in variables. If you need to reference a larger number of daily bars then we will have to store the daily bars in an array, requiring the use of ITERATIVE STATEMENTS.

The next issue we must consider are the functions, if any, you are calling. If you calling simple functions, ones that are easy to replicate inside the module like @TRUERANGE or @AVERAGE, then we are [nearly] home free. If you are calling more complex functions, like @RSI or @STDDEV then it may be necessary to write your system using two DATA SERIES, intraday for the actual fills and daily for the trading decisions.

For the purpose of this discussion, we are going to assume a larger number of bars but simple functions.

The basic logic here is used very frequently. What is unique about the first bar of each day? Only the first bar has a date greater than that of the previous bar. Every other bar has the same date as its predecessor. This is one important reason why computers store dates in YYMMDD format. They will always sort in numerical order. The relevant logic in this study is :

```
if  Date [00]  > Date [01]  then begin { detect new day }
end ; { first bar of a new day }
```

I have provided a couple of examples for your reading pleasure. See listing 6.02a

6.02a - Study : EZL.Synthetic Daily

This sample study is very straightforward and has no DEBUGGING STATEMENTS. It does contain sample buy and sell statements, as comments, that demonstrate how to use the logic in a trading system. The sample system would enter on the formation on an INTRADAY basis of a daily OUTSIDE VERTICAL BAR (OVB).

You can also refer to the SYSTEM by the same name. See listing 6.02b

6.02b - System : EZL.Synthetic Daily

The SYSTEM takes our daily logic from the study above one step further and creates TRENDLINES on the screen, marking the HIGH and LOW of the previous trading day, so we can visually see an OUTSIDE VERTICAL BAR (OVB) forming INTRADAY. This tool can be very useful for people who trade off very short time frame charts or who have many charts on the screen at one time.

3 Marking the first day of a week

Question ⇒ Mr. *EasyLanguage*, how do I write a PAINTBAR STUDY to mark every Monday?

Answer ⇒ To solve the question exactly as it was posed we would use something like :

```
if DayOfWeek (Date) = 01 then begin
  Plot1 (High, "Mon") ;   { BarHigh }
  Plot2 ( Low, "day") ;   { Bar Low }
end ;
```

However, my experience tells me that generally the user actually wants to mark the first bar of each new week, regardless of holidays. I will proceed with that assumption.

Know what assuming does? It makes and ASS out of U and ME. ASSUME. ASS U ME - get it?

This type of request is very common. The client wants to detect a regularly occurring condition. First I will provide the solution to this request. Next I will provide a solution that paints the last bar of the week.

To detect the first day of a week we test for a @DAYOFWEEK less than the @DAYOFWEEK of the previous bar.

6.03a - PaintBar : "EZL.Paint Mondays"

See listing 6.03a PaintBar: EZL.Paint Mondays

```
if  @DayOfWeek (Date[00]) <  @DayOfWeek (Date[01])  then ...
```

To detect the last day of a week we test for a @DAYOFWEEK = 5 or ((@DAYOFWEEK [0] <

@DayOfWeek [01] AND DayOfWeek [1] <> 5

6.03b - PaintBar : "EZL.Paint Fridays"

See listing 6.03b PaintBar: EZL.Paint Fridays

```
if  @DayOfWeek (Date[00])  =  05 or
   (@DayOfWeek (Date[01]) <>  05 and
    @DayOfWeek (Date[00]) <  @DayOfWeek (Date[01]))
then begin
```

Note that in order to paint the correct bar we use a variable named "Offset" that is zero (the current bar). However, if Friday was a holiday then "Offset" is one (the previous bar).

```
Offset  =  00 ;
if  ((@DayOfWeek (Date[01]) <>         05) and
     (@DayOfWeek (Date[00]) <  @DayOfWeek (Date[01])))
  then  Offset  = +01 ;
```

Please see the complete listing in the next section for how I applied this logic.

Later, I will provide an example (see EZL.Mark First Bar) that marks the first occurrence based on the @DataCompression of the chart.

4 Building Weekly bars out of Daily bars

Question ⇒ I am reading about a methodology using daily and weekly values. How do I build weekly bars out of daily bars?

Answer ⇒ The logic for this study (*PaintBar*) will be very similar to the earlier example of building Daily bars. Our goal is to detect the end of a calendar week. "If Now >= Last Bar of Week then ...". To detect a Friday is simple - `@DayOfWeek = 05`. To detect the first day of a week we test for @DayOfWeek today less than the @DayOfWeek of the previous bar.

In brief, we must first locate the first bar of a week. When a new week is found then we store the recently completed week into the Array and initialize the values for the first bar of the new week.

On each passing bar we store new intra-week highs and lows. The close of each bar is stored as well.

The "**Start**" variable is used to ensure that we only store a completed week. In other words, the first bar after MaxBarsBack might have been a Wednesday. We want to avoid storing this partial weekly bar into the array. Initially the value of Start is FALSE. Upon detecting a new week, the first thing we do is check to see if Start is TRUE. If it is TRUE then we store the completed week into the array. If Start is FALSE then we set it to TRUE. Next time we hit this logic it will be an entire week. There is also a "Week Counter" available. See listing 6.04 - - Study : **EZL.Synthetic Weekly**

6.04 - Study : EZL.Synthetic Weekly

```
Type : Study (Synthetic Bar)

Name : "EZL.Synthetic Weekly"

Notes: Create synthetic weekly bars from intraday data

       Plots synthetic weekly bar, also Commentary.
```

5 Marking the first bar of the higher time frame

Question ⇒ During a seminar you mentioned using the DataCompression function to create code that is self modifying. You lost me! How do I use DataCompression?

Answer ⇒ Sometimes we want to make trading decisions based on a higher time frame. The Daily and Weekly Bar examples demonstrate this concept. To complete this discussion I show how to detect Monthly and Yearly bars.

See listing 6.05 Below is a table of what this study will mark.

Type of Chart Search for Explanation

IntraDay (tick or minutes) First Bar of the Day To detect the first bar of the day we test for a Date greater than Date of the previous bar.

Daily First Day of the Week To detect the first day of a week we test for a @DayOfWeek less than the @DayOfWeek of the previous bar.

Weekly First Week of the Month To detect the first week of a month we test for a @DayOfMonth less than the @DayOfMonth of the previous bar.

Monthly First Month of the Year To detect the first month of a year we test for a @Month less than the @Month of the previous bar.

6 Playing a custom .WAV file from an Alert

Question ⇒ My system runs on hourly bars and I am not always in front of my screen when orders are generated. How do I create a study or system that will alert me by playing a .WAV file whenever a bar closes?

Answer ⇒ First let me go over how Alerts are used in *EasyLanguage*. The first step in implementing an ALERT STATEMENT is to test if ALERT-TESTING has been enabled and we are on the last bar of data. The KeyWord **CHECKALERT** will be true only if ALERTS have been enabled and if the data pointer is currently at the last bar of data on the chart. It is normally used in an IF...THEN BEGIN...END STATEMENT.

The actual alert is triggered by assigning a value of TRUE to the ALERT KEYWORD. It is possible to use a BOOLEAN ASSIGNMENT like :

```
if  CheckAlert  then  Alert = FastMA crosses above SlowMA ;
```

I prefer to use the IF Expression THEN Alert = TRUE ; method demonstrated below. The THEN clause can become a COMPOUND STATEMENT with the addition of a BEGIN...END ; BLOCK.

```
If  CheckAlert  then begin
  if  FastMA crosses above SlowMA  then Alert  =  TRUE ;
end ;
```

The logic could actually be simplified as in the example below but I prefer to use the first example. As I have mentioned before, there is no one right way.

```
If  CheckAlert and FastMA crosses above SlowMA
  then  Alert  =  TRUE ;
```

TradeStation 4.0 brought us a number of audio visual routines, one of which we will demonstrate here. Note that the alert structure described above is required to implement this logic. See listing 6.06 - Study : SKT.AUDIO ALERT

7 Demonstrating the use of the PRINT STATEMENT

Question ⇒ You make it look so easy. How do I use the PRINT STATEMENT?

Answer ⇒ An example demonstrating many of the classic uses of the PRINT STATEMENT including EXECUTION TRACKING, TEST DOCUMENTATION, DATA INFORMATION, VARIABLE & LOGIC DEBUGGING, etc.... See listing 6.07a for the STUDY and 6.07b for the USER FUNCTION.

6.07a - Study : skt.Print.Headers

```
Study    : skt.Print.Headers
```

6.07b - Function : skt.Print.Headers

```
Function: skt.Print.Headers
```

Output generated on first bar of data ("`if @BarNumber <= 01` ...")

```
==========================================================================
Report: 'skt.Print.Headers'                      Run Date : 04/05/99   1:24am

_____________-

Symbol        Comm#    Chart        First Bar          Last  Bar       Sample

____________________________________-

SPH9           149     Daily   06/10/97 16:00,   02/03/99 16:00,        1

One Point      =     0.0100     One Tick        =     0.1000
Min Move       =    10.0000     PriceScale      =   100
PointValue     =     2.5000     BigPointValue =   250.0000
```

Output generated on last bar of data ("if Date = @vrt.LastCalcDate ...")

```
==========================================================================
Report: 'skt.Print.Headers'                      Run Date : 04/05/99   1:24am
_____________-
Symbol        Comm#    Chart        First Bar          Last  Bar       Sample
____________________________________-
SPH9           149     Daily   06/10/97 16:00,   02/03/99 16:00,      406

One Point      =     0.0100     One Tick        =     0.1000
Min Move       =    10.0000     PriceScale      =   100
PointValue     =     2.5000     BigPointValue =   250.0000
```

Note that the first and last dates are known at the beginning of the run but the Sample Size (number of bars) is not known until the last bar.

8 Using Expert Commentary

Question ⇒ On the phone you suggested I use the EXPERT COMMENTARY TOOL to DEBUG my system. Will you please explain how I would do that?

Answer ⇒ I do not know exactly what you need to debug but I can certainly give you some helpful pointers. I am making up variables and conditions here. Replace the examples with what you are using in your program logic. Find a trouble bar and click to see what your code is doing. Remember, if you are using a system, all SIGNALS but the CLOSE ORDER are placed on the bar before they are filled. You may have to click one bar earlier to find the solution.

```
If  CheckCommentary  then begin

  CommentaryCL (Date:6:0, Time:5:0, ", ", Value1, ", ", Condtion1:6,
            ", Fast=", FastMA, ", Slow=", SlowMA,
            ", CrossUp=", FastMA Crosses Above SlowMA:6,
            ", CrossDn=", FastMA Crosses Below SlowMA:6) ;

end ; { only execute this code on the commentary bar you click on }
```

I have found Expert Commentary to be very useful both as a debugging tool, which is covered in Section 4, and to generate custom reports. In my own work, I use the Expert Commentary Tool as a programming aide and debugging tool, to generate custom reports and for actual natural language Commentary. See listing 6.08 for

6.08 - Study : EZL.Learn.Expt.Cmtry

9 Generating a Text Report

Question ⇒ My employer wants me to generate a probability report of the open to close movement on bars that meet a specific criteria. I need to be able to change the criteria easily. Can you show me how to do this?

Answer ⇒ During one of my *EasyLanguage* **Workshops I** created a simple report. It occurred to me that a set of generic routines could be created that would allow my clients to easily modify both the internal logic and the report captions.

The rows report where the bar opened in relation to the range of the previous bar. The columns report where the market closed in relation to the range of the previous bar.

6.09a - Study: EZL Row/Col Report

6.09b - Function: EZL.RowNum

6.09c - Function: EZL.Row_Label

6.09d - Function: EZL.ColNum

6.09e - Function: EZL.Col_Label

It might not do exactly what you asked for but it sure is a great example of applied logic! See listing 6.09a for the Study code. The User Functions are listings 6.09b, 6.09c, 6.09d and 6.09e.

	Totals	C[0]>H[1]	C[0]>75%[1]	C[0]>MdPt[1]	C[0]=MdPt[1]	C[0]<MdPt[1]	C[0]<25%[1]	C[0]<L[1]
Totals	217	76	28	31	1	27	17	37
O[0]>H[1]	45	27	5	6	0	5	2	0
O[0]>75%[1]	74	35	9	9	1	8	8	4
O[0]>MdPt[1]	39	10	5	5	0	6	3	10
O[0]=MdPt[1]	2	0	0	1	0	0	0	1
O[0]<MdPt[1]	26	3	7	3	0	3	1	9
O[0]<25%[1]	24	1	2	6	0	3	3	9
O[0]<L[1]	7	0	0	1	0	2	0	4

10 Generating a CSV file

Question ⇒ How do I create a CSV file. And Why?

Answer ⇒ By now it is simplistic to merely send output to the PRINT LOG WINDOW. When generating a CSV file use the PRINT STATEMENT with the to FILE KEYWORD (see page #55, 98) or the FILEAPPEND STATEMENT (see page #55).

By sending OUTPUT DATA to a CSV (COMMA SEPARATED VARIABLE) file it can easily be imported into an external program such as **Microsoft Excel** or **Access**. The advantage over a TXT file is that the fields will be automatically parsed into separate columns.

11 Defining Dual Bar Analysis

Question ⇒ I have heard you mention the DVBTI. What is it?

Answer ⇒ I have had the pleasure of working with Mr. Kent Calhoun, of KCI Seminars, for several years. One of the benefits he brings to the industry is a standardized vocabulary for describing **DUAL VERTICAL BAR ANALYSIS** (he labels this the DUAL VERTICAL BAR TREND INDICATOR or DVBTI for short). With his permission, I have shared this valuable gift with many of my clients and students.

When I was a young man, perhaps an old boy, my father explained to me that no two individuals can discuss a subject until they have agreed upon a vocabulary to describe that subject. This lesson has served me well ever since.

In brief, all DUAL VERTICAL BAR (who has ever heard of a HORIZONTAL BAR, I ask?) combinations may be broken into the five categories described below:

The Vocabulary of DUAL BAR PRICE ACTION

Bullish Bar

HIGHER HIGH and HIGHER LOW

```
if High[0]  > High[1] and Low [0]  > Low [1] then begin
  Plot1 (High, "Bullish") ; { Bar High }
  Plot2 ( Low, "Bullish") ; { Bar  Low }
end ; { Bullish Bar }
```

Bearish Bar

LOWER LOW and LOWER HIGH

```
if Low [0] <  Low [1] and High[0] < High[1] then begin
  Plot1 (High, "Bearish") ; { Bar High }
  Plot2 ( Low, "Bearish") ; { Bar  Low }
end ; { Bearish Bar }
```

Inside Bar

HIGHER or EQUAL LOW and LOWER or EQUAL HIGH. Can you say "POSSIBLE TREND REVERSAL"?

```
if Low [0] >= Low [1] and High[0] <= High[1] then begin
  Plot1 (High, "Inside") ; { Bar High }
  Plot2 ( Low, "Inside") ; { Bar  Low }
end ; { Inside Bar }
```

Outside Bar

HIGHER HIGH and LOWER LOW

```
if High[0]  > High[1] and Low [0] <  Low [1] then begin
  Plot1 (High, "Outside") ; { Bar High }
  Plot2 ( Low, "Outside") ; { Bar  Low }
end ; { Outside Bar }
```

Almost Outside Bar

HIGHER HIGH and EQUAL LOW or LOWER LOW and EQUAL HIGH

```
if (High[0]  > High[1] and Low [0]  = Low [1]) or
   (High[0]  = High[1] and Low [0] <  Low [1]) then begin
  Plot1 (High, "Near Out") ; { Bar High }
  Plot2 ( Low, "Near Out") ; { Bar  Low }
end ; { Almost Outside Bar }
```

When referring to a BULLISH BAR the term 'CONFIRMED' implies that the CLOSE is greater than the Close of the previous bar and the Close is greater than the MidRange ((High + Low) / 2) of the current bar. The bar is termed **'Divergent'** if either of these conditions is **not** met. In other words, the Close of the bar **failed** to confirm its Bullish price action. A Bearish bar is the inverse of this pattern.

6.11 - Study : EZL.DualBar Analysis

This study combines Expert Commentary and a Print Report. Below is an example of the output the study generates.

```
EZL.DualBar Analysis Indicator:

Price Action : Higher High - Higher Low
Description  : Bullish Confirmed Bar
Analysis     :

Report: EZL.DualBar Analysis
_______________________________________
Total number of bars in sample : 366
_______________________________________
   Bullish Bars     143      39.07%
      Confirmed      83      22.68%       58.04%
      Divergent      60      16.39%       41.96%
   Bearish Bars     124      33.88%
      Confirmed      52      14.21%       41.94%
      Divergent      72      19.67%       58.06%
   InSide  Bars      36       9.84%
   OutSide Bars      57      15.57%
   NearOut Bars       6       1.64%
_______________________________________
Totals              366     100.00%

end report (EZL.DualBar Analysis).
```

See listing 6.11 for the complete *EasyLanguage* code.

12 Generating advanced reports on a Black Box System

Question ⇒ I purchased a Trading System from one of the vendors listed on **Omega's** web page. The performance summary gives me a limited amount of information. Is there any way I can get more complete information on this system?

Answer ⇒ Many of my clients purchase **Black Box** Trading Systems from the many system vendors. When a system is offered without full disclosure of the methodology and/ or trading rules it is called a **Black Box System**. The system vendor usually provides some limited amount of performance information. Since we do not have access to the *EasyLanguage* code I had always assumed we could not obtain more detailed performance information other than by following the system in real-time.

One day it just came to me. Like a flash in the pan. I can use the INCLUDESYSTEM STATEMENT to combine the BLACK BOX SYSTEM with one or more CUSTOM REPORT SYSTEMS. An example can be found in Listing 6.12a,b,c.

Reports include: "skt.HI/LO TICK", "vrt.Final Report"

Functions used include: "skt.Print.Headers",

13 Controlling the execution of an INCLUDESYSTEM

Question ⇒ I am using an INCLUDESYSTEM to send data to a disk file. I am trying to toggle the INCLUDESYSTEM on and off using an Input. It does not work! Please help me!

Answer ⇒ The client sent me a CODE FRAGMENT that looked something like :

```
Inputs: DoReport (FALSE) ;

{ Attempt to control execution }
if  DoReport  then  IncludeSystem : "Final Report #1" ;
```

He complained that the INCLUDESYSTEM generated the disk file regardless of the value of the input. What was he missing? The INCLUDESYSTEM STATEMENT is a non-executable, (remember COMPILE or LINK TIME?) STATEMENT. The code he used is actually equivalent to :

```
Inputs: DoReport (FALSE) ;

{ Attempt to control execution }
if  DoReport  then ;
IncludeSystem : "Final Report #1" ;
```

Notice the empty IF...THEN STATEMENT, caused by the statement terminator immediately following the THEN KEYWORD.

An example of controlling the execution of an INCLUDESYSTEM can be seen in Listing 6.13.

6.13a - System : skt.File Append

6.13b - System : EZL.Timed Condition

6.13c - System : skt.File Append 2

14 Trading a Channel BreakOut

Question ⇒ I have read that many Money Managers use a Channel BreakOut System. How does this type of methodology work?

Answer ⇒ One of the common entry techniques is the Channel BreakOut. This term has been used to describe a number of channel types but many traders I know use the definition provided within the **Omega** System Library. This system enters upon a violation by price of the Highest High (buy order) or Lowest Low (sell order) of a specified number of bars (the period). Various filters and confirmation methods can be applied to adapt the system to your personal trading style. See Listing 6.16.

15 Replacing the built-in Trailing Stop orders

Question ⇒ I have seen complaints that the Trailing Stop in **TradeStation** is broken. How can I correct the Trailing Stop Exits so they work correctly?

Answer ⇒ There is nothing inherently wrong with the stops built into **TradeStation**. They may be misused in such a way that profitability is maximized. In other words, you can easily write a system that takes every opportunity to make a profit. Looks good on paper but it can be not be traded.

EasyLanguage places the Trailing Stop Order from a long position below the high of the highest bar assuming the dollar floor has been reached. The problem arises during historical testing when the stop order is within the range of the high bar. Since historically *EasyLanguage* has only four price fields available (open, high low and close) it does not place the stop below the absolute tick that met the floor requirement. As a result, your profit will be maximized even though your stop during real-time trading might have been placed earlier below the tick that fulfilled the floor. By writing our own exit orders as an IncludeSystem, we can ensure that the exit price is always an acceptable value. See listing 6.15

16 Using At$ in an Exit Order

Question ⇒ How and why do I use the AT$ operator?

Answer ⇒ The At$ KeyWord is used to anchor an exit price, through the life of the trade, at the price level of the bar of order generation.

The **AT$** operator is available only in SYSTEMS created in the *PowerEditor*.

The exit order containing the AT$ operator **must** be executed on the bar of order generation of the original entry order or the results **will be unpredictable!**

Assuming the exit order is executed on the bar of order generation, the NUMERIC EXPRESSION to the right of the AT$ operator will be locked.

17 Displaying SWING information as on-screen text

Question ⇒ You have previously shown me how to plot PIVOT POINTS and SWINGS. How can I display information about the change in price and amount of time between the pivot points?
Answer ⇒ I have a sample study that has been distributed to hundreds of my clients to demonstrate the use of LOOPS and ARRAYS. I have added to this study logic to compute and display the time between pivot points and the amount of movement in price of the SWING. This study demonstrates the DRAWING TOOL FUNCTIONS. See listing 6.17

A **PIVOT POINT** is one discreet point on the chart. The @SWINGHIGH, @SWINGHIGHBAR, @SWINGLOW and @SWINGLOWBAR FUNCTIONS are one popular method of defining a PIVOT POINT. A PIVOTPOINT does not have enough information to compute a size or length.

A **SWING** requires two PIVOT POINTS, one for each terminus of the SWING. See Listing #6.16.

18 Changing the color and/or size of plots

Question ⇒ I heard that **TradeStation 5.0** will allow me to change the size and color of a PLOT. Would you please explain how to do this?

Answer ⇒ Version 5.0 of *EasyLanguage* introduced many new functions. The two you are interested in are @SETPLOTSIZE and @SETPLOTCOLOR. Each require two inputs, the PLOT NUMBER (1…4) and a NUMERIC CONSTANT defining the target size or color. CONSULT the ON-LINE HELP available in the *PowerEditor* for a list of CONSTANT names and valid values.

The DUAL BAR ANALYSIS example from listing 6.11 from page 111 is one example of this technique.

19 Automatically draw parallel lines outside hand drawn TRENDLINES

Question ⇒ I know it can be done. How do I create parallel lines around a TRENDLINE drawn by hand on a chart?

Answer ⇒ The DRAWING TOOL FUNCTIONS introduced in **TradeStation Version 4.0** allow you to query for existing TRENDLINES on the chart. One of the inputs allows you to specify only lines drawn by the user. So, the first step is to locate any hand drawn TRENDLINES. This will give you a reference number for the TRENDLINE. Next we will use functions to query the start and end points. Each point has three critical pieces of information (date, time and price), six function calls in all. Having dutifully stored these six values you must now create two new lines, one adding a value to the start and end price, the other subtracting a value.

Sounds simple, right? See Listing 6.19 for the actual code that implements this idea.

20 ⇒ Protecting your *EasyLanguage* code

Question How do I protect my *EasyLanguage* code from prying eyes?

Answer ⇒ There are several different things you can do to protect your code. First, you can password protect the file. You should be certain you have an unprotected copy, or at least a printout, stored in a safe place. To the best of my knowledge, **Omega** will NOT help you recover lost passwords.

Inside your code you can do several additional types of protection. As you are probably aware, **TradeStation** requires a SECURITY BLOCK, or dongle as it is frequently called. You can test for a specific block, or a list of blocks, by using the @BLOCKNUMBER FUNCTION (see DATE and TIME FUNCTIONS in Section 3). I know, I cannot figure out why it is in the DATE and TIME FUNCTIONS either.

Additionally, you can control execution of all or part of your code based on the date of the bar being processed, the last bar on the chart and/or the current date based on the computer clock or your real-time data vendor.

Section 6

EasyLanguage Spoken Here

Program Listings

1 EasyLanguage Templates

When I began teaching my *EasyLanguage*™ workshops it immediately became apparent that some users are intimidated by the blank white screen of the *PowerEditor*. I have created a series of code modules the you can use as 'fill in the blank' templates.

#6.01a - Study — skt.EZL Template

```
{       Password
Type  : Study (Report)
Name  : skt.EZL Template
Notes: Samuel K. Tennis, EasyLanguage Template
        Your descriptive information goes here

Input: what inputs does it expect
Alert: does it generate any alerts
Uses : what user functions does it require
Calls: what DLL functions does it require

EasyLanguage interpretation provided
  by Samuel K. Tennis of Vista Research  1998, 1999
  Any unauthorized use of this material may constitute
  a violation of U.S. and International Copyright Laws.
}

{  ****     Declaration Statements      ****  }
Inputs: Price      (Close),
        CashStop    (1500) ;   { in dollars }

Vars   : App.Name ("skt.EZL Template") ;
Vars   : CashPnts (CashStop / BigPointValue),
         One.Point            (01 Point),
         One.Tick (MinMove * 01 Point) ;
Vars   : Dummy                     (00),
         le.Price            (+999999),          se.Price              (-999999),
         lx.Price            (-999999),          sx.Price              (+999999),
         lx.Limit            (+999999),          sx.Limit              (-999999),
         Cond01                (FALSE),          Cond02                  (FALSE) ;
```

```
{  ****    On first bar of data only    ****  }
if  (@BarNumber <= 01)  then begin
  Print ("") ;
  Print ("Study : '", App.Name, "'") ;
  Print ("————————————") ;
  Print ("") ;

  CashPnts = (CashStop / BigPointValue) ;
end ;

{  ****    Assignments on each and every bar of data    ****  }

{  ****    If conditions permit...    ****  }

{  ****    Process on each bar of data...    ****  }
Cond01 = FALSE ;
Cond02 = FALSE ;

{  ****  Position Information processing  ****  }
Vars  : MktPos (0) ;

MktPos  =  I_MarketPosition ;

if   MktPos <>  00  then ;

if   (MktPos  = +01)  then begin
  if  (MktPos[00] <> MktPos[01])  then begin
{*
 *    le.Price = +999999 ;
 *    lx.Price = MaxList (Lowest (Low, 3) - @Average (TrueRange, 05),
 *                        Lowest (Low, 3) - @Average (TrueRange, 30),
 *                        I_AvgEntryPrice - MMS.Pnts) ;
 *}
  end ; { first bar of new trade }
{*
 *  ExitLong  ("lx.MMStop#1") at lx.Price  Stop ;
 *  ExitLong  ("lx.Target#1") at lx.Limit Limit ;
 *}
end ; { currently Long }

if   (MktPos  = -01)  then begin
  if  (MktPos[00] <> MktPos[01])  then begin
  end ; { first bar of new trade }
{*
 *  ExitShort ("Sx.MMStop#1") at sx.Price  Stop ;
 *  ExitShort ("sx.Target#1") at Sx.Limit Limit ;
 *}
end ; { currently short }

if   (MktPos <>  00)  then ; { yet another example... }

{  ****  The Obligatory Plot Statement  ****  }
if  FALSE  then  Plot1 (Close, "Nyet") ;

{  ****  End of bar processing  ****  }
if  Cond01  then ;

if  Cond02  then begin
  Plot3 (High - One.Tick, "BarHi") ;
```

```
  Plot4 ( Low + One.Tick, "BarLo") ;
end ;

{  ****  On the last bar of data only  ****  }
if  (Date[00] = @vrt.LastCalcDate) and
    (Time[00] = @Sess1EndTime)
then begin
  Print ("Study : ", App.Name,
              " ('", @GetSymbolName, "',  ", @CommodityNumber:5:0, ")") ;
  Print (@vrt.FirstCalcDate:6:0, @vrt.FirstCalcTime:5:0, "  :  ",
         @vrt.LastCalcDate:6:0,  @vrt.LastCalcTime:5:0) ;
end ;
```

#6.01b - System — skt.EZL Template

```
{      Password
Type : System (Sample)
Name : skt.EZL Template
Notes: Samuel K. Tennis, Example of a fleshed out system.

Input: FastLen  (7) length of fast moving average
       SlowLen (14) length of slow moving average
       nTicks   (4) number of ticks
Alert: none
Uses : Highest
       Lowest
       Average
Calls: none

EasyLanguage interpretation provided
  by Samuel K. Tennis of Vista Research (c) 1998, 1999
  Any unauthorized use of this material may constitute
  a violation of U.S. and International Copyright Laws.
}

{
   ****    Declaration Statements    ****
}
Inputs: FastLen       (07),        SlowLen       (14),
        nTicks        (04) ;

Vars  : App.Name ("skt.EZL Template") ;
Vars  : FastMA        (00),        SlowMA        (00),
        Trend         (00),
        TrendUp       (00),        TrendUpOut    (00),
        TrendDn       (00),        TrendDnOut    (00),
        le.Price (+999999),        se.Price (-999999),
        lx.Price (-999999),        sx.Price (+999999),
        lx.Limit (+999999),        sx.Limit (-999999),
        nPoints  (MinMove * nTicks Points) ;
Vars  : OnePoint                 (01 Points),
        OneTick  (MinMove *       01 Points) ;

{ ———————————————————————————————————— }

if  (@BarNumber <= 01)  then begin
  Print ("") ;
  Print ("System: '", App.Name, "'") ;
  Print ("————————") ;
```

```
  Print ("") ;

  nPoints  = @MinMove * nTicks Points ;
end ; { first bar of data only }

{ ============================================================================ }
{ ———————————————————————————————————————— }
{*
        1         2         3         4         5         6         7
8
12345678901234567890123456789012345678901234567890123456789012345678901234567890
 ————+————+————+————+————+————+————+————+
        3         2    .    1         0         1         2         3
4
98765432109876543210987654321098765432101234567890123456789012345678901234567890
                                  ^Centered Text^
 *}
{ ———————————————————————————————————————— }
{ ============================================================================ }


{ ———————————————————————————————————————— }
{
    ****  Assignments on each and every bar of data  ****
}
FastMA  = @Average (Close,     FastLen) ;
SlowMA  = @Average (Close,     SlowLen) ;
nPoints = @Average (TrueRange,      15) ;
{
    ****  If conditions permit...  ****
}
if  (FastMA crosses above SlowMA)  then begin
  le.Price   = @Highest (Close, 05) + nPoints ;
  lx.Price   =  @Lowest (Close, 05) - nPoints ;
  lx.Limit   = @Highest ( High, 10) + nPoints * 3.00 ;
  Trend      = +01 ;
end ;

if  (FastMA crosses below SlowMA)  then begin
  se.Price   =  @Lowest (Close, 05) - nPoints ;
  sx.Price   = @Highest (Close, 05) + nPoints ;
  sx.Limit   =  @Lowest (  Low, 10) - nPoints * 3.00 ;
  Trend      = -01 ;
end ;

{ ———————————————————————————————————————— }
{
    ****  Process on each bar of data...  ****
}
if  (Trend  = +01)  then  Buy  ("le.#1") at le.Price stop ;
if  (Trend  = -01)  then  Sell ("se.#1") at se.Price stop ;
ExitLong  ("lx.#1") at lx.Price stop ;
ExitShort ("sx.#1") at sx.Price stop ;


if  (Trend             = +01) and
    (@MarketPosition <> +01)
then begin
  Buy        ("le.#2")    at le.Price stop ;
  ExitLong   ("lx.Stp#2") at lx.Price stop ;
```

```
  ExitLong  ("lx.Lmt#2") at lx.Limit stop ;
end ; { place entry order }

if  (Trend             = -01) and
    (@MarketPosition <> -01)
then begin
  Sell       ("se.#2")     at se.Price stop ;
  ExitShort ("sx.Stp#2") at sx.Price stop ;
  ExitShort ("sx.Lmt#2") at sx.Limit stop ;
end ; { place entry order }

if  (@MarketPosition >= +01)  then begin
  if  (@BarsSinceEntry <= +01)  then begin
    le.Price  = +999999 ;
    lx.Price  =  @Lowest (Close, 05) - nPoints ;
    lx.Limit  = @Highest ( High, 10) + nPoints * 3.00 ;
  end ; { first bar of new trade }

  ExitLong  ("lx.MMStop#1") at lx.Price  Stop ;
  ExitLong  ("lx.Target#1") at lx.Limit Limit ;
end ; { Currently  Long }

if  (@MarketPosition <= -01)  then begin
  if  (@BarsSinceEntry <= +01)  then begin
    se.Price  = -999999 ;
    sx.Price  = @Highest (Close, 05) + nPoints ;
    sx.Limit  =  @Lowest (  Low, 10) - nPoints * 3.00 ;
  end ; { first bar of new trade }

  ExitShort ("Sx.MMStop#1") at sx.Price  Stop ;
  ExitShort ("sx.Target#1") at sx.Limit Limit ;
end ; { Currently Short }

{ ——————————————————————————————— }
{*
 *      ****  End of bar processing  ****
 *}
if  (Trend  = +01)  then TrendUp  = TrendUp + 01 ;
if  (Trend  = +01) and (@MarketPosition <> +01)
  then  TrendUpOut  = TrendUpOut + 01 ;

if  (Trend  = -01)  then  TrendDn  = TrendDn + 01 ;
if  (Trend  = -01) and (@MarketPosition <> -01)
  then  TrendDnOut  = TrendDnOut + 01 ;

{ ——————————————————————————————— }
{*
 *   ****  On the last bar of data only  ****
 *}
if  Date  = @vrt.LastCalcDate  and  Time  = @Sess1EndTime  then begin
  Print ("System: ", App.Name,
            " ('", @GetSymbolName, "',  ", @CommodityNumber:6:0, ")") ;
  Print (@vrt.FirstCalcDate:6:0, @vrt.FirstCalcTime:5:0, "  :  ",
         @vrt.LastCalcDate:6:0,  @vrt.LastCalcTime:5:0) ;

  Print ("Up   : ", TrendUp, TrendUpOut, TrendUp / TrendUpOut, "%") ;
  Print ("Down : ", TrendDn, TrendDnOut, TrendDn / TrendDnOut, "%") ;
end ;

{
```

#6.01c - Function — skt.EZL Template

```
{       Password
Type  : User Function (Numeric, Boolean, String)
Name  : skt.EZL.Template
Notes: Samuel K. Tennis, Example of a fleshed out User Function.

Input: Price   (Close) Price field for study
       FastLen    (07) length of fast moving average
       SlowLen    (14) length of slow moving average
       nTicks     (04) number of ticks

Sample Usage :

  Trend = skt.EZL.Template (Close, 07, 14, 04) ;

EasyLanguage translation provided
  by Samuel K. Tennis
  of Vista Research (c) 1997, 1998, 1999

  Any unauthorized use of this material may constitute
  a violation of U.S. and International Copyright Laws.
}

{*
 *****     Declaration Statements     *****
 *}
Inputs: Price     (NumericSeries),
        FastLen   (NumericSimple),
        SlowLen   (NumericSimple),
        nTicks    (NumericSimple) ;

Vars   : App.Name ("skt.EZL.Template") ;
Vars   : FastMA          (00),          SlowMA          (00),
         Return          (00),
         nPoints  (MinMove * nTicks Points) ;
Vars   : OnePoint                (1 Points),
         OneTick  (MinMove *      1 Points) ;

{ ———————————————————————————————————— }

if  (@BarNumber <= +01)  then begin
  Print ("") ;
  Print ("Function: '", App.Name, "'") ;
  Print ("——————————————") ;
  Print ("") ;

  Return   =  00 ;
  nPoints  = @MinMove * nTicks Points ;
end ; { first bar of data only }

{ ====================================================================== }

{ ———————————————————————————————————— }
{*
         1         2         3         4         5         6         7
8
```

```
1234567890123456789012345678901234567890123456789012345678901234567890123456789 0
  ———+———+———+———+———+———+———+———+
          3         2         1         0         1         2         3
4
9876543210987654321098765432109876543210123456789012345678901234567890123456789 0
                                ^Centered Text^
 *}
{ ————————————————————————————————————— }


{*
 *  In this example we do not initialize the "Return" variable since we
 *  want want the Trend value to remain set until changed.
 *
 *  Return  = 00 ;  { reset return value each bar }
 *}

{*
 *****  Assignments on each and every bar of data  *****
 *}

FastMA  = @Average (Price,     FastLen) ;
SlowMA  = @Average (Price,     SlowLen) ;

{*
 *****  If conditions permit...  *****
 *}

if  (FastMA crosses above SlowMA)
  then  Return  = +01 ;

if  (FastMA crosses below SlowMA)
  then  Return  = -01 ;

{ ————————————————————————————————————— }

{*
 *****  Process on each bar of data...  *****
 *}

{ ————————————————————————————————————— }

{*
 *****  End of bar processing  *****
 *}

{ ————————————————————————————————————— }

{*
 *****  On the last bar of data only  *****
 *}

if  Date  = @vrt.LastCalcDate and
    Time  = @Sess1EndTime
then begin
  Print ("Function: '", App.Name, "' ('", @GetSymbolName,
               "', ", @CommodityNumber:6:0, ")") ;
  Print (@vrt.FirstCalcDate:6:0, @vrt.FirstCalcTime:5:0, "  :  ",
         @vrt.LastCalcDate:6:0,  @vrt.LastCalcTime:5:0) ;
end ;
```

```
{*
 *****  Return value for the function  *****
 *  You must change this assignment statement to your new function name
 *}

skt.EZL.Template  = Return ;

{
Custom Programming Services provided by:

                Samuel K. Tennis
                 Vista Research
                129 Staff Drive
        Ft. Walton Beach, Florida 32548
         voice :    1(850) 243-5105
         fax   :    1(850) 301-2884
         eMail :  skt@vista-research.com
           http://www.vista-research.com
}
```

2 Building Daily Bars Out Of Intraday Bars

#6.02a - Study — EZL.Synthetic Daily

```
{
Type : Study (synthetic bar)
Name : EZL.Synthetic Daily
Notes: Create synthetic daily bars from intraday data

Input: none
Alert: none
Calls: none
Uses : none

EasyLanguage interpretation provided
   by  Samuel K. Tennis
   of  Vista Research (c) 1998, 1999.
  Any unauthorized use of this material may constitute
  a violation of U.S. and International Copyright Laws.
}

Arrays: Day.Op [10] (00),        Day.HI [10] (00),
        Day.Lo [10] (00),        Day.Cl [10] (00) ;

Vars   : App.Name   ("EZL.Synthetic Daily") ;
Vars   : MaxSize      (10),        Loop         (00),
        Start     (FALSE) ;
Vars   : d.hi    (-999999),
        d.Lo    (+999999) ; { used in Alert statement }

if  Date [00]  > Date [01]  then begin
  if  Start  then begin
    for Loop = MaxSize DownTo 01 begin
      Day.Op [Loop] = Day.Op [Loop - 01] ;
      Day.HI [Loop] = Day.HI [Loop - 01] ;
      Day.Lo [Loop] = Day.Lo [Loop - 01] ;
```

```
      Day.Cl [Loop] = Day.Cl [Loop - 01] ;
    end ; { for loop }

    Plot1 [01] (Day.Op [00], "Open ") ;  {  Left Tic }
    Plot2 [01] (Day.Hi [00], "High ") ;  {  Bar High }
    Plot3 [01] (Day.Lo [00], " Low ") ;  {  Bar Low  }
    Plot4 [01] (Day.Cl [00], "Close") ;  { Right Tic }
  end ; { we have had at least one complete day }

  Day.Op [00] =  Open ;
  Day.Hi [00] =  High ;
  Day.Lo [00] =   Low ;
  Day.Cl [00] = Close ;

  if  Start = FALSE  then
    Start     =  TRUE ;
end ; { first bar of a new day }

if High  > Day.Hi [00] then Day.Hi [00] =  High ;
if Low  <  Day.Lo [00] then Day.Lo [00] =   Low ;
                            Day.Cl [00] = Close ;

if  Start  then begin
{*
 *   I do not want to reference a StudyBar value of an array so
 * I created two variables to store the intraday high and low.
 *}
  d.hi  = Day.Hi [00] ;
  d.lo  = Day.Lo [00] ;
  if  CheckAlert  then begin
    if  Day.Lo [00] <  Day.Lo [01] and
          d.hi [01] <= Day.Hi [01] and
          d.hi [00]  > Day.Hi [01]
      then  Alert  =  TRUE ;   { this high formed a daily OVB }
    if  Day.Hi [00]  > Day.Hi [01] and
          d.Lo [01] >= Day.Lo [01] and
          d.Lo [00] <  Day.Lo [01]
      then  Alert  =  TRUE ;   { this  low formed a daily OVB }
  end ; { alert processing }
{*
  if Day.Hi [00] <  Day.Hi [01] and Day.Lo [00] <  Day.Lo [01]
    then  Buy  ("le.OVB") at Day.Hi [01] + OneTick Stop ;

  if Day.Hi [00]  > Day.Hi [01] and Day.Lo [00]  > Day.Lo [01]
    then  Sell ("se.OVB") at Day.Lo [01] - OneTick Stop ;
 *}
end ; { at least one complete day }
```

#6.02b - System — EZL.Synthetic Daily

Examine this system carefully for examples of the use of TrendLine Drawing Tools.

```
{
Type : System (Top Level)
Name : EZL.Synthetic Daily
Notes: Create synthetic daily bars from intraday data.
```

```
Input: None
Alert: n/a
Calls: @MinMove
       @tl_New
       @TL_SetColor
       @TL_SetExtLeft
       @TL_SetExtRight
       @TL_SetEnd
Uses : None

EasyLanguage interpretation provided
    by  Samuel K. Tennis
    of  Vista Research (c) 1998, 1999.
  Any unauthorized use of this material may constitute
  a violation of U.S. and International Copyright Laws.
}

Arrays: Day.Op [10] (00),          Day.HI [10] (00),
        Day.Lo [10] (00),          Day.Cl [10] (00) ;

Vars   : App.Name ("EZL.Synthetic Daily") ;

Vars   : MaxSize     (10),         Loop         (00),
         Start    (FALSE),
         OnePoint (01 Point),
         OneTick  (@MinMove * 01 Point) ;

Vars   : tl_hiRef   (-01),         tl_hiErr     (00),
         tl_loRef   (-01),         tl_loErr     (00) ;


if  Date [00]  > Date [01]  then begin
  if  Start  then begin
    for Loop = MaxSize DownTo 01 begin
      Day.Op [Loop] = Day.Op [Loop - 01] ;
      Day.HI [Loop] = Day.HI [Loop - 01] ;
      Day.Lo [Loop] = Day.Lo [Loop - 01] ;
      Day.Cl [Loop] = Day.Cl [Loop - 01] ;
    end ; { for loop }
  end ;

  Day.Op [00] =  Open ;
  Day.Hi [00] =  High ;
  Day.Lo [00] =   Low ;
  Day.Cl [00] = Close ;

  if  Start = False  then
    Start     =  TRUE ;
end ; { first bar of a new day }

if  High  > Day.Hi [00]  then Day.Hi [00] =  High ;
if  Low   <  Day.Lo [00]  then Day.Lo [00] =   Low ;
                              Day.Cl [00] = Close ;

if  Start  then begin
  if  Date [00]  = Date [01] and
      Date [01] <> Date [02]
  then begin
    tl_hiRef = @tl_New (Date [01], Time [01], Day.Hi [01],
```

```
                        Date [00], Time [00], Day.Hi [01]) ;
    if  tl_hiRef <> -01  then begin
      tl_hiErr = @TL_SetColor    (TL_hiRef, Tool_White) ;
      tl_hiErr = @TL_SetExtLeft  (TL_hiRef, FALSE) ;
      tl_hiErr = @TL_SetExtRight (TL_hiRef, FALSE) ;
    end ;

    tl_loRef = @tl_New (Date [01], Time [01], Day.Lo [01],
                        Date [00], Time [00], Day.Lo [01]) ;
    if  tl_loRef <> -01  then begin
      tl_loErr = @TL_SetColor    (TL_loRef, Tool_White) ;
      tl_loErr = @TL_SetExtLeft  (TL_loRef, FALSE) ;
      tl_loErr = @TL_SetExtRight (TL_loRef, FALSE) ;
    end ;
  end
  else
    if  Date [00] = Date [01]  then begin
      if  tl_hiRef <> -01  then begin
        tl_hiErr = @TL_SetEnd      (TL_hiRef, Date, Time, Day.Hi [01]) ;
      end ;

      if  tl_loRef <> -01  then begin
        tl_loErr = @TL_SetEnd      (TL_loRef, Date, Time, Day.Lo [01]) ;
      end ;
    end ;

  if  Day.Hi [00] <  Day.Hi [01] and
      Day.Lo [00] <  Day.Lo [01]
    then  Buy  ("le.OVB") at Day.Hi [01] + OneTick Stop ;

  if  Day.Hi [00]  > Day.Hi [01] and
      Day.Lo [00]  > Day.Lo [01]
    then  Sell ("se.OVB") at Day.Lo [01] - OneTick Stop ;
end ; { at least one complete day }
```

03 Marking The First Day Of A Week

#6.03a - PaintBar — EZL.Paint Mondays

The one and only bar on which the day of the week (0...6) will be smaller than the day of the week of the previous bar is on the first bar of a new week.

```
{
Type  : PaintBar
Name  : EZL.Paint Mondays
Notes : Paint the first bar of each calendar week.

The one and only bar on which the day of the week (0..6) becomes smaller…

EasyLanguage translation provided
  by Samuel K. Tennis
  of Vista Research (c) 1998, 1999
}

if  @DayOfWeek (Date [00]) <  @DayOfWeek (Date [01])
```

```
then begin
  Plot1 (High, "Monday") ; { BarHigh }
  Plot2 ( Low, "Monday") ; { Bar Low }

  if  CheckAlert  then  Alert  =  TRUE ;
end ; {  }
```

#6.03b - PaintBar — EZL.Paint Fridays

```
{
Type   : PaintBar
Name   : EZL.Paint Fridays
Notes : Paint the last bar of each calendar week.

EasyLanguage translation provided
  by Samuel K. Tennis
  of Vista Research (c) 1997, 1999
}

{*
 *  In most cases it will find a bar for Friday.  However, when Friday is
 *  a holiday it will paint the last day of the week.
 *}
Vars   : Offset (00) ;

if  @DayOfWeek (Date[00])  =  05 or
   (@DayOfWeek (Date[01]) <>  05 and
    @DayOfWeek (Date[00]) <  @DayOfWeek (Date[01]))
then begin
  Offset  = 00 ;
  if  ((@DayOfWeek (Date[01]) <>          05) and
       (@DayOfWeek (Date[00]) <  @DayOfWeek (Date[01])))
  then  Offset  = +01 ;

  Plot1[Offset] (High [Offset], "Friday") ;
  Plot2[Offset] ( Low [Offset], "Friday") ;

  if  CheckAlert  then  Alert  =  TRUE ;
end ; {  }
```

4 Building Weekly Bars Out Of Daily Bars

Sophisticated example using LOOPS and ARRAYS. Demonstrates the use of COUNTER and FLAG ASSIGNMENT STATEMENTS.

#6.04 - Study : EZL.Synthetic Weekly

```
{
Type : Study (synthetic bar)
Name : EZL.Synthetic Weekly
Notes: Create synthetic weekly bars from intraday data

Input: none
```

```
Alert: none
Calls: @DayOfWeek
Uses : none

EasyLanguage interpretation provided
   by  Samuel K. Tennis
   of  Vista Research (c) 1998, 1999.
  Any unauthorized use of this material may constitute a
  violation of U.S. and International Copyright Laws.
}

Arrays: Week.Op [10] (00),        Week.HI [10] (00),
        Week.Lo [10] (00),        Week.Cl [10] (00) ;

Vars  : App.Name  ("EZL.Synthetic Weekly") ;

Vars  : MaxSize       (10),        Loop          (00),
        Week.Cnt      (00),        Start      (FALSE) ;

{*
 *   Day Of Week (Monday = 01) is less than
 * the Day Of Week of the previous bar (Friday = 05)
 *}
if  @DayOfWeek (Date [00]) <  @DayOfWeek (Date [01])
then begin

  if  Start  then begin  { Have we completed at least one day yet? }

{ store ("Bubble Up") values of previous weeks }
    for Loop = MaxSize DownTo 01 begin
      Week.Op [Loop] = Week.Op [Loop - 01] ;
      Week.HI [Loop] = Week.HI [Loop - 01] ;
      Week.Lo [Loop] = Week.Lo [Loop - 01] ;
      Week.Cl [Loop] = Week.Cl [Loop - 01] ;
    end ; { for loop }
    Week.Cnt  = Week.Cnt + 01 ;  { increment week counter }

{ Zero element still contains the completed weeks values }
    Plot1 [01] (Week.Op [00], "Open ") ;
    Plot2 [01] (Week.Hi [00], "High ") ;
    Plot3 [01] (Week.Lo [00], " Low ") ;
    Plot4 [01] (Week.Cl [00], "Close") ;
  end ; { if start, at least one complete week }

{ assign Zero element values on first bar of new day }
  Week.Op [00] =  Open ;
  Week.Hi [00] =  High ;
  Week.Lo [00] =   Low ;
  Week.Cl [00] = Close ;

  if  Start  = FALSE  then
    Start      =  TRUE ;  { begin a new week }
end ; { First bar of new week }

{ Store Higher Highs, Lower Lows and most recent close }
if  High  > Week.Hi [00]  then  Week.Hi [00] =  High ;
if   Low <  Week.Lo [00]  then  Week.Lo [00] =   Low ;
                                Week.Cl [00] = Close ;

if  Start and Week.Cnt  > 01  then begin
```

```
{*
  if  Week.Hi [00] <  Week.Hi [01] and
      Week.Lo [00] <  Week.Lo [01]
    then  Buy  ("le.OVB") at Week.Lo [01] Stop ;

  if  Week.Hi [00]  > Week.Hi [01] and
      Week.Lo [00]  > Week.Lo [01]
    then  Sell ("se.OVB") at Week.Lo [01] Stop ;
 *}
end ; { at least one complete day }

if  CheckCommentary  then begin
  CommentaryCL (" [00] ",
                Week.Op[00], Week.Hi[00], Week.Lo[00], Week.Cl[00]) ;
  CommentaryCL (" [01] ",
                Week.Op[01], Week.Hi[01], Week.Lo[01], Week.Cl[01]) ;
end ; { Expert Commentary }
```

5 Marking The First Bar Of The Higher Time Frame

#6.05 - Study — EZL.Mark First Bar

```
{
Type  : Study (PaintBar)
Name  : EZL.Mark First Bar
Notes : Example using DataCompression function

Inputs:
Alert : None
Calls : EasyLanguage User Functions
Uses  : DLL Function Calls

EasyLanguage translation provided
  by Samuel K. Tennis
  of Vista Research (c) 1997, 1998, 1999

  Any unauthorized use of this material may constitute
  a violation of U.S. and International Copyright Laws.
}

Vars  : Line1  (00),
        Line2  (00) ;

Line1 = 00 ;
Line2 = 00 ;

if  @DataCompression      <=                    01  and
              Date [00]  >              Date [01]
then begin
  Line1 = High [00] ;
  Line2 =  Low [00] ;
end ; { IntraDay - first bar of new day }

if  @DataCompression       =                    02  and
    DayOfWeek  (Date [00]) <  DayOfWeek  (Date [01])
then begin
  Line1 = High [00] ;
```

```
  Line2 =  Low [00] ;
end ; { Daily - first bar of new week }

if  @DataCompression       =                     03  and
    DayOfMonth (Date [00]) <  DayOfMonth (Date [01])
then begin
  Line1 = High [00] ;
  Line2 =  Low [00] ;
end ; { Weekly - first bar of new month }

if  @DataCompression       =                     04  and
    Year       (Date [00])  > Year       (Date [01])
then begin
  Line1 = High [00] ;
  Line2 =  Low [00] ;
end ; { Monthly - first bar of new year }

if  Line1 <> 00  then begin
  Plot1 (Line1, "BarHi") ;
  Plot2 (Line2, "BarLo") ;
end ; { Paint the bar }
```

6 Playing A Custom .WAV File From An Alert

#6.06 - Study — EZL.Audio Alert

```
{
Type   : Study (Alert w/ Sound)
Name   : EZL.Audio Alert
Notes  : Play a wave file upon triggering an Alert.

  sFile is the Drive, Path and FileName of your sound file.

EasyLanguage translation provided
  by Samuel K. Tennis
  of Vista Research (c) 1997, 1999
}

Inputs: sFile ("C:\Windows\msRemind.WAV") ;
Vars   : Cond1 (FALSE) ;

{*
 *  Put your alert condition here!
 *}
Cond1 = (Date = @vrt.LastCalcDate and
         Time = @vrt.LastCalcTime) ;

{*
 *  This executes the actual Alert and plays the WAV file
 *}
if  CheckAlert  then begin
  if  Cond1  then begin
{*
 *  If you do NOT want the Alert window to open then omit this line.
 *}
    Alert  =  TRUE ;
```

```
      if  @PlaySound (sSFile)  then ;
    end ; {  }
  end ; { is the alert enabled? }

  {*
   *  The obligatory plot statement
   *}
  if  FALSE  then  Plot1 (Close, "") ;
```

7 Demonstrating The Use Of The PRINT STATEMENT

#6.07a - Study — skt.Print.Headers

```
{
Type   : Study (Sample Report)
Name   : skt.Print.Headers
Notes  : Demonstrates use of @skt.Print.Headers & "skt_0002.DLL"

EasyLanguage translation provided
  by Samuel K. Tennis
  of Vista Research (c) 1997, 1999
}

Vars   : App.Name ("skt.Print.Headers") ;
Vars   : OnePoint            (01 Point),
         OneTick  (MinMove * 01 Point) ;
{*
 *
 *}
if  @BarNumber <= 01 or
   (Date = vrt.LastCalcDate and Time = vrt.LastCalcTime)
then begin
  if  @skt.Print.Headers (App.Name)  then ;

  Print ("One Point     = ", OnePoint      :04:04,
    "     One Tick      = ", OneTick       :04:04) ;
  Print ("Min Move      = ", @MinMove      :04:04,
    "     PriceScale    = ", @PriceScale   :04:00) ;
  Print ("PointValue    = ", @PointValue   :04:04,
    "     BigPointValue = ", @BigPointValue:04:04) ;

  if  FALSE  then  PLot1 (Close, "") ; { obligatory Plot Statement }
end ;

{
Custom Programming Services provided by:

               Samuel K. Tennis
                Vista Research
               129 Staff Drive
        Ft. Walton Beach, Florida 32548
         voice :    1(850) 243-5105
         fax   :    1(850) 301-2884
         eMail :  skt@vista-research.com
           http://www.vista-research.com
```

#6.07b - Function: skt.Print.Headers

This User Function is called from many of my Custom Reports. It requires several functions found in a proprietary DLL (Dynamic Link Library) available from Vista Research.

```
{
Type : User Function (Print Report)
Name : skt.Print.Headers
Notes: Prints standardized report header, requires "skt_0002.DLL".

03/24/99  skt
  Since this report prints the sample size by using the value of @CurrentBar
it should really be called at the same time that the report is generated
rather than on the first bar of data.  Note that it requires the use of one
of my DLL utility sets.

Calls: GetSymbolName
       LeftStr
       Spaces
       StrLen
       NumToStr
       DataCompression
       BarInterval
       vrt.FirstCalcDate
       vrt.FirstCalcTime
       vrt.LastCalcDate
       vrt.LastCalcTime

Uses : "C:\UserDLL\skt_0002.DLL", "TypeOfChart2"
       "C:\UserDLL\skt_0002.DLL", "dll_MMDDYY"
       "C:\UserDLL\skt_0002.DLL", "dll_HHMMpm"
       "C:\UserDLL\skt_0002.DLL", "dll_HHMM"

Not
Used : "C:\UserDLL\skt_0002.DLL", "TypeOfChart"
       "C:\UserDLL\skt_0002.DLL", "dll_MMDDYYYY"
       "C:\UserDLL\skt_0002.DLL", "dll_Format"
       "C:\UserDLL\skt_0002.DLL", "dll_FormatPrice"

EasyLanguage interpretation provided by
  Samuel K. Tennis of Vista Research (c) 1998, 1999
  Any unauthorized use of this material constitutes
  a violation of U.S. and International Copyright Laws.
}


DefineDllFunc: "C:\UserDLL\skt_0002.DLL", LPSTR, "TypeOfChart2", Int, Int ;
DefineDllFunc: "C:\UserDLL\skt_0002.DLL", LPSTR, "dll_MMDDYY",   Long ;
DefineDllFunc: "C:\UserDLL\skt_0002.DLL", LPSTR, "dll_HHMMpm",   Int ;
DefineDllFunc: "C:\UserDLL\skt_0002.DLL", LPSTR, "dll_HHMM",     Int ;

Inputs: App.Name (StringSimple) ;
Vars  : Hyphens (
"————————————————————————————————————"),
        Equals  (
"======================================================================="),
        Header1 (
"Symbol      Comm#   Chart      First Bar        Last  Bar      Sample"),
        Str0          (""),
```

```
        Str1          (""),
        Str2          ("") ;
Vars  : MaxSymbolName (10),
        MaxCommNumLen (06) ;

{ ————————————————————————————————————— }

Print ("") ;
Print (Equals) ;

Str1 = "Report: '" + App.Name + "'" ;
Str2 = "Run Date : " + dll_MMDDYY (@CurrentDate)
               + " " + dll_HHMMpm (@CurrentTime) ;
Str0 = Str1 + @Spaces (@StrLen (Equals) -
                      (@StrLen (Str1) + @StrLen (Str2))) + Str2 ;

  Print (Str0) ;
  Print (@LeftStr (Hyphens, @StrLen (App.Name) + 10)) ;

Print (Header1) ;
Print (Hyphens) ;
Str0 = @GetSymbolName + Spaces (MaxSymbolName - @StrLen (@GetSymbolName)) ;
Str1 = @NumToStr (@CommodityNumber, 0) ;
Str2 = @Spaces   (MaxCommNumLen - @StrLen (Str1)) + Str1 ;
Str0 = Str0 + Str2 + "   " + TypeOfChart2 (@DataCompression, @BarInterval) +
"  " ;
Str1 = @NumToStr (@CurrentBar, 0) ;
Str2 = @Spaces   (MaxCommNumLen - @StrLen (Str1)) + Str1   ;
Str0 = Str0 + "  " + dll_MMDDYY (@vrt.FirstCalcDate) +
              "  " + dll_HHMM   (@vrt.FirstCalcTime) +
            ",   " + dll_MMDDYY (@vrt.LastCalcDate)  +
              "  " + dll_HHMM   (@vrt.LastCalcTime)  +
            ",   " + Str2  ;
  Print (Str0) ;
  Print ("") ;

skt.Print.Headers  = TRUE ;

{ ————————————————————————————————————— }
```

8 Using Expert Commentary

The study below plots the price levels for a CHANNEL BREAKOUT. It also demonstrates the manipulation of CHARACTER STRINGS, the use of the PRINT STATEMENT and the advanced usage of EXPERT COMMENTARY.

#6.08 - Study — EZL.Learn.Expt.Cmtry

```
{
Type : Study (Commentary Report)
Name : EZL.Learn.Expt.Cmtry
Notes: Learn to use Expert Commentary in your EasyLanguage code.

Input: None
Alert: None
Uses : skt.Return.Headers
```

```
       NumToStr
Calls: None

05/23/98  skt
     Code updated slightly to better demonstrate some string manipulation
features.

EasyLanguage interpretation provided by Samuel K. Tennis
  of Vista Research (c) 1998, 1999
  Any unauthorized use of this material may constitute
  a violation of U.S. and International Copyright Laws.
}

Vars   : App.Name ("EZL.Learn.Expt.Cmtry") ;
Vars   : hi1      (00),          hi2      (00),
         hi3      (00),          hi4      (00) ;
Vars   : hbe.str ("\hb\he"),
         hb.str  (""),           he.str   (""),
         my.str  ("") ;

if  @BarNumber <=  01  then begin
  hb.Str =  @LeftStr (hbe.str, 3) ;
  he.Str = @RightStr (hbe.str, 3) ;
end ; { by using this trick I can catenate characters w/ highlighting }

my.Str   = "" ;

{*  Suggested Naming Convention and Control of Orders
 * Buy        ("le.#1")          at market ; { on the first tic of the next
bar }
 * ExitLong   ("lx.#1")       on the close ; { on the last tic of this bar }
 * Sell       ("se.#1") at se.Price  stop ; { or worse order }
 * ExitShort ("sx.#1") at sx.Price limit ; { or better order }
 *}

{ ==================== }
{*
 * Store bar number of four most recent swing Highs
 *}

Inputs: Strength (03) ;
Vars  : Length   (Strength + 01) ;

if  SwingHighBar (01,  High, Strength, Length)  > -01  then begin
  hi4 = hi3 ;
  hi3 = hi2 ;
  hi2 = hi1 ;
  hi1 = BarNumber [Strength] ;

  if  hi4  > -01 and      hi3  > -01 and
      hi2  > -01 and      hi1  > -01 and
     (BarNumber - hi4  > -01 and BarNumber - hi4 <  MaxBarsBack) and
     (BarNumber - hi3  > -01 and BarNumber - hi3 <  MaxBarsBack) and
     (BarNumber - hi2  > -01 and BarNumber - hi2 <  MaxBarsBack) and
     (BarNumber - hi1  > -01 and BarNumber - hi1 <  MaxBarsBack) and
      High [BarNumber - hi4]  >  High [BarNumber - hi3] and
      High [BarNumber - hi3]  >  High [BarNumber - hi2] and
      High [BarNumber - hi2]  >  High [BarNumber - hi1]
  then begin
    Print        (Date:6:0, Time:5:0, "  Holaliyah!!!  ", BarNumber:6:0) ;
```

```
      My.Str = Text (Date:6:0, Time:5:0, "  Holaliyah!!!  ", BarNumber:6:0) ;
    end ;
  end ;

  { ===================== }
  {*
   * Typical "Channel BreakOut" orders
   *}
  Vars  : le.Price (+999999),        lx.Price (-999999),
          se.Price (-999999),        sx.Price (+999999) ;

  le.Price = Highest (High,  28) ; {   Blue   }
  sx.Price = Highest (High,  14) ; {   Cyan   }
  lx.Price =  Lowest ( Low,  14) ; { Magenta }
  se.Price =  Lowest ( Low,  28) ; {   Red    }

  Plot1 (le.Price, "le.Price") ;
  Plot2 (sx.Price, "sx.Price") ;
  Plot3 (lx.Price, "lx.Price") ;
  Plot4 (se.Price, "se.Price") ;

  { ===================== }

  #BeginCmtryOrAlert  { compiler directive }

  Vars  : st ("") ;

  if  CheckCommentary  then begin
  {*
    CommentaryCL (skt.Return.Header (App.Name)) ;
   *}
    Commentary ("The 'CL' appended to end of 'CommentaryCL' statement adds");
    Commentary ("a 'CarriageReturn / LineFeed' (CR/LF) pair to your text.") ;
    CommentaryCL ;

    Commentary   ("I  can have as many line breaks ",
                  "in my character string as I want and ",
                  "it does NOT effect how the text is displayed. ",
                "  If I want to insert blank lines ",
                  NewLine,
               "  (or to terminate this line) ",
                  NewLine,
                  "I do so with the '", hb.str, "NewLine", he.str, "' com-
mand.",
                  NewLine, NewLine) ;

    CommentaryCL ("Any text you put inside \hbspecial characters\he "
                + "will be highlighted.") ;

    st = " le = " + NumToStr (le.Price, 04)
      + ", lx = " + NumToStr (lx.Price, 04)
      + ", se = " + NumToStr (se.Price, 04)
      + ", sx = " + NumToStr (sx.Price, 04) ;

    if  My.Str  > " " then my.Str  = NewLine + NewLine + my.Str ;

    CommentaryCL (NewLine,
         "You can display numeric values along with string literals.",
                 NewLine,
                " hi1 = ", hi1:5:0, ", hi2 = ", hi2:5:0,
```

```
            ", hi3 = ", hi3:5:0, ", hi4 = ", hi4:5:0,
             NewLine,
 "And you can fill a string variable and display it in your commentary.",
             NewLine, "'", st, "'", my.Str) ;
{*
 * Demonstrate use of Expert Commentary Tool to obtain specific data using
 * the Print Statement.  Contrast with hard coding each sample period.
 *
 * BarNumber can be as high as 13,000  { ":5", five whole number places }
 * but can not have no fractional part. { ":0", with zero decimals. }
 *}
  Print (" hi1 = ", hi1:5:0, ", hi2 = ", hi2:5:0,
       ", hi3 = ", hi3:5:0, ", hi4 = ", hi4:5:0) ;
  Print (st) ;
end ;

#end ; { compiler directive }

{
Custom Programming Services provided by:

               Samuel K. Tennis
                Vista Research
               129 Staff Drive
        Ft. Walton Beach, Florida 32548
         voice :    1(850) 243-5105
         fax   :    1(850) 301-2884
         eMail :  skt@vista-research.com
           http://www.vista-research.com
}
```

09 Generating A Text Report

A GENERIC TEXT REPORT designed to allow the non-programmer to modify the conditions and legends of the report. I created this during one of my *EasyLanguage* Workshops in response to a request from a student. It allows you to easily specify a description of the target bar. Examples might be Inside Bars, Outside Bars, bars with increasing momentum or, as coded right now, an RSI greater than 65.

#6.09a - Study — EZL Row/Col Report

```
{
Type  : Study (Report)
Name  : EZL Row/Col Report
Notes : Generates a report to Print Log and CSV file.

EasyLanguage translation provided
  by Samuel K. Tennis
  of Vista Research (c) 1998, 1999

  Any unauthorized use of this material may constitute
  a violation of U.S. and International Copyright Laws.
}
```

```
{*
 * The user can enable and disable these features from the chart.
 *}
Inputs: DoReport (FALSE),    { Send output to Print Log Window }
        DiskFile (FALSE)  ; { Send output to CSV file on disk }
{*
 * If you alter the size of the array be sure to change the
 * MaxRows and/or MaxCols variables below.
 *}
Arrays: Specs [10, 10] (0) ;
{*
 * The user MIGHT want to alter the report name and/or filename below.
 *}
Vars   : App.Name ("EZL Row/Col Report"),
         fName    ("C:\UserDLL\RowCol.CSV") ;

Vars   : Match (FALSE),
         MaxRows  (10),        MaxCols  (10),
         UseRows  (10),        UseCols  (10),
         Row       (0),        Col       (0) ;
Vars   : Hyphens  ("——————————————————————————————") ;


if  @BarNumber <= 1  then begin
  Hyphens  = Hyphens + Hyphens ;

  UseRows  = @EZL.RowNum ; { request number of rows being used }
  UseCols  = @EZL.ColNum ; { request number of cols being used }

  if UseRows > MaxRows then UseRows = MaxRows ;
  if UseCols > MaxCols then UseCols = MaxCols ;
end ;

{*
 *  Step #1: Enter below your Custom Pattern Logic or User Function
 *
 * Match  =  High [0] <  High [1] and
 *            Low [0] <   Low [1] and
 *           Open [0] <  Close[0] ;
 *}

Match  = RSI (Close, 14) > 65 ;

if  Match  then begin
  Plot1 (High - 1 point, "Match") ;
  Plot2 ( Low + 1 point, "Match") ;
end ; { paint the bar }

{*
 * Step #2: Offset Match by appropriate number of bars.
 *}
if  Match[01]  then begin
  Row = EZL.RowNum ; { what row does this item belong to? }
  Col = EZL.ColNum ; { what col does this item belong to? }

  Specs [  0,   0] = Specs [  0,   0] + 1 ; { Count - running total }
```

```
    Specs [Row,    0] = Specs [Row,    0] + 1 ; { Count - all this row }
    Specs [   0, Col] = Specs [   0, Col] + 1 ; { Count - all this col }
    Specs [Row, Col] = Specs [Row, Col] + 1 ; { Count - this pattern }
  end ;

  {*
   * Nothing below here should need to be changed
   *}

  Vars   : LoopX  (0),          LoopY  (0),
           st0    (""),         st1    ("") ;

  if Date = @vrt.LastCalcDate and Time = @vrt.LastCalcTime
  then begin
    st1 = " ," ;
    for  LoopY = 0 to @MinList (UseCols, MaxCols) begin
      st1 = st1 + @EZL.Col_Label (LoopY) ;
      if LoopY <  @MinList (UseCols, MaxCols)
        then st1 = st1 + "," ;
    end ;

  {* *}
    if DoReport then begin
  {* Currently requires proprietary DLL *}
      if @skt.Print.Headers (App.Name) then ;

      Print (st1) ;
      Print (LeftStr (Hyphens, StrLen (st1))) ;
    end ;
  {* *}
    if  DiskFile  then  FileAppend (fName, st1 + NewLine) ;
  {* *}

    for LoopX = 0 to @MinList (UseRows, MaxRows)
    begin
      st1  = @EZL.Row_Label (LoopX) + "," ;
      for  LoopY = 0 to @MinList (UseCols, MaxCols)
      begin
        st0 = @NumToStr (Specs [LoopX, LoopY], 00) ;
        if @StrLen (st0) < 3 then st0 = Spaces (03 - @StrLen (st0)) + st0 ;

        st1 = st1 + st0 ;
        if LoopY < MinList (UseCols, MaxCols) then st1 = st1 + "," ;
      end ; { loop - items }

  {* *}
      if DoReport then Print (st1) ;
  {* *}
      if DiskFile then FileAppend (fName, st1 + NewLine) ;
  {* *}
    end ; { loop - rows }
  end ; { On Last Bar Of Data }
```

The rows report the relation of the Open of this bar to the Range of the previous bar.

#6.09b - Function — EZL.RowNum

```
{
Type  : UserFunction (Numeric)
Name  : EZL.RowNum
Notes : Compute the row number used to stuff the array.

EasyLanguage translation provided
  by Samuel K. Tennis
  of Vista Research (c) 1998, 1999

  Any unauthorized use of this material may constitute
  a violation of U.S. and International Copyright Laws.
}

Vars : MidRng (00),        Rng.75 (00),        Rng.25 (00),
       MaxRow (07),        Return (00) ;


Return = +00 ;
MidRng = (High +    Low) * 0.50 ; { center of range }
Rng.75 = (High + MidRng) * 0.50 ; { upper 75% of range }
Rng.25 = ( Low + MidRng) * 0.50 ; { lower 25% of range }

if  @BarNumber <= 01  then Return  = MaxRow
else begin
       Return = +00 ;            { +0 - Default }
  if Open [00]  >  High [01]
  then Return = +01              { +1 - Open above high }
  else
  if Open [00]  > Rng.75[01]
  then Return = +02              { +2 - Open above 75% }
  else
  if Open [00]  > MidRng[01]
  then Return = +03              { +3 - Open above midrange }
  else
  if Open [00]  = MidRng[01]
  then Return = +04              { +4 - Open equal to midrange }
  else
  if Open [00] <    Low [01]
  then Return = +07              { +7 - Open below low }
  else
  if Open [00] <  Rng.25[01]
  then Return = +06              { +6 - Open below 25% }
  else
  if Open [00] <  MidRng[01]
  then Return = +05              { +5 - Open below midrange }
  else Return = -01 ;            { error }
end ; { Allow one bar to pass... }

EZL.RowNum  = Return ;
```

#6.09c - Function — EZL.Row_Label

```
{
Type   : UserFunction (String)
Name   : EZL.Row_Label
Notes  : Return string literal for requested row number.

EasyLanguage translation provided
  by Samuel K. Tennis
  of Vista Research (c) 1998, 1999

  Any unauthorized use of this material may constitute
  a violation of U.S. and International Copyright Laws.
}

Inputs: RowNum (NumericSimple) ;
Vars  : Return ("") ;


Return = "Default" ;

if  @BarNumber >= 00  then begin
  if     RowNum    = +00
  then  Return     = "Totals"          { +0 - Totals }
  else if  RowNum = +01
  then  Return     = "O[0]>H[1]"       { +1 - Open above high }
  else if  RowNum = +02
  then  Return     = "O[0]>75%[1]"     { +2 - Open above 75% }
  else if  RowNum = +03
  then  Return     = "O[0]>MdPt[1]"    { +3 - Open above MidPoint }
  else if  RowNum = +04
  then  Return     = "O[0]=MdPt[1]"    { +4 - Open equal to MidPoint }
  else if  RowNum = +07
  then  Return     = "O[0]<L[1]"       { +7 - Open below low }
  else if  RowNum = +06
  then  Return     = "O[0]<25%[1]"     { +6 - Open below 25% }
  else if  RowNum = +05
  then  Return     = "O[0]<MdPt[1]"    { +5 - Open below MidPoint }
  else  Return = "Error"   ;           { error }
end ; { Allow one bar to pass... }

EZL.Row_Label  = Return ;

{
Custom Programming Services provided by:

               Samuel K. Tennis
                Vista Research
               129 Staff Drive
       Ft. Walton Beach, Florida 32548
        voice :     1(850) 243-5105
        fax   :     1(850) 301-2884
        eMail :  skt@vista-research.com
          http://www.vista-research.com
}
```

The columns report the relation of the Close to the Range of the previous bar.

#6.09d - Function — EZL.ColNum

```
{
Type  : UserFunction (Numeric)
Name  : EZL.ColNum
Notes : Compute the column number used to stuff the array.

The events must be exclusive, else it reports last one that hit.
Because of the cascading IF it will return the first one found.  Always.

EasyLanguage translation provided
  by Samuel K. Tennis
  of Vista Research (c) 1998, 1999
  Any unauthorized use of this material may constitute
  a violation of U.S. and International Copyright Laws.
}

Vars : MidRng (00),        Rng.75 (00),        Rng.25 (00),
       MaxCol (07),        Return (00) ;

Return = +00 ;

MidRng = (High +    Low) * 0.50 ; { center of range }
Rng.75 = (High + MidRng) * 0.50 ; { upper 75% of range }
Rng.25 = ( Low + MidRng) * 0.50 ; { lower 25% of range }

if  @BarNumber <= 01  then  Return  = MaxCol
else begin
        Return = +00 ;          { +0 - Default }
  if  Close[00]  >  High [01]
  then  Return = +01            { +1 - Close above previous high }
  else
  if  Close[00]  > Rng.75[01]
  then  Return = +02            { +2 - Close above previous 75% }
  else
  if  Close[00]  > MidRng[01]
  then  Return = +03            { +3 - Close above previous midrange }
  else
  if  Close[00]  = MidRng[01]
  then  Return = +04            { +4 - Close equal to previous midrange }
  else
  if  Close[00] <    Low [01]
  then  Return = +07            { +7 - Close below previous low }
  else
  if  Close[00] <  Rng.25[01]
  then  Return = +06            { +6 - Close below previous 25% }
  else
  if  Close[00] <  MidRng[01]
  then  Return = +05            { +5 - Close below previous midrange }
  else  Return = -01 ;          { error }
end ; { Allow one bar to pass... }

EZL.ColNum  = Return ;
```

```
{
Custom Programming Services provided by:

               Samuel K. Tennis
                Vista Research
               129 Staff Drive
        Ft. Walton Beach, Florida 32548
         voice :    1(850) 243-5105
         fax   :    1(850) 301-2884
         eMail :  skt@vista-research.com
           http://www.vista-research.com
}
```

#6.09e - Function: EZL.Col_Label

```
{
Type  : UserFunction (String)
Name  : EZL.Col_Label
Notes : Returns the label for requested column.

EasyLanguage translation provided
  by Samuel K. Tennis
  of Vista Research (c) 1998, 1999

  Any unauthorized use of this material may constitute
  a violation of U.S. and International Copyright Laws.
}

Inputs: ColNum (NumericSimple) ;
Vars  : Return ("") ;

Return  = "Default" ;
if  @BarNumber >= 00  then begin
  if  ColNum = +00
  then  Return = "Totals"         { +0 - Column for Totals }
  else
  if  ColNum = +01
  then  Return = "C[0]>H[1]"      { +1 - Close above previous high }
  else
  if  ColNum = +02
  then  Return = "C[0]>75%[1]"    { +2 - Close above previous 75% }
  else
  if  ColNum = +03
  then  Return = "C[0]>MdPt[1]"   { +3 - Close above previous MidPoint }
  else
  if  ColNum = +04
  then  Return = "C[0]=MdPt[1]"   { +4 - Close equal to previous MidPoint
}
  else
  if  ColNum = +07
  then  Return = "C[0]<L[1]"      { +7 - Close below previous low }
  else
  if  ColNum = +06
  then  Return = "C[0]<25%[1]"    { +6 - Close below previous 25% }
  else
  if  ColNum = +05
```

```
    then  Return = "C[0]<MdPt[1]"    { +5 - Close below previous MidPoint }
    else  Return = "Error" ;         { error }
  end ; { Allow one bar to pass... }

  EZL.Col_Label  = Return ;

  {
  Custom Programming Services provided by:

                  Samuel K. Tennis
                   Vista Research
                  129 Staff Drive
           Ft. Walton Beach, Florida 32548
            voice :     1(850) 243-5105
            fax   :     1(850) 301-2884
            eMail :  skt@vista-research.com
              http://www.vista-research.com
  }
```

10 Generating a .CSV File

The process of generating a .CSV file has been included in several other listings.

11 Defining Dual Bar Analysis

This study provides, as well as very valuable information, an example of using ASSIGNMENT STATEMENTS like FLAGS and COUNTERS, generating a custom report with sophisticated output statements.

#6.11 - Study — EZL.DualBar Analysis

```
{
Type : Study
Name : EZL.DualBar Analysis
Notes: How to properly analyze two vertical bars.

10/20/97  skt
    Must limit/stretch numbers to correct width.

EasyLanguage interpretation provided by Samuel K. Tennis
  of Vista Research (c) 1998, 1999
  Any unauthorized use of this material may constitute
  a violation of U.S. and International Copyright Laws.
}

Inputs: nTicks       (05) ;

Vars  : App.Name     ("EZL.DualBar Analysis") ;

Vars  : nPoints      (MinMove * nTicks points) ;
Vars  : Bearish.Cnt (00),        Bullish.Cnt (00),
        BearCnf.Cnt (00),        BullCnf.Cnt (00),
        BearDvg.Cnt (00),        BullDvg.Cnt (00),
```

```
        Outside.Cnt (00),          Inside.Cnt   (00),
        NearOut.Cnt (00),          Total.Cnt    (00) ;
Vars  : St.Desc     (""),          St.Labl      (""),
        St.Anal     (""),          st           (""),
        Equals  (
"=========================================================================="),
        Hyphens ("————————————————————————") ;


St.Desc     =  "" ; { describe the price action }
St.Labl     =  "" ; { label the bar }
St.Anal     =  "" ; { Analysis }

Total.Cnt   = Total.Cnt   + 01 ;
{*
 *  Bullish Bar
 *}
if  High  > High[01]  and  Low   > Low [01]
then begin
  if  CheckCommentary  then begin
    St.Desc = "Higher High - Higher Low" ;
    St.Labl = "Bullish" ;
    St.Anal = "" ;
{* *}
    if  Close  > (High +  Low) * 0.50 and Close  > Close[01]
      then St.Labl      = St.Labl      + " Confirmed"
      else St.Labl      = St.Labl      + " Divergent" ;
{* *}
    St.Labl = St.Labl + " Bar" ;
  end ; { On Commentary Bar }

{*
 * Counting done regardless of Commentary
 *}
  Bullish.Cnt = Bullish.Cnt + 01 ;
  if    Close  > (High +  Low) * 0.50 and Close  > Close[01]
    then BullCnf.Cnt = BullCnf.Cnt + 01
    else BullDvg.Cnt = BullDvg.Cnt + 01 ;

  Plot1 (Low  - nPoints, "BullishBar") ;
end ; {  }

{*
 *  Bearish Bar
 *}
if   Low <   Low [01]  and  High <  High[01]
then begin
  if  CheckCommentary  then begin
    St.Desc = "Lower Low - Lower High" ;
    St.Labl = "Bearish" ;
    St.Anal = "" ;
{* *}
    if  Close <  (High +  Low) * 0.5 and Close <  Close[01]
      then St.Labl      = St.Labl      + " Confirmed"
      else St.Labl      = St.Labl      + " Divergent" ;
{* *}
    St.Labl = St.Labl + " Bar" ;
  end ; { On Commentary Bar }

{*
```

```
  * Counting done regardless of Commentary
  *}
   Bearish.Cnt = Bearish.Cnt + 01 ;

   if  Close <  (High +  Low) * 0.5 and Close <  Close[01]
     then  BearCnf.Cnt = BearCnf.Cnt + 01
     else  BearDvg.Cnt = BearDvg.Cnt + 01 ;

   Plot2 (High + nPoints, "BearishBar") ;
 end ; {  }

 {*
  *  Inside Bar
  *}
 if  Low  >= Low [01]  and  High <= High[01]
 then begin
   if CheckCommentary then begin
     St.Desc = "Higher Low, Lower High" ;
     St.Labl = "Inside Bar" ;
     St.Anal = "Possible Trend Reversal" ;
   end ; { On Commentary Bar }

 {*
  * Counting done regardless of Commentary
  *}
   Inside.Cnt  =  Inside.Cnt + 01 ;

   Plot3 (High,            "inORoutBar") ;
   Plot4 (Low,             "inORoutBar") ;
 end ;

 {*
  *  Outside Bar
  *}
 if   Low <   Low [01]  and  High  > High[01]
 then begin
   if CheckCommentary then begin
     St.Desc = "Lower Low, Higher High" ;
     St.Labl = "Outside Bar" ;
     St.Anal = "" ;
   end ; { On Commentary Bar }

 {*
  * Counting done regardless of Commentary
  *}
   Outside.Cnt = Outside.Cnt + 01 ;

   Plot3 (High,            "inORoutBar") ;
   Plot4 (Low,             "inORoutBar") ;
 end ;
 {*
  *  Almost Outside Bar
  *}
 if (Low   =  Low[01]  and  High  > High[01]) or
    (Low   <  Low[01]  and  High  = High[01])
 then begin
   if CheckCommentary then begin
     St.Desc = "Almost Lower Low, Higher High" ;
     St.Labl = "Nearly Outside Bar" ;
     St.Anal = "" ;
```

```
  end ; { On Commentary Bar }

{*
 * Counting done regardless of Commentary
 *}
  NearOut.Cnt = NearOut.Cnt + 01 ;
end ;

{*
 *  Generate Expert Commentary (see Expert Commentary Tool)
 *  on the selected bar of data
 *}

if  CheckCommentary  then begin
  Commentary (NewLine + "Price Action : " + st.Desc +
              NewLine + "Description  : " + st.Labl +
              NewLine + "Analysis     : " + St.Anal) ;

{*
 *  In this section we are using the Commentary Statement.  Notice how the
 *  entire report is catenated into one string variable and then sent to
 *  the screen at one time.
 *}
  st = NewLine + NewLine + "Report: " + App.Name + NewLine
          + Hyphens + NewLine ;
  st = st + "Total number of bars in sample : "
          +  NumToStr (Total.Cnt, 0) + NewLine ;
  st = st + Hyphens + NewLine ;
  st = st + "  Bullish Bars " +
       @skt.nChars (@NumToStr ( Bullish.Cnt, 0), 6)
          + "   " +
       @skt.nChars (@NumToStr ((Bullish.Cnt /   Total.Cnt) * 100.0, 2), 9)
          + "%" + NewLine ;
  st = st + "     Confirmed " +
       @skt.nChars (@NumToStr ( BullCnf.Cnt, 0), 6) + "   " +
       @skt.nChars (@NumToStr ((BullCnf.Cnt /   Total.Cnt) * 100.0, 2), 9)
          + "%   " +
       @skt.nChars (@NumToStr ((BullCnf.Cnt / Bullish.Cnt) * 100.0, 2), 9)
          + "%" + NewLine ;
  st = st + "     Divergent " +
       @skt.nChars (@NumToStr ( BullDvg.Cnt, 0), 6)
          + "   " +
       @skt.nChars (@NumToStr ((BullDvg.Cnt /   Total.Cnt) * 100.0, 2), 9)
          + "%   " +
       @skt.nChars (@NumToStr ((BullDvg.Cnt / Bullish.Cnt) * 100.0, 2), 9)
          + "%" + NewLine ;

  st = st + "  Bearish Bars " +
       @skt.nChars (@NumToStr ( Bearish.Cnt, 0), 6) + "   " +
       @skt.nChars (@NumToStr ((Bearish.Cnt /   Total.Cnt) * 100.0, 2), 9)
          + "%" + NewLine ;
  st = st + "     Confirmed " +
       @skt.nChars (@NumToStr ( BearCnf.Cnt, 0), 6) + "   " +
       @skt.nChars (@NumToStr ((BearCnf.Cnt /   Total.Cnt) * 100.0, 2), 9)
          + "%   " +
       @skt.nChars (@NumToStr ((BearCnf.Cnt / Bearish.Cnt) * 100.0, 2), 9)
          + "%" + NewLine ;
  st = st + "     Divergent " +
       @skt.nChars (@NumToStr ( BearDvg.Cnt, 0), 6) + "   " +
       @skt.nChars (@NumToStr ((BearDvg.Cnt /   Total.Cnt) * 100.0, 2), 9)
```

```
            + "%   " +
         @skt.nChars (@NumToStr ((BearDvg.Cnt / Bearish.Cnt) * 100.0, 2), 9)
            + "%" + NewLine ;

    st = st + "  InSide  Bars " +
         @skt.nChars (@NumToStr (  Inside.Cnt, 0), 6) + "   " +
         @skt.nChars (@NumToStr (( Inside.Cnt /   Total.Cnt) * 100.0, 2), 9)
            + "%" + NewLine ;

    st = st + "  OutSide Bars " +
         @skt.nChars (@NumToStr ( Outside.Cnt, 0), 6) + "   " +
         @skt.nChars (@NumToStr ((Outside.Cnt /   Total.Cnt) * 100.0, 2), 9)
            + "%" + NewLine ;

    st = st + "  NearOut Bars " +
         @skt.nChars (@NumToStr ( NearOut.Cnt, 0), 6)
            + "   " +
         @skt.nChars (@NumToStr ((NearOut.Cnt /   Total.Cnt) * 100.0, 2), 9)
            + "%" + NewLine ;
    st = st + Hyphens + NewLine ;
    st = st + "Totals            " +
         @skt.nChars (@NumToStr ((Bullish.Cnt + Bearish.Cnt +
                  Outside.Cnt +  Inside.Cnt + NearOut.Cnt), 0), 6)
            + "   " +
         @skt.nChars (@NumToStr (((Bullish.Cnt /   Total.Cnt) * 100.0 +
                                  (Bearish.Cnt /   Total.Cnt) * 100.0 +
                                  (Outside.Cnt /   Total.Cnt) * 100.0 +
                                  ( Inside.Cnt /   Total.Cnt) * 100.0 +
                                  (NearOut.Cnt /   Total.Cnt) * 100.0), 2), 9)
            + "%" + NewLine ;

    st = st + NewLine + "end report (" + App.Name + ")." + NewLine ;
    CommentaryCL (st) ;
  end ; { On Commentary Bar }
  {*
   *  Generate a print report (see Print Log Window) on the last bar of data
   *}
  if  Date = @vrt.LastCalcDate and Time = @vrt.LastCalcTime {@Sess1EndTime}
  then begin
  {*
   * If this line generates an error then you do not have the supporting
   * Utility Set(s) and the accompanying DLL(s) required.
   * Simply replace with the commented out headers below.
   * Print ("") ;
   * Print ("Report: '", App.Name. "'") ;
   * Print ("————————————————") ;
   *}
    if  @skt.Print.Headers (App.Name)  then ;
    Print ("Total number of bars in sample : ", Total.Cnt:1:0) ;
    Print ("——————————————————") ;
    Print ("  Bullish Bars ", Bullish.Cnt:5:0,
                             (Bullish.Cnt /   Total.Cnt) * 100.0:5:2, "%") ;
    Print ("     Confirmed ", BullCnf.Cnt:5:0,
                             (BullCnf.Cnt /   Total.Cnt) * 100.0:5:2, "%   ",
                             (BullCnf.Cnt / Bullish.Cnt) * 100.0:5:2, "%") ;
  {*
   *  Unlike the Commentary Statement, each individually line must be output.
   *  When using the Print Statement I do not accumulate multiple lines in a
   *  single string variable.
   *  The print Log Window is limited to about 79 characters in width.
```

```
*}
 Print ("     Divergent ", BullDvg.Cnt:5:0,
                          (BullDvg.Cnt /   Total.Cnt) * 100.0:5:2, "%  ",
                          (BullDvg.Cnt / Bullish.Cnt) * 100.0:5:2, "%") ;
 Print ("  Bearish Bars ", Bearish.Cnt:5:0,
                          (Bearish.Cnt /   Total.Cnt) * 100.0:5:2, "%") ;
 Print ("     Confirmed ", BearCnf.Cnt:5:0,
                          (BearCnf.Cnt /   Total.Cnt) * 100.0:5:2, "%  ",
                          (BearCnf.Cnt / Bearish.Cnt) * 100.0:5:2, "%") ;
 Print ("     Divergent ", BearDvg.Cnt:5:0,
                          (BearDvg.Cnt /   Total.Cnt) * 100.0:5:2, "%  ",
                          (BearDvg.Cnt / Bearish.Cnt) * 100.0:5:2, "%") ;
 Print ("  InSide  Bars ",  InSide.Cnt:5:0,
                          ( Inside.Cnt /   Total.Cnt) * 100.0:5:2, "%") ;
 Print ("  OutSide Bars ", OutSide.Cnt:5:0,
                          (Outside.Cnt /   Total.Cnt) * 100.0:5:2, "%") ;
 Print ("  NearOut Bars ", NearOut.Cnt:5:0,
                          (NearOut.Cnt /   Total.Cnt) * 100.0:5:2, "%") ;
 Print ("———————————————") ;
 Print ("Totals         ", (Bullish.Cnt +  Bearish.Cnt + Outside.Cnt
                                     + Inside.Cnt + NearOut.Cnt):5:0,
                    ((Bullish.Cnt /   Total.Cnt) * 100.0 +
                     (Bearish.Cnt /   Total.Cnt) * 100.0 +
                     (Outside.Cnt /   Total.Cnt) * 100.0 +
                     ( Inside.Cnt /   Total.Cnt) * 100.0 +
                     (NearOut.Cnt /   Total.Cnt) * 100.0):5:2, "%") ;
 Print ("") ;
 Print (Equals) ;
 Print ("end report (", App.Name, ").") ;
end ;
```

12 Generating Advanced Performance Reports On A Black Box System

For this example, our BLACK BOX SYSTEM will be #6.14: "EZL.CHANNEL BREAKOUT". Our "ADVANCED PERFORMANCE REPORTS" will be #6.12b: "skt.Hi/Lo Tick" and #6.12c: "VRT.FINAL REPORT"

#6.12a - System — EZL.Black Box Report

```
{
Type  : System (Top Level)
Name  : EZL.Black Box Report
Notes : Generate Report on a Black Box System

EasyLanguage interpretation provided
   by  Samuel K. Tennis
   of  Vista Research (c) 1998, 1999
  Any unauthorized use of this material may constitute
  a violation of U.S. and International Copyright Laws.
}

Vars  : App.Name ("EZL.Black Box Report") ;

Inputs: le.Bars        (14),        se.Bars        (14),
        lx.Bars        (14),        sx.Bars        (14),
```

```
        le.Ticks         (05),         se.Ticks        (05),
        lx.Ticks         (05),         sx.Ticks        (05) ;
Inputs: en.Mode          (00) ;

IncludeSystem: "EZL.Channel BreakOut",
        le.Bars,           se.Bars,
        lx.Bars,           sx.Bars,
        le.Ticks,          se.Ticks,
        lx.Ticks,          sx.Ticks,
        en.Mode ;

Inputs: enBars  (03) ;

IncludeSystem: "skt.Hi/Lo Tick",   enBars, "EZL.Channel BreakOut" ;

Inputs: DoReport   (TRUE),        Dsk.File  (FALSE) ;

IncludeSystem: "vrt.Final Report", DoReport, Dsk.File, "EZL.Channel
BreakOut" ;
```

#6.12b - System — skt.Hi/Lo Tick

```
{
Type : System (Include Report)
Name : skt.Hi/Lo Tick
Notes:

Easy Language interpretation provided by Samuel K. Tennis
  of Vista Research (c) 1998, 1999
  Any unauthorized use of this material constitutes
  a violation of U.S. and International Copyright Laws.
}

Inputs: enBars        (03),
        SysName ("Default") ;

Arrays: Position [02]  ("") ;

Vars  : App.Name      ("skt.Hi/Lo Tick") ;
Vars  : Trend         (00),        enTick       (00),
        hiTick        (00),        loTick       (00),
        hi.Sum        (00),        lo.Sum       (00),
        hi.Buy        (00),        lo.Buy       (00),
        hi.Sel        (00),        lo.Sel       (00) ;

{ ————————————————————————————————————————— }

if  (@BarNumber <= 01)  then begin
  Position [00] = "Short" ;
  Position [01] = " Flat" ;
  Position [02] = " Long" ;

  Print ("               Entry              Exit") ;
  Print (" Pos,  Date, Time,  Price,  Date, Time,  Price,  loTik, hiTik") ;
end ;

if  @MarketPosition = +01 and @BarsSinceEntry = 00
then begin
```

```
   if  Trend  < +01  then begin
 {*
 "MktPos, EnDate, EnTime, EnPrice, ExDate, ExTime, ExPrice, loTik, hiTik"
  *}
     Print (Position [@MarketPosition (01) + 01],
            @EntryDate (01):7:0, @EntryTime (01):5:0, " ",
            @vrt.Format (@EntryPrice (1)),            " ",
            @ExitDate (01):7:0, @ExitTime  (01):5:0,  " ",
            @vrt.Format  (@ExitPrice (1)),            " ",
            @vrt.Format (enTick - loTick),            ", ",
            @vrt.Format (hiTick - enTick)) ;

    hi.Sum = hi.Sum + (enTick - loTick) ;
    lo.Sum = lo.Sum + (hiTick - enTick) ;
    hi.Sel = hi.Sel + (enTick - loTick) ;
    lo.Sel = lo.Sel + (hiTick - enTick) ;

    Trend  =   +01 ;
    enTick = Close ;
    hiTick =  High ;
    loTick =   Low ;
  end
  else begin
  end ;
end ;

if  @MarketPosition = -01 and @BarsSinceEntry = 00
then begin
  if  Trend >  -01  then begin
    Print (Position [@MarketPosition (01) + 01],
           @EntryDate (01):7:0, @EntryTime (1):5:0, " ",
          @vrt.Format (@EntryPrice (01)),           " ",
            @ExitDate (01):7:0,  @ExitTime (1):5:0, " ",
          @vrt.Format  (@ExitPrice (01)),           " ",
          @vrt.Format (hiTick - enTick),            ", ",
          @vrt.Format (enTick - loTick)) ;

    hi.Sum = hi.Sum + (hiTick - enTick) ;
    lo.Sum = lo.Sum + (enTick - loTick) ;
    hi.Buy = hi.Buy + (hiTick - enTick) ;
    lo.Buy = lo.Buy + (enTick - loTick) ;

    Trend  =   -01 ;
    enTick = Close ;
    hiTick =  High ;
    loTick =   Low ;
  end
  else begin
{  }
  end ;
end ;

if  @MarketPosition <>     00 and
    @BarsSinceEntry <= enBars
then begin
  if High  > hiTick then hiTick = High ;
  if Low   <  loTick then loTick =  Low ;
end ;

if @MarketPosition  =  00 and @BarsSinceExit   = 00 then begin
```

```
    Trend = 00 ;
  end ;

  if                          Date = @vrt.LastCalcDate and
     (@DataCompression   > 01 or Time = @vrt.LastCalcTime)
  then begin
    Print ("") ;
    Print ("System : '", App.Name, "' (", SysName, ")") ;
    Print ("             UpSide        DnSide") ;
    Print (" All : ", hi.Sum:6:4, ", ", lo.Sum:7:4) ;
    Print (" Buy : ", hi.Buy:6:4, ", ", lo.Buy:7:4) ;
    Print ("Sell : ", hi.Sel:6:4, ", ", lo.Sel:7:4) ;
    Print ("") ;
  end ;

  { ———————————————————————————————————— }
```

#6.12c - System — vrt.Final Report

This INCLUDESYSTEM is more of an example to get you thinking than the finished ultimate in trading research. I have to leave something for you to do, after all!

```
{
Type  : System (Include, Report)
Name  : vrt.Final Report
Notes: Note that this system uses the "next bar" modifier it may prevent
  real time order generation when using end of day data.  It should run
  satisfactorily, once the market has opened, on a realtime data feed.

(Highest (High, 5) - Lowest (Low, 5)) / Average (TrueRange, 15)
(Highest (High, 5) - Lowest (Low, 5)) / (Average (High, 15) - Lowest (Low,
5))

    (Highest (High, 10) - Lowest (Low, 10))[00] /
    (Highest (High, 10) - Lowest (Low, 10))[05]

    (1 - (Average (TrueRange, 10) [00] /
           iff (BarNumber > 5, (Average (TrueRange, 10))[05], 1 Point)) ;

Easy Language interpretation provided by Samuel K. Tennis
  of Vista Research (c) August 1997, 1999
  Any unauthorized use of this material constitutes
  a violation of U.S. and International Copyright Laws.
}

Inputs: DoReport   (TRUE),
        Dsk.File   (FALSE),
        Sys.Name   ("SysName goes here...")  ;

Vars  : HiHi      (-999999),       LoLo      (+999999),
        HiRng     (-999999),       loRng     (+999999),
        ClSum          (00),       RngSum         (00) ;
Vars  : st             (""),       Dummy          (00) ;

Arrays: Position [02] ("") ;


if  @BarNumber <= 01  then begin
```

```
   Position [00] = "Short" ;
   Position [01] = " Flat" ;
   Position [02] = " Long" ;
end ;

if High   > HiHi  then HiHi   = High ;
if  Low  <  LoLo  then LoLo   =  Low ;
                       ClSum  = ClSum   + Close ;

if Range  > HiRng then HiRng  = Range ;
if Range <  loRng and
   Range  >  0.00 then loRng  = Range ;
                       RngSum = RngSum  + Range ;


Vars  : EquityPeak  (00),
        eqBarsDown  (00) ;

eqBarsDown = @vrt.LongestEquityDip ;

if      DoReport
   and  Date next bar = @vrt.LastCalcDate
   and (Time next bar = @vrt.LastCalcTime or @DataCompression  > 01)
then begin

{
============================================================================
}

Vars  : nnn   (00),
        ppp   (00) ;

  Print ("") ;
  Print ("Report: 'vrt.TimeInMarket' ") ;
  Print ("————————————") ;
  nnn = (AvgBarsWinTrade * NumWinTrades) + (AvgBarsLosTrade * NumLosTrades)
;

  ppp = (nnn / CurrentBar) * 100 ;
  Print (Date:6:0, CurrentBar:6:0, ", ", nnn:6:0,
         ppp:6:2, (AvgBarsWinTrade * NumWinTrades):6:0,
                  (AvgBarsLosTrade * NumLosTrades):6:0) ;
  Print ("") ;
  Print (
"      Bars Flat,        Bars Long,     Bars Not Flat,        Bars Short") ;
  Print (
"————————————————————————————————————") ;
{*
  Print ("      ", BarsFlat   :5:0,
           "    ", BarsLong   :5:0,
         "      ", BarsNotFlat:5:0,
           "    ", BarsShort  :5:0) ;
 *}
  Print ({Date:6:0, CurrentBar:5:0, " : ",}
        (CurrentBar - vrt.TimeInMarket ( 0)):6:0, ", ",
       ((CurrentBar - vrt.TimeInMarket ( 0)) / CurrentBar) * 100:4:2, "%, ",
                      vrt.TimeInMarket (+1) :6:0, ", ",
                     (vrt.TimeInMarket (+1)  / CurrentBar) * 100:4:2, "%, ",
                      vrt.TimeInMarket ( 0) :6:0, ", ",
                     (vrt.TimeInMarket ( 0)  / CurrentBar) * 100:4:2, "%, ",
```

```
                        vrt.TimeInMarket (-1) :6:0, ", ",
                       (vrt.TimeInMarket (-1)  / CurrentBar) * 100:4:2, "%") ;
  Print ("") ;

{
==================================================================================
}

Vars   : MaxBarsFlat    (00) ;
Vars   : MaxBarsFlat.dt (00) ;

  MaxBarsFlat = @vrt.LongestFlat ;

if MaxBarsFlat <> MaxBarsFlat[1] then MaxBarsFlat.dt = Date ;

  Print ("") ;
  Print ("Report: 'vrt.LongestFlat'") ;
  Print ("——————————") ;
  Print (Date:6:0, CurrentBar:6:0, MaxBarsFlat:6:0,
        (MaxBarsFlat / CurrentBar) * 100.0:5:2, "%") ;

{
==================================================================================
}

{*
  Print ("") ;
  if  EqBarsDown <> EqBarsDown[1]  then begin
    Print (Date      :6:0,   Time      :5:0,
         " Longest Equity Dip ",
           EqPrevPeak:6:2,   EqPrevBars:6:0,
           EquityPeak:6:2,   EqBarsDown:6:0) ;
  end ;
*}

  Print ("") ;
  Print ("Report: 'vrt.LongestEquityDip'") ;
  Print ("——————————————") ;
  Print ("  Of ", CurrentBar:6:0, " bars : ",
          EqBarsDown:6:0, (EqBarsDown / CurrentBar) * 100.0:5:2,
         "% (trading days)") ;

{
==================================================================================
}

  Print ("") ;
  Print ("System Report : '", Sys.Name,
      "'  Run Date: ", @CurrentDate:6:0, ", ", @CurrentTime:5:0) ;
  Print ("——————————————————") ;
  Print ("") ;
  Print ("SymName= '",   @GetSymbolName,
     "',  CommNum= ",    @CommodityNumber:6:0,
      ",  DelivMo= ",    @DeliveryMonth  :3:0,
      ",  DelivYr= ",     @DeliveryYear  :3:0) ;

  Print ("DataCmp= ",    @DataCompression:4:0,
      ",  BarInt=  ",    @BarInterval    :5:0,
      ",  PrScale= ",    @PriceScale,
      ",  MinMove= ",    @MinMove        :4:0) ;
```

```
  Print ("One Pt = ",              01 Point :1:4,
" ($", BigPointValue *            01 Point :1:2, ")",
       ", One Tic= ",   MinMove * 01 Point :1:4,
" ($", BigPointValue * (MinMove * 01 Point):1:2, ")",
        ", PtVal=$",             PointValue :1:2,
        ", BPVal=$",          BigPointValue :1:2) ;

  Print ("Limit =  ",   DailyLimit      :6:2,
      ",  Margin=  ",   Margin          :6:2,
      ",  Commis=  ",   Commission      :6:2,
      ",  Slip  =  ",   Slippage        :6:2) ;

  Print ("") ;
  Print (
   "Sess1=  ", Sess1StartTime:6:0, Sess1FirstBarTime:6:0, Sess1EndTime:6:0,
",  Sess2= ",  Sess2StartTime:6:0, Sess2FirstBarTime:6:0, Sess2EndTime:6:0)
;

  Print ("First bar= ", vrt.mmddyy (vrt.FirstCalcDate),
                 ", ",               vrt.FirstCalcTime:5:0,
       ",  Last bar= ", @vrt.mmddyy  (@vrt.LastCalcDate),
                 ", ",                 @vrt.LastCalcTime :5:0,
        ",  Samples= ", @CurrentBar:5:0) ;

  Print ("") ;
  Print (                "Mkt High : ",   @vrt.Format (HiHi),
            ",            Mkt  Low : ",   @vrt.Format (LoLo),
                   ",  Avg Close : ",   @vrt.Format (ClSum  / @CurrentBar)
) ;
  Print (                " Hi Rng   :  ",  @vrt.Format (HiRng),
"                        Avg Rng    :   ", @vrt.Format (RngSum / @CurrentBar),
                 @vrt.Format ((RngSum / @CurrentBar) * @BigPointValue)) ;
  Print ("") ;

  if  @MaxContracts    >  00  then begin
    if  @TotalTrades <>  00  then Dummy = @TotalTrades
                           else Dummy = 1 ;

    Print ("    NetProf     GrProfit     GrLosses    MaxDDown") ;
    Print ("————————————————————————————") ;
    Print (NetProfit:8:2,    ",",    @GrossProfit  :9:2,  ",",
@GrossLoss:9:2,
                             ",", @NetProfit / Dummy,   @MaxIDDrawDown:8:2)
;

    Print ("") ;
    Print (" TotTrds     #WinTrds     #LosTrds     PcntProf     MktCnt") ;
    Print ("——————————————————————————————") ;
    Print (@TotalTrades  :8:0, ",", @NumWinTrades:12:0, ",",
          @NumLosTrades:12:0, ", ",
          (@NumWinTrades / Dummy) * 100 {PercentProfit}, "%,",
          @MaxContracts :8:0) ;

    Print ("") ;
    Print ("   BEStop   MoneyMgt   Profit       ** Trailing  Stop **") ;
    Print ("    Floor    StopAmt   Target     Amount    Floor  Percent,
MBB") ;
    Print ("————————————————————————————————") ;
    Print (@BreakEvenStopFloor:6:2, "   ",
```

```
            @MoneyMgtStopAmt    :6:2,
            @ProfitTargetStop  :6:2, "   ",
            @TrailingStopAmt    :6:2,
            @TrailingStopFloor :6:2,
            @TrailingStopPct    :6:2,
            @MaxBarsBack        :7:0) ;
   Print ("") ;
 end ; { MaxContracts }

 if  Dsk.File  then begin
   st =      Text (NewLine + "System Report : '", Sys.Name,
       "',  Run Date: ", @CurrentDate:6:0, ", ", @CurrentTime:5:0, NewLine,
       "-------------------", NewLine) ;

   st = st + Text ("SymName= ,'",  @GetSymbolName,
                 "', CommNum= ,",  @CommodityNumber :6:0,
                  ", DelivMo= ,",  @DeliveryMonth   :3:0,
                  ", DelivYr= ,",  @DeliveryYear    :3:0, NewLine) ;

   st = st + Text ("DataCmp= ,",   @DataCompression :4:0,
                   ", BarInt= ,",  @BarInterval     :5:0,
                  ", PrScale= ,",  @PriceScale,
                  ", MinMove= ,",  @MinMove         :4:0, NewLine) ;

   st = st + Text ("One Pt= ,",    01 Point         :1:4,
                 ", One Tic= ,", @MinMove * 01 Point :1:4,
                   ", PtVal= ,",   @PointValue      :1:4,
                   ", BPVal= ,",   @BigPointValue   :1:2, NewLine) ;

   st = st + Text ("Limit= ,",     @DailyLimit      :1:2,
                 ", Margin= ,",    @Margin          :1:2,
                 ", Commis= ,",    @Commission      :1:2,
                   ", Slip= ,",    @Slippage        :1:2, NewLine) ;

   st = st + NewLine
           + Text ("Sess1= ,", @Sess1StartTime   :6:0,
                           ",", @Sess1FirstBarTime:6:0,
                           ",", @Sess1EndTime     :6:0,
                 ",  Sess2= ,", @Sess2StartTime   :6:0,
                           ",", @Sess2FirstBarTime:6:0,
                           ",", @Sess2EndTime     :6:0)
           + NewLine ;

   st = st + Text ("First bar= ,", @vrt.mmddyy (@vrt.FirstCalcDate),
                             ",", @vrt.FirstCalcTime:5:0,
                  ", Last bar= ,", @vrt.mmddyy  (@vrt.LastCalcDate),
                             ",", @vrt.LastCalcTime :5:0,
                   ", Samples= ,", @CurrentBar       :5:0)
           + NewLine ;

   st = st + NewLine
           + Text ("Mkt High :,", @vrt.Format (HiHi),
                ",  Mkt  Low :,", @vrt.Format (LoLo),
               ",  Avg Close :,", @vrt.Format (ClSum  / @CurrentBar))
           + NewLine ;

   st = st + Text (" Hi Rng  :,", @vrt.Format (HiRng), ",",
                 "  Avg Rng :,", @vrt.Format (RngSum / @CurrentBar))
           + NewLine ;
```

```
    if  @MaxContracts  > 00  then begin
      st = st + NewLine
              +       "NetProf, GrProfit, GrLosses, MaxDDown "
              + NewLine ;
      st = st + Text (@NetProfit    :8:2, ",",
                      @GrossProfit  :9:2, ",",
                      @GrossLoss    :9:2, ",",
                      @MaxIDDrawDown:8:2)
              + NewLine ;

      if  @TotalTrades <> 00  then Dummy  = @TotalTrades
                              else Dummy  = 01 ;
      st = st + " TotTrds, #WinTrds, #LosTrds, PcntProf, MktCnt"
              + NewLine ;
      st = st + Text (@TotalTrades:8:0,    ",",
                      @NumWinTrades:12:0, ",",
                      @NumLosTrades:12:0,  ",",
                     (@NumWinTrades / Dummy) * 100 {PercentProfit}, "%,",
                      @MaxContracts:8:0) ;
      st = st + NewLine + NewLine
              + "BEStop, MoneyMgt, Profit, ** Trailing , , Stop **"
              + NewLine
              + "Floor, StopAmt, Target, ** Amount,  Floor, Percent **, MBB"
              + NewLine ;
      st = st + Text (@BreakEvenStopFloor:6:2,    ", ",
                      @MoneyMgtStopAmt   :6:2,    ", ",
                      @ProfitTargetStop  :6:2,    ", ",
                      @TrailingStopAmt   :6:2,    ", ",
                      @TrailingStopFloor :6:2,    ", ",
                      @TrailingStopPct   :6:2,    ", ",
                      @MaxBarsBack       :6:0)
              + NewLine ;
    end ;
    FileAppend ("C:\Temp\Final.csv", st) ;
  end ; { DiskFile selected }
end ;
```

13 Controlling The Execution Of An IncludeSystem

The Top Level System "skt.File Append" calls two IncludeSystems: "EZL.Timed Condition" and "skt.File Append #2".

#6.13a - System — skt.File Append

```
{
Type   : System (Top Level)
Name   : skt.File Append
Notes  : Demonstrate use of "FileAppend" command.

EasyLanguage translation provided
  by Samuel K. Tennis
  of Vista Research (c) 1997, 1999
}

Inputs: Fast.Len      (60),        Slow.Len     (120),
        le.Bars       (20),        se.Bars       (20) ;
```

```
IncludeSystem: "EZL.Timed Condition", Fast.Len, Slow.Len, le.Bars,
se.Bars ;


Inputs: Dsk.File  (FALSE) ;

IncludeSystem: "skt.FileAppend #2", Dsk.File ;
```

#6.13b - System — EZL.Timed Condition

```
{
Type : System (Top Level)
Name : EZL.Timed Condition
Notes: EZL Sem 08/23/98

Input: Fast.Len  (10) Length of fast moving average
       Slow.Len  (30) Length of slow moving average
       le.Bars   (20) Number of bars for long  entry
       se.Bars   (20) Number of bars for short entry
Alert: n/a
Calls: vrt.CrossOver
       MarketPosition
       Average
       Highest
        Lowest
       FastK
       FastD
       MRO
Uses : n/a

EasyLanguage interpretation provided
   by  Samuel K. Tennis
   of  Vista Research (c) 1998, 1999.
  Any unauthorized use of this material may constitute
  a violation of U.S. and International Copyright Laws.
}

Inputs: Fast.Len      (10),        Slow.Len      (30),
        le.Bars       (20),        se.Bars       (20) ;

Vars  : App.Name ("EZL.Timed Condition") ;

Vars  : Fast.MA       (00),        Slow.MA       (00),
        XOver         (00),
        BuyMode    (FALSE),        SelMode    (FALSE) ;

Vars  : nPoints  (MinMove * 04 Points),
        le.Price (+999999),        lx.Price (-999999),
        se.Price (-999999),        sx.Price (+999999),
        Stoc.Cnt      (00) ;

 {*
  * Compute moving averages
  *}
Fast.MA = @Average (Close, Fast.Len) ;
```

```
Slow.MA = @Average (Close, Slow.Len) ;

{*
 * Test for crossover
 *}
XOver  = @VRT.CrossOver (Fast.MA, Slow.MA, 0.00) ;

{*
 * Upon cross above set buy mode ON, sell mode OFF
 *}
if  XOver  = +01  then begin
  BuyMode  =  TRUE ;
  SelMode  = FALSE ;
  le.Price = @Highest (High, 24) + nPoints ;
  lx.Price =  @Lowest (Low,  14) - nPoints ;
  Stoc.Cnt =  00 ;
  se.Price = -999999 ;
  sx.Price = +999999 ;
end ;

{*
 * Upon cross above set buy mode OFF, sell mode ON
 *}
if  XOver  = -01  then begin
  SelMode  =  TRUE ;
  BuyMode  = FALSE ;
  se.Price =  @Lowest (Low,  24) - nPoints ;
  sx.Price = @Highest (High, 14) + nPoints ;
  Stoc.Cnt =  00 ;
  le.Price = +999999 ;
  lx.Price = -999999 ;
end ;
{*
 * if Buy enabled and cross was within le.Bars (20) bars
 *}
if  BuyMode and @MRO (XOver = +01, le.Bars, 01) <> -01
then begin
  if  @FastK (14) crosses above @FastD (14)
    then  Stoc.Cnt = Stoc.Cnt + 01 ;

  if  Stoc.Cnt  > 03
    then  Buy  ("le.Main") at le.Price stop ;
end ;
{*
 * Sell enabled and cross within se.Bars (20) bars
 *}
if  SelMode and @MRO (XOver = -01, le.Bars, 01) <> -01
then begin
  if  @FastK (14) crosses below @FastD (14)
    then  Stoc.Cnt = Stoc.Cnt + 01 ;

  if  Stoc.Cnt  > 03
    then  Sell ("se.Main") at se.Price stop ;
end ;

if  @MarketPosition  = +01  then begin
```

```
    ExitLong  ("lx.Main") at lx.Price stop ;
  end ;

  if  @MarketPosition  = -01  then begin
    ExitShort ("sx.Main") at sx.Price stop ;
  end ;

  if  CheckCommentary  then begin
    CommentaryCL (Date:6:0, Time:5:0, Fast.MA, Slow.MA, XOver, Stoc.Cnt,
  NewLine,
                  "  Buy  Side : ", BuyMode, le.Price, lx.Price, NewLine,
                  "  Sell Side : ", SelMode, se.Price, sx.Price, NewLine) ;
  end ;
```

#6.13c - System — skt.File Append #2

```
  {
  Type  : System (Include)
  Name  : skt.FileAppend #2
  Notes : Demonstrate the FileAppend function...
          Created for John C. Connely

  EasyLanguage translation provided
    by Samuel K. Tennis
    of Vista Research (c) 1997, 1999
  }

  Inputs: Dsk.File (FALSE) ;
  Vars  : st          (""),
          FileName ("C:\Temp\FileApnd.CSV") ;

  if  (Date = @vrt.LastCalcDate and
       Time = @vrt.LastCalcTime)
  then begin
    st  = "" ;
    if  Dsk.File  then begin
      st = st + NewLine
         + "BEStop, MoneyMgt, Profit, ****, Trailing Stop , ****"
         + NewLine
         + "Floor, StopAmt, Target, ** Amount,  Floor, Percent **, MBB"
         + NewLine ;
      st = st + Text (BreakEvenStopFloor:6:2,   ", ",
                      MoneyMgtStopAmt   :6:2,   ", ",
                      ProfitTargetStop  :6:2,   ", ",
                      TrailingStopAmt   :6:2,   ", ",
                      TrailingStopFloor :6:2,   ", ",
                      TrailingStopPct   :6:2,   ", ",
                      MaxBarsBack       :6:0) + NewLine ;

      FileAppend (FileName, st) ;
    end ; { Disk file selected }
  end ; { Last bar of data }
```

14 Trading A Channel Breakout

The CHANNEL BREAKOUT SYSTEM included below is used by the BLACK BOX REPORT example earlier in this section.

#6.14 - System : EZL.Channel BreakOut

```
{
Type   : System
Name   : EZL.Channel BreakOut
Notes  : Example of Channel Breakout w/ Entry and Exit Orders

Easy Language translation provided
  by Samuel K. Tennis
  of VISTA Research and Trading, Inc. (c) 1997

EasyLanguage interpretation provided
   by  Samuel K. Tennis
   of  Vista Research (c) 1998, 1999
  Any unauthorized use of this material may constitute
  a violation of U.S. and International Copyright Laws.
}

Inputs: le.Bars        (14),         se.Bars        (14),
        lx.Bars        (14),         sx.Bars        (14),
        le.Ticks       (05),         se.Ticks       (05),
        lx.Ticks       (05),         sx.Ticks       (05) ;
Inputs: en.Mode        (00) ;

Vars  : App.Name   ("EZL.Channel BreakOut") ;
Vars  : le.Price   (+999999),         se.Price   (-999999),
        lx.Price   (-999999),         sx.Price   (-999999),
        le.Points (MinMove * le.Ticks Points),
        se.Points (MinMove * se.Ticks Points),
        lx.Points (MinMove * lx.Ticks Points),
        sx.Points (MinMove * sx.Ticks Points) ;

{*
 *  Assign values each bar
 *}
le.Price = Highest (High, le.Bars) + le.Points ;
se.Price =  Lowest ( Low, se.Bars) - se.Points ;
lx.Price =  Lowest ( Low, lx.Bars) - lx.Points ;
sx.Price = Highest (High, sx.Bars) + sx.Points ;
{*
 *  If we are not currently long
 *}
if  @MarketPosition <> +01  then begin
  if  en.Mode  > -01  then
    Buy      ("le.ChanBrk#0") at le.Price stop ;
  ExitShort ("sx.ChanBrk#0") at le.Price stop ;
end ;
{*
 *  If we are not currently short
```

```
 *}
if  @MarketPosition <> -01  then begin
  if  en.Mode <  +01  then
    Sell    ("se.ChanBrk#0") at se.Price stop ;
  ExitLong  ("lx.ChanBrk#0") at se.Price stop ;
end ;
{*
 *  If we ARE currently long
 *}
if  @MarketPosition  = +01  then begin
  if  Highest (High, 05) <  Highest (High, le.Bars) then
    Buy     ("le.ChanBrk#1") at le.Price stop ;
  ExitLong  ("lx.ChanBrk#1") at lx.Price stop ;
end ;
{*
 *  If we ARE currently short
 *}
if  @MarketPosition  = -01  then begin
  if  Lowest ( Low, 05)  >  Lowest ( Low, se.Bars)  then
    Sell    ("se.ChanBrk#1") at se.Price stop ;
  ExitShort ("sx.ChanBrk#1") at sx.Price stop ;
end ;

{
Custom Programming Services provided by:

               Samuel K. Tennis
                Vista Research
               129 Staff Drive
        Ft. Walton Beach, Florida 32548
         voice :    1(850) 243-5105
         fax   :    1(850) 301-2884
         eMail :  skt@vista-research.com
           http://www.vista-research.com
}
```

15 *Replacing The Built-In Trailing Stop Orders.*

#6.15 - System : vrt.Trailing Stop %

```
{
Type : System (Include)
Name : vrt.Trailing Stop %
Notes: Replace built in n Percent Trailing Stop.

Purpose: Demonstrate the use of the IncludeSystem statement.

12/27/97 skt  Corrected error - MinPoints was using mult. instead of div.

EasyLanguage interpretation provided
   by  Samuel K. Tennis
   of  Vista Research (c) 1998, 1999
  Any unauthorized use of this material may constitute
```

```
  a violation of U.S. and International Copyright Laws.
}

Inputs: MinFloor   (10000),        Percent     (0.50) ;

Vars   : App.Name  ("vrt.Trailing Stop %") ;
Vars   : HiHi      (-999999),       LoLo       (+999999),
         lx.Price  (-999999),       sx.Price   (+999999),
         tsPoints       (00),       MinPoints (MinFloor / BigPointValue)
;


if  @BarNumber <= 01
then begin
  Print ("System : '", App.Name, "' (",
          MinFloor:1:2, ", ", Percent:1:4, ") ;") ;
end ;

if  @MarketPosition   = +01  then begin
{ we have just entered the market }
  if  @BarsSinceEntry{0} = 00  then  HiHi   = High [00] ;
  if  @BarsSinceEntry{0} = 01  then  HiHi   = High [01] ;
  if   High  > HiHi            then  HiHi   = High [00] ;

  if  HiHi - @EntryPrice  > MinPoints
  then begin
    tsPoints = (HiHi - @EntryPrice) * Percent ;
    lx.Price =  HiHi - tsPoints ;

    ExitLong  ("lx.tStop%") at lx.Price stop ;
  end ;
end ;

if  @MarketPosition{0}  = -01  then begin
{ we have just entered the market }
  if  @BarsSinceEntry{0} = 00  then  LoLo  =  Low [00] ;
  if  @BarsSinceEntry{0} = 01  then  LoLo  =  Low [01] ;
  if  Low   <  LoLo            then  LoLo  =  Low [00] ;

  if  @EntryPrice - LoLo  > MinPoints
  then begin
    tsPoints = (@EntryPrice - LoLo) * Percent ;
    sx.Price =  LoLo  + tsPoints ;

    ExitShort ("sx.tStop%") at sx.Price stop ;
  end ;
end ;
{*
if CheckCommentary then begin
  CommentaryCL (MarketPosition:3:0, BarsSinceEntry:3:0, EntryPrice,
MinPoints,
                NewLine,
               ", HiHi=",   HiHi,     ", LoLo=",   LoLo,
               ", tsPnts=", tsPoints,
               ", lx.Pri=", lx.Price, ", sx.Pri=", sx.Price) ;
end ; { debugging commentary }
```

```
*}

{
Custom Programming Services provided by:

                Samuel K. Tennis
                 Vista Research
                129 Staff Drive
         Ft. Walton Beach, Florida 32548
          voice :     1(850) 243-5105
          fax   :     1(850) 301-2884
          eMail :  skt@vista-research.com
            http://www.vista-research.com
}
```

16 Using At$ In An Exit Order

#6.16 - System : EZL.Control Signals

```
{
Type : System
Name : EZL.Control Signals
Notes: Logical control over signal execution

You can use the optimizer to test this system.
  If Use is non-zero then signal is active
  If Mode is -1 then take sell signals only
  If Mode is  0 then take all signals
  If Mode is +1 then take buy signals only

  En.UseA  [+00..+01:01]
  En.ModeA [-01..+01:01]
  En.UseB  [+00..+01:01]
  En.ModeB [-01..+01:01]

Input: En.UseA
       En.ModeA
       En.UseB
       En.ModeB
Alert: none
Calls: none
Uses : none

EasyLanguage interpretation provided
   by  Samuel K. Tennis
   of  Vista Research (c) 1998, 1999
  Any unauthorized use of this material may constitute
  a violation of U.S. and International Copyright Laws.
}

Inputs: En.UseA  (00),  { numeric value allows for optimizing signals }
        En.ModeA (00),  { +01=Buy only;  00=All trades; -01=Sell only }
        En.UseB  (00),  { numeric value allows for optimizing signals }
        En.ModeB (00) ; { +01=Buy only;  00=All trades; -01=Sell only }
```

```
Vars   : App.Name ("EZL.Control Signals") ;

if  en.UseA <> 00  then begin
  if  en.ModeA  > -01  then begin
    Buy  ("le.Main#A") at market ;
  end ; { Long entry enabled (Not Short Entry Only) }

  if  en.ModeA <  +01  then begin
    Sell ("se.Main#A") at market ;
  end ; { Short entry enabled (Not Long Entry Only) }
end ; { Signal #A is enabled }

if  en.UseB <> 00  then begin
  if  en.ModeB  > -01  then begin
    Buy  ("le.Main#B") at Market ;
  end ; { Long entry enabled (Not Short Entry Only) }

  if  en.ModeB <  +01  then begin
    Sell ("se.Main#B") at Market ;
  end ; { Short entry enabled (Not Long Entry Only) }
end ; { Signal #B is enabled }

{* Exit Orders *}

Inputs: ex.UseA  (00),  { numeric value allows for optimizing signals }
        ex.ModeA (00) ; { +01=LExit only; 00=All exits;-01=SExit only }

ExitLong  ("lx.At$") all Contracts
                     from Entry ("le.Main#A")
                     at$  Lowest ( Low, 03) stop ;

ExitShort ("sx.At$") all Contracts
                     from Entry ("se.Main#A")
                     at$ Highest (High, 03) stop ;

{
Custom Programming Services provided by:

               Samuel K. Tennis
                Vista Research
               129 Staff Drive
        Ft. Walton Beach, Florida 32548
         voice :    1(850) 243-5105
         fax   :    1(850) 301-2884
         eMail :  skt@vista-research.com
           http://www.vista-research.com
}
```

17 Displaying Swing Information As On-Screen Text

#6.17 - Study :"EZL.Swing High/Low"

```
{
Type : Study
Name : EZL.Swing High/Low
Notes: Track swings, including trend, using Arrays

02/01/99  skt
    Swing High/Low #7 created for Andrew Ro and Worth Ware...
  This version uses "Phantom Swing" logic.

06/09/98  skt
  Put in logic to track the trend of the market.

Properties:
  MaxBars   100
  Scaling   Price
  Layout    Color    Type      Width      Pen       Label
  ____________________________________
 *   Plot1     Red     Line   Thinnest    Solid
    Plot3   Green    Point       Thin    Solid    "Trend Up"
    Plot4     Red    Point       Thin    Solid    "Trend Dn"

NOTE: MaxBarsBack must be large enough to encompass the
      second most recent swing and Strength bars before it.

NOTE: If you are using version 2.02 or 2.03 of TradeStation,
      then you must change the calls to LowestBar and HighestBar
      to LowestBarSimple and HighestBarSimple.

EasyLanguage translation provided
  by Samuel K. Tennis
  of Vista Research (c) 1998, 1999
}

Inputs: Strength      (04),
        Sho.TLin   (FALSE),
        Sho.Text   (FALSE),
        Sho.Trnd   (FALSE),
        Debug      (FALSE) ;

Arrays: hiSwing [10] (-01),        loSwing [10] (-01) ;
Vars  : MaxSwings     (10) ;

Vars  : Length (Strength + 01),
        LastSwing     (00),
        Loop          (00),        Dummy          (00),
        SWHbar        (00),        SWH2bar        (00),
        SWLbar        (00),        SWL2bar        (00) ;
Vars  : swSiz         (00),        swCum          (00),
        swSum         (00),        swCnt          (00),
        Trend         (00) ;

Vars  : tl_Ref       (-01),        tl_Err         (00),
        Dummy1        (00),        Dummy2         (00) ;
Vars  : tx_Str        (""),
```

```
        tx_Ref       (-01),        tx_Err       (-01) ;


SWHbar   = SwingHighBar (01, High, Strength, Length) ;
SWLbar   = SwingLowBar  (01, Low,  Strength, Length) ;

if  SWHbar <> -01 and SWLbar <> -01  then begin
{
  SWHbar = -01 ;
  SWLbar = -01 ;
}
  if  LastSwing = +01  then  SWHbar  = -01 ;
  if  LastSwing = -01  then  SWLbar  = -01 ;
end ; { invalidate two swings on one bar? }

if  SWHbar  > -01  then begin
  if  LastSwing[01] <> -01  then begin
    if  hiSwing[00]  > 00
      then dummy = VRT.BarOffset (hiSwing[00])
      else dummy = -01 ;

    if  Dummy  >  00  then begin
      SWL2bar = LowestBar (Low,  (Dummy - SWHbar) - 01)[SWHbar + 01] ;

      for Loop  = MaxSwings DownTo 01 begin
        loSwing[Loop]  = loSwing[Loop - 01] ;
      end ;
      loSwing[00]  = CurrentBar - SWL2bar ;

      swSiz  = High [VRT.BarOffset (hiSwing[00])] -
                 Low [VRT.BarOffset (loSwing[00])] ;
      swSum  = swSum + swSiz ;
      swCnt  = swCnt + 01 ;
      swCum  = swCum + swSiz ;
{*
      swCum  = swCum + ( Low [VRT.BarOffset (loSwing[00])] -
                         High [VRT.BarOffset (hiSwing[00])]) ;
 *}
{*
    if  DeBug  then
      Print (Date:6:0, Time:5:0, " swlo ", swSiz:3:4,
             High[VRT.BarOffset (hiSwing[00])]:5:2,
             Low [VRT.BarOffset (loSwing[00])]:5:2,
             swCnt:5:0, swSum, swSum / swCnt:4:4, swCum) ;
 *}
      Dummy1 = vrt.BarOffset (hiSwing[00]) ;
      Dummy2 = vrt.BarOffset (loSwing[00]) ;

      if  Sho.TLin  then begin
        tl_Ref = TL_New (Date [Dummy1], Time [Dummy1], High [Dummy1],
                         Date [Dummy2], Time [Dummy2], Low  [Dummy2]) ;
        if  tl_Ref  > -01  then begin
          tl_Err  = TL_SetExtLeft  (tl_Ref, FALSE) ;
          tl_Err  = TL_SetExtRight (tl_Ref, FALSE) ;
          tl_Err  = TL_SetColor    (tl_Ref, Tool_Blue)  ;
        end ;
```

```
        end ;

        if  Sho.Text  then begin
          tx_Str  = NumToStr (AbsValue (Dummy1 - Dummy2), 00)
            + "," + vrt.Format (swSiz)
            + "," + vrt.Format ( Low [Dummy2]) ;

          tx_Ref = Text_New (Date[Dummy2], Time[Dummy2],
                             Low [Dummy2], tx_Str) ;

          if  tx_Ref <  -20 or tx_Ref  > -01  then begin
            tx_Err  = Text_SetColor (tx_Ref, Tool_Blue) ;
            tx_Err  = Text_SetStyle (tx_Ref,   02,  00) ;
          end ;
        end ;
      end ;
    {*
      else
        if  DeBug  then
          Print (Date:6:0, Time:6:0, SWHbar:4:0, SWH2bar:4:0,
               " Missed SwingHigh!") ;
     *}
     end ;

     for Loop = MaxSwings DownTo 01 begin
       hiSwing[Loop] = hiSwing[Loop - 01] ;
     end ;
     hiSwing[00] = CurrentBar - SWHbar ;

     swSiz  = High [VRT.BarOffset (hiSwing[00])] -
                Low [VRT.BarOffset (loSwing[00])] ;
     swSum  = swSum + swSiz ;
     swCnt  = swCnt + 01 ;
     swCum  = swCum + swSiz ;

     if  High [VRT.BarOffset (hiSwing[00])]  > High [VRT.BarOffset
    (hiSwing[01])]
     then begin
       Trend  = +01 ;
       if  Sho.Trnd  then
         Plot3 ( Low [VRT.BarOffset (loSwing[01])], "Trend Up") ;
     end ;
    {*
     if  DeBug  then
       Print (Date:6:0, Time:5:0, " SwHi ", swSiz:3:4,
              High[VRT.BarOffset (hiSwing[00])]:5:2,
              Low [VRT.BarOffset (loSwing[00])]:5:2,
              swCnt:5:0, swSum, swSum / swCnt:4:4, swCum, Trend:5:0) ;
     *}
     Dummy1 = vrt.BarOffset (loSwing[00]) ;
     Dummy2 = vrt.BarOffset (hiSwing[00]) ;

     if  Sho.TLin  then begin
       tl_Ref = TL_New (Date  [Dummy1], Time  [Dummy1], Low  [Dummy1],
                        Date  [Dummy2], Time  [Dummy2], High [Dummy2]) ;
       if  tl_Ref  > -01  then begin
```

```
      tl_Err   = TL_SetExtLeft  (tl_Ref, FALSE) ;
      tl_Err   = TL_SetExtRight (tl_Ref, FALSE) ;
      tl_Err   = TL_SetColor    (tl_Ref, Tool_Blue)  ;
    end ;
  end ;

  if  Sho.Text  then begin
    tx_Str   = NumToStr (AbsValue (Dummy1 - Dummy2), 00)
      + "," + vrt.Format (swSiz)
      + "," + vrt.Format (High [Dummy2]) ;

    tx_Ref = Text_New (Date[Dummy2], Time[Dummy2], High[Dummy2], tx_Str)
;

    if  tx_Ref <  -20 or tx_Ref  > -01  then begin
      tx_Err   = Text_SetColor (tx_Ref,  Tool_Red) ;
      tx_Err   = Text_SetStyle (tx_Ref,   02,  01) ;
    end ;
  end ;

  LastSwing = +01 ;
end ;

if  SWLbar > -01  then begin
  if  LastSwing[01] <> +01  then begin
    if (loSwing[00] > 00)
      then dummy = VRT.BarOffset (loSwing[00])
      else dummy = -01 ;

    if  Dummy >  00  then begin
      SWH2bar = HighestBar(High, (Dummy - SWLbar) - 01)[SWLbar + 01] ;

      for Loop = MaxSwings DownTo 1 begin
        hiSwing[Loop] = hiSwing[Loop - 01] ;
      end ;
      hiSwing[00] = CurrentBar - SWH2bar ;

      swSiz = High [VRT.BarOffset (hiSwing[00])] -
               Low [VRT.BarOffset (loSwing[00])] ;
      swSum = swSum + swSiz ;
      swCnt = swCnt + 01 ;
      swCum = swCum + swSiz ;
{*
    if  DeBug  then
      Print (Date:6:0, Time:5:0, " swhi ", swSiz:3:4,
             High[VRT.BarOffset (hiSwing[00])]:5:2,
             Low [VRT.BarOffset (loSwing[00])]:5:2,
             swCnt:5:0, swSum, swSum / swCnt:4:4, swCum) ;
 *}
      Dummy1 = vrt.BarOffset (loSwing[00]) ;
      Dummy2 = vrt.BarOffset (hiSwing[00]) ;

      if  Sho.TLin  then begin
        tl_Ref = TL_New (Date [Dummy1], Time [Dummy1], Low  [Dummy1],
                         Date [Dummy2], Time [Dummy2], High [Dummy2]) ;
```

```
          if  tl_Ref  > -01  then begin
            tl_Err  = TL_SetExtLeft  (tl_Ref, FALSE) ;
            tl_Err  = TL_SetExtRight (tl_Ref, FALSE) ;
            tl_Err  = TL_SetColor    (tl_Ref, Tool_Blue)  ;
          end ;
        end ;

        if  Sho.Text  then begin
          tx_Str  = NumToStr (AbsValue (Dummy1 - Dummy2), 00)
            + "," + vrt.Format (swSiz)
            + "," + vrt.Format (High [Dummy2]) ;

          tx_Ref  = Text_New (Date [Dummy2], Time [Dummy2],
                              High[SWH2bar], tx_Str) ;
          if  tx_Ref <  -20 or tx_Ref  > -01  then begin
            tx_Err  = Text_SetColor (tx_Ref,  Tool_Red) ;
            tx_Err  = Text_SetStyle (tx_Ref,   02,  01) ;
          end ;
        end ;
      end ;
  {*
      else
        if  DeBug  then  Print (Date:6:0, Time:6:0, SWLbar:4:0,
  SWL2bar:4:0,
                              " Missed SwingLow!") ;
   *}
    end ;

    for Loop = MaxSwings DownTo 1 begin
      loSwing[Loop] = loSwing[Loop - 1] ;
    end ;
    loSwing[00] = CurrentBar - SWLbar ;

    swSiz = High [VRT.BarOffset (hiSwing[00])] -
             Low [VRT.BarOffset (loSwing[00])] ;
    swSum = swSum + swSiz ;
    swCnt = swCnt + 01 ;
    swCum = swCum + swSiz ;
  {*
    swCum = swCum + ( Low [VRT.BarOffset (loSwing[00])] -
                     High [VRT.BarOffset (hiSwing[00])]) ;
   *}
    if  Low [VRT.BarOffset (loSwing[00])] < Low [VRT.BarOffset
  (loSwing[01])]
    then begin
      Trend  = -01 ;
      if  Sho.Trnd
        then Plot4 (High [VRT.BarOffset (hiSwing[01])], "Trend Dn") ;
    end ;
  {*
    if  DeBug  then
      Print (Date:6:0, Time:5:0, " SwLo ", swSiz:3:4,
             High[VRT.BarOffset (hiSwing[00])]:5:2,
             Low [VRT.BarOffset (loSwing[00])]:5:2,
             swCnt:5:0, swSum, swSum / swCnt:4:4, swCum, Trend:5:0) ;
   *}
```

```
  Dummy1 = vrt.BarOffset (hiSwing[00]) ;
  Dummy2 = vrt.BarOffset (loSwing[00]) ;

  if  Sho.TLin  then begin
    tl_Ref = TL_New (Date [Dummy1], Time [Dummy1], High [Dummy1],
                     Date [Dummy2], Time [Dummy2], Low  [Dummy2]) ;

    if  tl_Ref  > -01  then begin
      tl_Err  = TL_SetExtLeft  (tl_Ref, FALSE) ;
      tl_Err  = TL_SetExtRight (tl_Ref, FALSE) ;
      tl_Err  = TL_SetColor    (tl_Ref, Tool_Blue)  ;
    end ;
  end ;

  if  Sho.Text  then begin
    tx_Str  = NumToStr (AbsValue (Dummy1 - Dummy2), 00)
      + "," + vrt.Format (swSiz)
      + "," + vrt.Format ( Low [Dummy2]) ;

    tx_Ref = Text_New (Date[SWLbar], Time[SWLbar],  Low[SWLbar], tx_Str)
;
    if  tx_Ref <  -20 or tx_Ref  > -01  then begin
      tx_Err  = Text_SetColor (tx_Ref, Tool_Blue) ;
      tx_Err  = Text_SetStyle (tx_Ref,   02,  00) ;
    end ;
  end ;
{*
Date-line = horizontal/x-coordinate
Hright     0      Drawn right of the date-line
Hleft      1      Drawn left of the date-line
Hcenter    2      Drawn centered on the date-line

Price-line = vertical/y-coordinate
Vbelow     0      Drawn below the price-line
Vabove     1      Drawn above the price-line
Vcenter    2      Drawn centered on the price-line
 *}
  LastSwing = -01 ;
end ;

{*
 *  If we wait for the next swing high / low then our trend reversal
 *  might be delayed quite some time (and price).
 *  By removing the lines marked w/ "{ ** }" you get plots until the
 *  swing is confirmed and the trend is changed.
 *}

if  Trend <  +00 and High  > High [VRT.BarOffset (hiSwing[00])]
  then  Trend  = +00 ;

if  Trend  > +00 and  Low <   Low [VRT.BarOffset (loSwing[00])]
  then  Trend  = +00 ;

{*
 *  By inserting the lines below we can see the price level required
 *  to reverse the trend.
```

```
 *}

if  Sho.Trnd and Trend[00] = +01 and Trend[01] = +01
  then Plot3 ( Low [VRT.BarOffset (loSwing[00])], "Trend Up") ;

if  Sho.Trnd and Trend[00] = -01 and Trend[01] = -01
  then Plot4 (High [VRT.BarOffset (hiSwing[00])], "Trend Dn") ;

{*
if  DeBug  then
  Print (Date:6:0,
         hiSwing[00]:5:0, hiSwing[01]:5:0, hiSwing[02]:5:0,
         loSwing[00]:5:0, loSwing[01]:5:0, loSwing[02]:5:0) ;
 *}

{
Custom Programming Services provided by:

               Samuel K. Tennis
                Vista Research
               129 Staff Drive
        Ft. Walton Beach, Florida 32548
         voice :    1(850) 243-5105
         fax   :    1(850) 301-2884
         eMail :  skt@vista-research.com
           http://www.vista-research.com
}
```

18 *Changing The Color An/Or Size Of Plots*

19 *Automatically Draw Parallel Lines Outside TrendLines*

#6.19 - Study : EZL.Trend Line Bands

```
{
Type : Study
Name : EZL.Trend Line Bands
Notes: Written for David Worstine, N.Y. City TS User Group Leader.

    NoMore is allows you to use the Expert Commentary Tool to prevent the
  study from updating itself beyond the bar you click the mouse on.
    Why?  Who knows.  In this application it does not serve much purpose
  but it is a valueable technique that allows you to get mouse input into
  your Easy Language code.

EasyLanguage interpretation provided
   by  Samuel K. Tennis
   of  Vista Research (c) 1998, 1999
  Any unauthorized use of this material may constitute
  a violation of U.S. and International Copyright Laws.
```

```
}

Arrays: tl_Ref [10, 10] (-01) ;

Vars  : App.Name ("EZL.Trend Line Bands") ;
Vars  : NoMore  (-01),        TrndCnt  (00) ;

Vars  : MaxRows  (10),        MaxCols  (10),        Loop     (00) ;
Vars  : tlErr   (-01),        tlRef   (-01),        tlVal    (00),
        Pref     (02) ;        { 2 = First Trend Line created by user }
Vars  : hiMax   (-01),        loMax   (-01) ;
Vars  : st0      (""),        st1      (""),
        st2      (""),        st3      ("") ;


if  @BarNumber <= 01  then begin
  Print ("") ;
  Print ("Study: '" + App.Name + "'") ;
  Print ("——————————————") ;
  Print ("") ;

  Loop     =  00 ;
  TrndCnt  =  00 ;
  tlRef    =  TL_GetFirst (Pref) ;
  while (tlRef > -01 and Loop <= MaxRows) begin
    TrndCnt = TrndCnt + 01 ;

    tl_Ref[Loop, 00] = tlRef ;              { trend line reference number
}
    tl_Ref[Loop, 01] =   -01 ;         { High trend line reference number
}
    tl_Ref[Loop, 02] =   -01 ;         {  Low trend line reference number
}

    tl_Ref[Loop, 03] = TL_GetBeginDate (tlRef) ;                { BegDate
}
    tl_Ref[Loop, 04] = TL_GetBeginTime (tlRef) ;                { BegTime
}
    tl_Ref[Loop, 05] = TL_GetBeginVal  (tlRef) ;                { BegPrice
}
    tl_Ref[Loop, 06] = TL_GetEndDate   (tlRef) ;                { EndDate
}
    tl_Ref[Loop, 07] = TL_GetEndTime   (tlRef) ;                { EndTime
}
    tl_Ref[Loop, 08] = TL_GetEndVal    (tlRef) ;                { EndPrice
}

    tl_Ref[Loop, 09] =                           -01 ;          { MaxVal
}

    tlRef = TL_GetNext (tlRef, Pref) ;                { get next trend line
}
    Loop = Loop + 01 ;                            { increment loop counter
}
  end ; { while loop }
end ; { first bar of data  }
```

```
if  TrndCnt  > 00  then begin
  Loop  =  00 ;
  while (TL_Ref[Loop, 00]  > -01) begin
    if  NoMore <   00               and
        (Date  > TL_Ref[Loop, 03]   or        { date later than BegDate OR
}
        (Date  = TL_Ref[Loop, 03]   and        { date equal to BegDate AND
}
         Time >= TL_Ref[Loop, 04])) and { time equal or later than BegTime
}
        (Date <  TL_Ref[Loop, 06]   or       { date earlier than EndDate OR
}
        (Date  = TL_Ref[Loop, 06]   and        { date equal to EndDate AND
}
         Time <= TL_Ref[Loop, 07]))      ime less than or equal to EndTime
}
    then begin
      hiMax   =  -01 ;
      loMax   =  -01 ;
      tlVal   = TL_GetValue (tl_Ref[Loop, 00], Date, Time) ;
      if  High  - tlVal  > TL_Ref[Loop, 09]  then  hiMax =  High - tlVal
;
      if  tlVal -   Low  > TL_Ref[Loop, 09]  then  loMax = tlVal -   Low
;

      if  (hiMax  > TL_Ref[Loop, 09] or loMax  > TL_Ref[Loop, 09])
      then begin
        TL_Ref[Loop, 09] = MaxList (hiMax, loMax) ;
{* delete old trend line(s) if new 'MaxVal' is found *}
        if TL_Ref[Loop, 01]  > -01
          then  tlErr = tl_Delete (TL_Ref[Loop, 01]) ;
        if TL_Ref[Loop, 02]  > -01
          then  tlErr = tl_Delete (TL_Ref[Loop, 02]) ;
{* draw the new high side trend line. *}
        TL_Ref[Loop, 01] = TL_New (TL_Ref[Loop, 03],  TL_Ref[Loop, 04],
                                   TL_Ref[Loop, 05] + TL_Ref[Loop, 09],
                                   TL_Ref[Loop, 06],  TL_Ref[Loop, 07],
                                   TL_Ref[Loop, 08] + TL_Ref[Loop, 09]) ;
{* if no error then change the color and extend right. *}
        if  TL_Ref[Loop, 01]  > -01  then begin
          tlErr = TL_SetColor    (TL_Ref[Loop, 01], Tool_White) ;
          tlErr = TL_SetExtLeft  (TL_Ref[Loop, 01], FALSE) ;
          tlErr = TL_SetExtRight (TL_Ref[Loop, 01],  TRUE) ;
        end ;
{* draw the new low side trend line. *}
        TL_Ref[Loop, 02] = TL_New (TL_Ref[Loop, 03],  TL_Ref[Loop, 04],
                                   TL_Ref[Loop, 05] - TL_Ref[Loop, 09],
                                   TL_Ref[Loop, 06],  TL_Ref[Loop, 07],
                                   TL_Ref[Loop, 08] - TL_Ref[Loop, 09]) ;
{* if no error then change the color and extend right. *}
        if TL_Ref[Loop, 02]  > -01 then begin
          tlErr = TL_SetColor    (TL_Ref[Loop, 02], Tool_White) ;
          tlErr = TL_SetExtLeft  (TL_Ref[Loop, 01], FALSE) ;
          tlErr = TL_SetExtRight (TL_Ref[Loop, 02],  TRUE) ;
        end ;
```

```
      end ; { if }
    end ; {  }
    Loop = Loop + 01 ; { increment loop counter }
  end ; { while loop }
end ; { there was at least one trend line detected on the chart }

if  CheckCommentary  then begin
  NoMore = +01 ;
{*
 * CommentaryCL (swLo, loBarNo, loDate, loTime, loPrice, loMax) ;
 * CommentaryCL (swHi, hiBarNo, hiDate, hiTime, hiPrice, hiMax) ;
 *}
end ; {  }
{*
 *    Right now there is nothing I want to see plotted but a study
 *  MUST contain a plot statement.
 *}
if false then plot1 (Close, "c") ;
{*
 *  Print a report on the last bar of data.
 *}
if  Date = vrt.LastCalcDate and Time = vrt.LastcalcTime  then begin
  if  TrndCnt  > 00  then begin
    Print (
  "Cnt  Ref#    Date   Time  Price  to  Date   Time  Price MaxVal") ;
    Print ("--------------------------------") ;
    for Loop = 00 to TrndCnt - 01 begin

      st0 = vrt.Format (tl_Ref [Loop, 05]) ;
      if  strLen (st0) <  07
        then  st1 = Spaces (07 - StrLen (st0)) + st0
        else  st1 = st0 ;

      st0 = vrt.Format (tl_Ref [Loop, 08]) ;
      if  strLen (st0) <  07
        then  st2 = Spaces (07 - StrLen (st0)) + st0
        else  st2 = st0 ;

      st0 = vrt.Format (tl_Ref [Loop, 09]) ;
      if  strLen (st0) <  07
        then  st3 = Spaces (07 - StrLen (st0)) + st0
        else  st3 = st0 ;

      Print (          Loop    :3:0, " ",
               tl_Ref [Loop, 00]:4:0, "   ",  { Ref Num  }
   vrt.mmddyy (tl_Ref [Loop, 03]),            { BegDate  }
               tl_Ref [Loop, 04]:5:0, " ",    { BegTime  }
             st1,                    "    ",  { BegPrice }
   vrt.mmddyy (tl_Ref [Loop, 06]),            { EndDate  }
               tl_Ref [Loop, 07]:5:0, " ",    { EndTime  }
             st2, st3) ;                      { EndPrice, MaxVal }
{*
      Print (          Loop    :3:0, " ",
               tl_Ref [Loop, 00]:4:0, "   ",  { Ref Num  }
   vrt.mmddyy (tl_Ref [Loop, 03]),            { BegDate  }
               tl_Ref [Loop, 04]:5:0, " ",    { BegTime  }
```

```
      vrt.Format (tl_Ref [Loop, 05]),      "     ", { BegPrice }
      vrt.mmddyy (tl_Ref [Loop, 06]),             { EndDate  }
                  tl_Ref [Loop, 07]:5:0, " ",     { EndTime  }
      vrt.Format (tl_Ref [Loop, 08]),             { EndPrice }
      vrt.Format (tl_Ref [Loop, 09])) ;           { MaxVal   }
    *}
      end ;
      Print ("————————————————————————————————") ;
      Print ("A total of ", TrndCnt:1:0, " manual Trend Lines were found.")
;
    end
    else Print ("No manually drawn trend lines detected on this chart.") ;

end ; { on last bar of data }

{
Custom Programming Services provided by:

               Samuel K. Tennis
                Vista Research
               129 Staff Drive
        Ft. Walton Beach, Florida 32548
         voice :     1(850) 243-5105
         fax   :     1(850) 301-2884
         eMail :  skt@vista-research.com
           http://www.vista-research.com
}
```

20 *Protecting Your Easylanguage Code.*

#6.20 - System : vrt.Date Protection

```
{       Password
Type : System
Name : vrt.Date Protection
Notes: How to protect your EasyLangauge code
       Prepared initially for my client and friend Mr. Sam Halim

EasyLanguage interpretation provided
   by  Samuel K. Tennis
   of  Vista Research (c) 1998, 1999
  Any unauthorized use of this material may constitute
  a violation of U.S. and International Copyright Laws.
}

{*
 *  CurrentDate is the date of the DataFeed or Computer Clock
 *  LastcalcDate is the last bar loaded in the chart
 *}
if     ((@CurrentDate  <  990615) and  (@LastCalcDate <  990610))
{*
 *  Date is a price field and refers to the current StudyBar
 *}
   or ((Date          >= 980101) and  (Date          <= 981231))
```

```
{*
 * Product is used to determin TradeStation, or SuperCharts
 *}
   or ((@Product       =    010)
{*
 * BlockNumber returns the number of the SecurityBlock
 *}
  and ((@BlockNumber   = 004028)
   or  (@BlockNumber   = 009813)))
then begin
{*
 *  This may surround your system logic, a part of it or
 *  only the system orders.  Your choice...
 *}
end ;

{
Custom Programming Services provided by:

               Samuel K. Tennis
                Vista Research
               129 Staff Drive
        Ft. Walton Beach, Florida 32548
         voice :    1(850) 243-5105
         fax   :    1(850) 301-2884
         eMail :  skt@vista-research.com
           http://www.vista-research.com
}
```

21 StudyBar Related Functions

#6.21 - Function: VRT.BarOffset

Pass in a @CurrentBar Value and it returns a StudyBar Value relative to @BarNumber. For example, if you stored the value of CurrentBar on bar number 100 and on this bar BarNumber has a value of 120 then @vrt.BarOffset will return a value of 20 (120 - 100). If the result would yield a MaxBarsBack Error the function returns a value of zero (00).

```
{
Type : User Function (StudyBar)
Name : VRT.BarOffset
Notes: Returns difference from CurrentBar.

Provided by Samuel K. Tennis
         of VISTA Research and Trading, Inc.
        (c) all rights reserved, 1994, 1995, 1998.

EasyLanguage interpretation provided
   by  Samuel K. Tennis
   of  Vista Research (c) 1998, 1999
  Any unauthorized use of this material may constitute
  a violation of U.S. and International Copyright Laws.
}
```

```
Inputs: BarIn  (NumericSimple) ;
Vars  : Return (0) ;

Return    = 00 ;

if  @BarNumber >=       BarIn  then  Return   = @BarNumber - BarIn ;

if  Return    <            00  or
    Return     > MaxBarsBack  then  Return   = 00 ;

VRT.BarOffset  = Return ;

{
Custom Programming Services provided by:

               Samuel K. Tennis
                Vista Research
               129 Staff Drive
        Ft. Walton Beach, Florida 32548
         voice :    1(850) 243-5105
         fax   :    1(850) 301-2884
         eMail :  skt@vista-research.com
           http://www.vista-research.com
}
```

22 String Related Functions

#6.22a - Function: vrt.HHMM

This Function receives a Numeric Time Field and returns a formatted String Value in HHMM format (delimited with a colon).

```
{
Type : User Function (String)
Name : vrt.HHMM
Notes: Returns the Time in hh:mm format.

EasyLanguage interpretation provided
   by  Samuel K. Tennis
   of  Vista Research (c) 1998, 1999
  Any unauthorized use of this material may constitute
  a violation of U.S. and International Copyright Laws.
}

Inputs: xTime (NumericSimple) ;
Vars  : hh     (00),        mm     (00),
        st.hh  (""),        st.mm  (""),
        Return ("") ;

hh      =        @IntPortion  (xTime * 0.01) ;
mm      = Round (@FracPortion (xTime * 0.01) * 100.0, 00) ;
{
Print (xTime, hh, mm, FracPortion (xTime * 0.01),
                    FracPortion (xTime * 0.01) * 100.0, xTime * 0.01) ;
}
```

```
st.hh     = @NumToStr (hh, 00) ;
st.mm     = @NumToStr (mm, 00) ;
if  @StrLen (st.hh) <  02  then  st.hh   = "0" + st.hh ;
if  @StrLen (st.mm) <  02  then  st.mm   = "0" + st.mm ;
Return    = st.hh + ":" + st.mm ;

vrt.HHMM = Return ;

{
Custom Programming Services provided by:

               Samuel K. Tennis
                Vista Research
               129 Staff Drive
        Ft. Walton Beach, Florida 32548
         voice :     1(850) 243-5105
         fax   :     1(850) 301-2884
         eMail :   skt@vista-research.com
           http://www.vista-research.com
}
```

#6.22b - Function: vrt.MMDDYY

This function converts a Numeric Date Value into a String Value in MM/DD/YY format (delimited with slashes).

```
{
Type   : User Function (String)
Name   : vrt.MMDDYY
Notes  : Converts the numeric date input into a delimited string.
Return: Date as a string "mm/dd/yy".

EasyLanguage interpretation provided
   by  Samuel K. Tennis
   of  Vista Research (c) 1998, 1999
  Any unauthorized use of this material may constitute
  a violation of U.S. and International Copyright Laws.
}

Inputs: tDate (NumericSimple) ;
Vars  : chDD   (""),         chMM   (""),
        chYY   (""),         RetStr ("") ;
Vars  : dd     (00),         mm     (00),        yy     (00) ;

{ ------------------------------------------- }

dd = @Round       (@FracPortion (tDate *    0.01) * 100.0, 00) ;
mm = @IntPortion (@FracPortion (tDate * 0.0001) * 100.0) ;
yy = @IntPortion                (tDate * 0.0001) ;

chDD  = @NumToStr (DD, 00) ;
chMM  = @NumToStr (MM, 00) ;
chYY  = @NumToStr (YY, 00) ;

if  @StrLen (chDD) <  02  then  chDD  = "0" + chDD ;
if  @StrLen (chMM) <  02  then  chMM  = "0" + chMM ;
{*
chYY = "19" + chYY ;
 *}
```

```
RetStr = chMM + "/" + chDD + "/" + chYY ;

vrt.mmddyy = RetStr ;

{ ———————————————————————————————————————— }

{
Custom Programming Services provided by:

                Samuel K. Tennis
                 Vista Research
                129 Staff Drive
         Ft. Walton Beach, Florida 32548
          voice :    1(850) 243-5105
          fax   :    1(850) 301-2884
          eMail :  skt@vista-research.com
            http://www.vista-research.com
}
```

#6.22c - Function: vrt.Format

Pass this User Function a Price Value and it returns a formatted String Value. The function uses PriceScale and the value of one Point. It does NOT round to the nearest tick.

```
{
Type   : User Function (String)
Name   : vrt.Format
Notes  : Converts decimal price into formatted string.
Return: Formatted Price as String

History:
  08/29/96 skt
    Modified to support negative numbers.

EasyLanguage translation provided
  by Samuel K. Tennis
  of Vista Research (c) 1998, 1999
}

Inputs: Price (NumericSimple) ;

Vars   : RetStr (""),
         st0    (""),          st1    (""),
         st2    (""),          st3    ("") ;


st0 = "" ;  { Working Storage Fields }
st1 = "" ;
st2 = "" ;
st3 = "" ;

Value1 = IntPortion  (@AbsValue (Price)) ; { Integer portion }
Value2 = FracPortion (@AbsValue (Price)) ; { Decimal portion }
Value3 = Round (Value2 / 01 Point, 00) ;   { what / why ???? }
```

```
if  Price <  00  then  st0  = "-"  else  st0  = " " ;

st1  = NumToStr (Value1, 00) ;

if @PriceScale  > 01 then begin
  st3 = NumToStr (Value3, 0) ;
  if  @PriceScale  > 00010  and  StrLen (st3) = 001  then st3 = "0" + st3
;
  if  @PriceScale  > 00100  and  StrLen (st3) = 002  then st3 = "0" + st3
;
  if  @PriceScale  > 01000  and  StrLen (st3) = 003  then st3 = "0" + st3
;
  if  @PriceScale  > 10000  and  StrLen (st3) = 004  then st3 = "0" + st3
;

  st2        = "?" ;
  if (@PriceScale  =  002) or (@PriceScale  =  004) or
     (@PriceScale  =  008) or (@PriceScale  =  016) or
     (@PriceScale  =  032) or (@PriceScale  =  064) or
     (@PriceScale  =  128) or (@PriceScale  =  256)
    then st2 = "^"      { price as a fraction }
    else st2 = "." ;    { price as a decimal }
end ;

RetStr = st0 + st1 + st2 + st3 ;

VRT.Format  = RetStr ;

{
Custom Programming Services provided by:

               Samuel K. Tennis
                Vista Research
               129 Staff Drive
        Ft. Walton Beach, Florida 32548
         voice :    1(850) 243-5105
         fax   :    1(850) 301-2884
         eMail :  skt@vista-research.com
           http://www.vista-research.com
}
```

#6.22d - Function: skt.nChars

Pass in a String Value and a number for the length in characters. It returns the String Value padded with spaces so it is "MinChars" in length.

```
{
Type : User Function (String)
Name : skt.nChars
Notes: Pad input price w/ spaces to meet MinChars length.

EasyLanguage interpretation provided by Samuel K. Tennis
  of VISTA Research and Trading, Inc. (c) 1998
  Any unauthorized use of this material constitutes
  a violation of U.S. and International Copyright Laws.
```

```
EasyLanguage interpretation provided
   by  Samuel K. Tennis
   of  Vista Research (c) 1998, 1999
  Any unauthorized use of this material may constitute
  a violation of U.S. and International Copyright Laws.
}

Inputs: Price     (StringSimple),
        MinChars (NumericSimple) ;

Vars  : Return ("") ;


Return = Price ;

if  @StrLen (Price) <  MinChars
  then  Return  = @Spaces (MinChars - @StrLen (Price)) + Price ;

skt.nChars = Return ;

{
Custom Programming Services provided by:

               Samuel K. Tennis
                Vista Research
               129 Staff Drive
        Ft. Walton Beach, Florida 32548
         voice :     1(850) 243-5105
         fax   :     1(850) 301-2884
         eMail :  skt@vista-research.com
           http://www.vista-research.com
}
```

#6.22e - Function: skt.Bool.str

Similar to the @IFF Built-In Function but it returns a value of type String, you pass it a Boolean Value and it returns " TRUE" or "FALSE".

```
{       Password
Type  : User Function (String)
Name  : skt.Bool.str
Return: " True" / "False"
Notes : Immediate IF - Returns one of two strings based on Bool.Val.
Immediate IF - Returns one of two strings based on 'Bool.Exp' input
value.

Input: Bool.Exp (TrueFalseSimple)  Any valid Boolean expression.
Alert: None
Uses : None
Calls: None

Sample Usage:
  BoolStr = skt.iff.Str (MarketPosition  >  0) ;
  Print ("The sell order generated is an ", PosStr, " Order.") ;
ation of U.S. and International Copyright Laws.
```

```
EasyLanguage interpretation provided
   by  Samuel K. Tennis
   of  Vista Research (c) 1998, 1999
  Any unauthorized use of this material may constitute
  a violation of U.S. and International Copyright Laws.
}

Inputs: Bool.Val (TrueFalseSimple) ;

Vars  : Return               (""),
        t.String         (" True"),
        f.String         ("False") ;


if  Bool.Val  then  Return  = t.String
              else  Return  = f.String ;

skt.Bool.str  = Return ;

{
Custom Programming Services provided by:

               Samuel K. Tennis
                Vista Research
               129 Staff Drive
        Ft. Walton Beach, Florida 32548
         voice :    1(850) 243-5105
         fax   :    1(850) 301-2884
         eMail :  skt@vista-research.com
           http://www.vista-research.com
}
```

#6.22f - Function: skt.IFF.str

Similar to the @IFF Built-In Function but it returns a value of type String. The three Inputs are the Boolean Value that controls the function, the String Value returned if TRUE and the String Value to return if FALSE.

```
{      Password
Type : User Function (String)
Name : skt.IFF.str
Notes: Immediate IF - Returns one of two strings based on 'Bool.Exp'
input value.

Input: Bool.Exp (TrueFalseSimple) Any valid Boolean expression.
       t.String    (StringSimple)  String returned if Bool.Exp is  TRUE.
       f.String    (StringSimple)  String returned if Bool.Exp is FALSE.
Alert: None
Uses : None
Calls: None

Sample Usage:

  PosStr = skt.iff.Str (MarketPosition  >  0, "SAR", "Entry") ;
  Print ("The sell order generated is an ", PosStr, " Order.") ;
```

```
EasyLanguage interpretation provided
   by  Samuel K. Tennis
   of  Vista Research (c) 1998, 1999
  Any unauthorized use of this material may constitute
  a violation of U.S. and International Copyright Laws.
}

Inputs: Bool.Val (TrueFalseSimple),
        t.String     (StringSimple),
        f.String     (StringSimple) ;
Vars  : Return                 ("") ;


if  Bool.Val  then  Return  = t.String
              else  Return  = f.String ;

skt.IFF.str  = Return ;

{
Custom Programming Services provided by:

               Samuel K. Tennis
                Vista Research
               129 Staff Drive
        Ft. Walton Beach, Florida 32548
         voice :     1(850) 243-5105
         fax   :     1(850) 301-2884
         eMail :   skt@vista-research.com
           http://www.vista-research.com
}
```

#6.22g - Function: skt.Month.Name

Returns the Month Name (a String) for the input date.

```
{
Type   : User Function (String)
Name   : skt.Month.Name
Notes  : Returns month name of input date.


EasyLanguage translation provided
  by Samuel K. Tennis
  of VISTA Research and Trading, Inc. (c) 1998

EasyLanguage interpretation provided
   by  Samuel K. Tennis
   of  Vista Research (c) 1998, 1999
  Any unauthorized use of this material may constitute
  a violation of U.S. and International Copyright Laws.
}

Inputs: tDate (NumericSimple) ;
Arrays: MonName     [13]  ("") ;
Vars  : RetStr            (""),
        MonVal            (01) ;
```

```
{ ————————————————————————————————————— }

if  @BarNumber <= 01  then begin
  MonName [00]  = "Error. " ;
  MonName [01]  = "January" ;
  MonName [02]  = "February" ;
  MonName [03]  = "March" ;
  MonName [04]  = "April" ;
  MonName [05]  = "May" ;
  MonName [06]  = "June" ;
  MonName [07]  = "July" ;
  MonName [08]  = "August" ;
  MonName [09]  = "September" ;
  MonName [10]  = "October" ;
  MonName [11]  = "November" ;
  MonName [12]  = "December" ;
  MonName [13]  = "Error. " ;
end ; {  }

RetStr  = MonName [00] ;
MonVal  = @Month (tDate) ;

if  MonVal  > 00 and MonVal <= 12
  then RetStr  = MonName [MonVal] ;

skt.Month.Name  = RetStr ;

{ ————————————————————————————————————— }

{
Custom Programming Services provided by:

               Samuel K. Tennis
                Vista Research
               129 Staff Drive
        Ft. Walton Beach, Florida 32548
         voice :    1(850) 243-5105
         fax   :    1(850) 301-2884
         eMail :  skt@vista-research.com
           http://www.vista-research.com
}
```

23 Date & Time Related Functions

#6.23a - Function: VRT.AddDate

Add (or subtract) a number of days to the base date in YYMMDD format.

```
{
Type   : User Function
Name   : VRT.AddDate
Notes  :

Return: Adjusted date in YYMMDD format.
```

```
Inputs: xDate  - date in YYMMDD.
        nDays  - Number of days to add
                  (pass a negative number to subtract).
Usage :
  if (Date[0] > VRT.AddDate (EntryDate(0), +5)) then ...

EasyLanguage interpretation provided
   by  Samuel K. Tennis
   of  Vista Research (c) 1997, 1999
  Any unauthorized use of this material may constitute
  a violation of U.S. and International Copyright Laws.
}

Inputs: xDate (NumericSimple),  { Date in YYMMDD format }
        nDays (NumericSimple) ; { days to add or subt. }


VRT.AddDate = JulianToDate (DateToJulian (xDate) + nDays) ;

{
  To break the procedure down into easy to chew steps,
    below is the expanded code.

  1)  Convert calendar date to julian.

Value1  = DateToJulian (xDate) ;

  2)  Add the input nDays to our converted date.

Value2  = Value1 + nDays ;

  3)  Convert the sum back to YYMMDD format.

Value4  = JulianToDate (Value3) ;

  4)  Assign return value to the function name.

VRT.AddDate = Value4 ;
}

{
Custom Programming Services provided by:

               Samuel K. Tennis
                Vista Research
               129 Staff Drive
         Ft. Walton Beach, Florida 32548
          voice :    1(850) 243-5105
          fax   :    1(850) 301-2884
          eMail :  skt@vista-research.com
            http://www.vista-research.com
}
```

#6.23b - Function: VRT.AddTime

Add (or subtract) a number of minutes to the base time in 24 hour (Military) format.

```
{
Type : User Function
Name : VRT.AddTime
Notes: Add minutes to current time

Inputs : xTime   - time in 24 hour format.
         Minutes - Number of minutes to add
                   (pass a negative number to subtract).
Returns: Adjusted time in 24 hour format.
         No test for the return valkue being within session time(s).
Usage  :
  if (Time[0] > vrt.AddTime (Sess1StartTime, +30))
    then ...

  if (Time[0] < vrt.AddTime (Sess1EndTime, -2 * BarInterval))  then ...

EasyLanguage interpretation provided
   by  Samuel K. Tennis
   of  Vista Research (c) 1998, 1999
  Any unauthorized use of this material may constitute
  a violation of U.S. and International Copyright Laws.
}

Inputs : xTime   (NumericSimple),    { time in 24 hour format }
         Minutes (NumericSimple) ;   { minutes to add or subt. }

VRT.AddTime = MinutesToTime (TimeToMinutes (xTime) + Minutes) ;

{*
  Explanation: To break the procedure down into easy to chew steps,
               below is the expanded code.

  1)  Convert 24 hour time to minutes since midnight.

Value1  = TimeToMinutes (xTime) ;

  2)  Add the input Minutes to our converted time.
     (note that a negative value would effectivly be subtracted).

Value2  = Value1 + Minutes ;

  3)  Convert the sum back to 24 hour format.

Value3  = MinutesToTime (Value3) ;

  4)  Assign the return value to the function name.

VRT.AddTime = Value3 ;
 *}

{
Custom Programming Services provided by:

               Samuel K. Tennis
                Vista Research
```

```
                129 Staff Drive
         Ft. Walton Beach, Florida 32548
          voice :    1(850) 243-5105
          fax   :    1(850) 301-2884
          eMail :  skt@vista-research.com
            http://www.vista-research.com
}
```

#6.23c - Function: vrt.FirstCalcDate

Returns the date of the first bar on the chart.

```
{       Password
Type : User Function (Numeric / Date)
Name : vrt.FirstCalcDate
Notes:

EasyLanguage interpretation provided
   by  Samuel K. Tennis
   of  Vista Research (c) 1998, 1999
  Any unauthorized use of this material may constitute
  a violation of U.S. and International Copyright Laws.
}

Vars  : dBarNum  (-01),        Return  (Date) ;

if  BarNumber  = 01  and  dBarNum <= 00
then begin
  Return  =      Date ;
  dBarNum = BarNumber ;
end ;

vrt.FirstCalcDate = Return ;

{
Custom Programming Services provided by:

               Samuel K. Tennis
                Vista Research
               129 Staff Drive
         Ft. Walton Beach, Florida 32548
          voice :    1(850) 243-5105
          fax   :    1(850) 301-2884
          eMail :  skt@vista-research.com
            http://www.vista-research.com
}
```

#6.23d - Function: vrt.FirstCalcTime

Returns the time of the first bar on the chart.

```
{
Type : User Function (Numeric / Time)
Name : vrt.FirstCalcTime
Notes:
```

```
EasyLanguage interpretation provided
   by  Samuel K. Tennis
   of  Vista Research (c) 1998, 1999
  Any unauthorized use of this material may constitute
  a violation of U.S. and International Copyright Laws.
}


Vars  : dBarNum  (-01),        Return  (Time) ;

if  BarNumber  = 01  and  dBarNum <=  00
then begin
  Return  =      Time ;
  dBarNum = BarNumber ;
end ;

vrt.FirstCalcTime = Return ;

{
Custom Programming Services provided by:

               Samuel K. Tennis
                Vista Research
               129 Staff Drive
        Ft. Walton Beach, Florida 32548
         voice :    1(850) 243-5105
         fax   :    1(850) 301-2884
         eMail :  skt@vista-research.com
           http://www.vista-research.com
}
```

#6.23e - Function: vrt.LastCalcDate

Returns the date of the last bar on the chart.

```
{
Type : User Function (Numeric / Date)
Name : vrt.LastCalcDate
Notes:

EasyLanguage interpretation provided
   by  Samuel K. Tennis
   of  Vista Research (c) 1998, 1999
  Any unauthorized use of this material may constitute
  a violation of U.S. and International Copyright Laws.
}

Vars  : Return (00) ;

Return = JulianToDate (LastCalcJDate) ;

vrt.LastCalcDate = Return ;

{
Custom Programming Services provided by:
```

```
              Samuel K. Tennis
               Vista Research
              129 Staff Drive
       Ft. Walton Beach, Florida 32548
        voice :     1(850) 243-5105
        fax   :     1(850) 301-2884
        eMail :  skt@vista-research.com
          http://www.vista-research.com
}
```

#6.23f - Function: vrt.LastCalcTime

Returns the time of the last bar on the chart.

```
{
Type : User Function (Numeric / Time)
Name : vrt.LastCalcTime
Notes:

EasyLanguage interpretation provided
   by  Samuel K. Tennis
   of  Vista Research (c) 1998, 1999
  Any unauthorized use of this material may constitute
  a violation of U.S. and International Copyright Laws.
}

Vars  : Return (00) ;

Return = MinutesToTime (LastCalcMMTime) ;

vrt.LastCalcTime = Return ;

{
Custom Programming Services provided by:

              Samuel K. Tennis
               Vista Research
              129 Staff Drive
       Ft. Walton Beach, Florida 32548
        voice :     1(850) 243-5105
        fax   :     1(850) 301-2884
        eMail :  skt@vista-research.com
          http://www.vista-research.com
}
```

24 *System Related Functions*

A medley of User Functions that should be of special interest to system developers.

#6.24a - Function: vrt.LongestEquityDip

What is the longest period of time between an equity peak and the next time the system makes a new equity high.

```
{
```

```
Type : User Function (Numeric)
Name : vrt.LongestEquityDip
Notes: What is the longest period between new equity highs?

11/03/97  skt  The function should not be used to generate a report.

EasyLanguage interpretation provided
   by  Samuel K. Tennis
   of  Vista Research (c) 1998, 1999
  Any unauthorized use of this material may constitute
  a violation of U.S. and International Copyright Laws.
}

{
Inputs: Position     (NumericSimple) ;
Vars  : BarsLong     (00),         BarsShort   (00) ;
}
Vars  : Equity       (00),
        EqNewPeak    (00),         BarsDown    (00),
        EqPrevPeak   (00),         EqPrevBars  (00),
        EquityPeak   (00),         EqBarsDown  (-1) ;

{ ————————————————————————————————————— }

Equity  = NetProfit ;

if  Equity[00]  > Equity[01]  then begin
  if  Equity[00]  > EqNewPeak  then begin
{
    EqPrevBars = EqBarsDown ;
    EqPrevPeak = EquityPeak ;
}
    EqNewPeak = Equity ;
    if  BarsDown  > EqBarsDown  then begin
      EqPrevBars = EqBarsDown ;
      EqPrevPeak = EquityPeak ;
      EquityPeak = EqNewPeak ;
      EqBarsDown = BarsDown ;
    end ;
    BarsDown    =            00 ;
  end ;
end
else BarsDown   = BarsDown + 01 ;

vrt.LongestEquityDip = EqBarsDown ;

{*
if  EqBarsDown <> EqBarsDown[1]  then begin
  Print (Date      :6:0,   Time      :5:0,
       " Longest Equity Dip ",
         EqPrevPeak:6:2,   EqPrevBars:6:0,
         EquityPeak:6:2,   EqBarsDown:6:0) ;
end ;

if  Date  = vrt.LastCalcDate and
   (Time  = vrt.LastCalcTime or DataCompression  > 1)
then begin
  Print ("") ;
  Print ("Report: 'vrt.LongestEquityDip'") ;
  Print ("———————————————") ;
```

```
    Print (Date       :6:0,   Time       :5:0,
           EquityPeak:6:2,   EqBarsDown:6:0) ;
end ;
*}

{ ---------------------------------------- }

{
Custom Programming Services provided by:

               Samuel K. Tennis
                Vista Research
               129 Staff Drive
        Ft. Walton Beach, Florida 32548
         voice :     1(850) 243-5105
         fax   :     1(850) 301-2884
         eMail :  skt@vista-research.com
           http://www.vista-research.com
}
```

#6.24b - Function: vrt.TimeInMarket

Out of all the trading days in the sample period, on how many of those bars was the system in the market?

```
{
Type : User Function (Numeric)
Name : vrt.TimeInMarket
Notes: Returns the percent of time this system is in the market.
       Reports percent of time system is in market.

11/03/97  skt  The function should not be used to generate a report.

EasyLanguage interpretation provided
   by  Samuel K. Tennis
   of  Vista Research (c) 1998, 1999
  Any unauthorized use of this material may constitute
  a violation of U.S. and International Copyright Laws.
}

Inputs: Position    (NumericSimple) ;

Vars  : Return      (0),
        BarsFlat    (0),        BarsNotFlat (0),
        BarsLong    (0),        BarsShort   (0) ;

{ ---------------------------------------- }

if  @MarketPosition <> 00  then begin
  BarsNotFlat = BarsNotFlat + 01 ;

  if MarketPosition = +01 then BarsLong  = BarsLong   + 01 ;
  if MarketPosition = -01 then BarsShort = BarsShort  + 01 ;
end
else BarsFlat = BarsFlat + 01 ;

if  Position  = -01  then Return = BarsShort ;
if  Position  =  00  then Return = BarsNotFlat ;
if  Position  = +01  then Return = BarsLong ;
```

```
vrt.TimeInMarket = Return ;

{ ——————————————————————————————————— }

{**
Vars   : nnn (00),         ppp (00) ;

if   (Date   = vrt.LastCalcDate) and
     (Time   = vrt.LastCalcTime or DataCompression  > 01) and
     (Position  = 00)
then begin
  Print ("") ;
  Print ("Report: 'vrt.TimeInMarket': (", Position:2:0,")") ;
  Print ("————————————") ;
  nnn = (AvgBarsWinTrade * NumWinTrades) + (AvgBarsLosTrade * NumLosTrades)
;

  ppp = (nnn / Currentbar) * 100 ;
  Print (Date:6:0,         nnn:6:0,         ppp:6:2,
         (AvgBarsWinTrade * NumWinTrades):6:0,
         (AvgBarsLosTrade * NumLosTrades):6:0) ;

Print (" Bars Flat,   Long, Not Flat,  Short") ;
Print ("     ", BarsFlat   :5:0,          "    ", BarsLong   :5:0,
       "     ", BarsNotFlat:5:0,          "    ", BarsShort  :5:0) ;
{*
  Print (Date:6:0, CurrentBar:5:0, " : ",
  vrt.TimeInMarket (-1):8:0, ", ", (vrt.TimeInMarket (-1) /
CurrentBar)*100:6:2, "%, ",
  vrt.TimeInMarket ( 0):8:0, ", ", (vrt.TimeInMarket ( 0) /
CurrentBar)*100:6:2, "%, ",
  vrt.TimeInMarket (+1):8:0, ", ", (vrt.TimeInMarket (+1) /
CurrentBar)*100:6:2, "%") ;
 *}
end ;
 **}

{ ——————————————————————————————————— }

{
Custom Programming Services provided by:

               Samuel K. Tennis
                Vista Research
               129 Staff Drive
        Ft. Walton Beach, Florida 32548
         voice :    1(850) 243-5105
         fax   :    1(850) 301-2884
         eMail :  skt@vista-research.com
           http://www.vista-research.com
}
```

#6.24c - Function: vrt.LongestFlat

Returns the greatest number of days between any two trades. An improvement would be to track the ten largest flat periods. Another idea, how much of the time are you in the market compared to the time flat. Just thinking out loud…

```
{
Type : User Function
Name : vrt.LongestFlat
Notes: What is the longest period between trades?

11/03/97  skt  The function should not be used to generate a report.

EasyLanguage interpretation provided
   by  Samuel K. Tennis
   of  Vista Research (c) 1998, 1999
  Any unauthorized use of this material may constitute
  a violation of U.S. and International Copyright Laws.
}

{
Inputs: Position      (NumericSimple) ;
Vars  : BarsLong      (00),         BarsShort    (00) ;
}
Vars  : BarsFlat      (00),         MaxBarsFlat (-01) ;


{ ————————————————————————————— }

if  @MarketPosition  =      00  and
   (@ExitDate (01)  <> Date[00] or
   (@ExitDate (01)   = Date[00] and @ExitTime (01)  <> Time[00]))
then begin
  BarsFlat  = BarsFlat + 01 ;
end ;

if  (@MarketPosition <> 00)  then begin
  if  BarsFlat <> 00  then begin
    if  BarsFlat  > MaxBarsFlat  then  MaxBarsFlat  = BarsFlat ;
  end ;

  BarsFlat  = 00 ;
end ;

vrt.LongestFlat = MaxBarsFlat ;

{**
if  MaxBarsFlat[0] <> MaxBarsFlat[1]
  then Print (Date:6:0, Time:5:0, "  Update Max Bars Flat ",
MaxBarsFlat:6:0) ;


if (Date  = vrt.LastCalcDate) and
   (Time  = vrt.LastCalcTime or DataCompression  > 01)
then begin
  Print ("") ;
  Print ("Report: 'vrt.LongestFlat'") ;
  Print ("——————————") ;
  Print (Date:6:0, CurrentBar:6:0, MaxBarsFlat:6:0, CurrentBar /
MaxBarsFlat) ;
end ;
 **}

{ ————————————————————————————— }

{
```

```
Custom Programming Services provided by:

                Samuel K. Tennis
                 Vista Research
                129 Staff Drive
         Ft. Walton Beach, Florida 32548
          voice :     1(850) 243-5105
          fax   :     1(850) 301-2884
          eMail :  skt@vista-research.com
            http://www.vista-research.com
}
```

#6.24d - Function: vrt.TradesToday

Returns the number of trades entered on the target date.

```
{
Type  : User Function (Numeric)
Name  : vrt.TradesToday
Notes : Returns the number of entries on specified date.

Inputs: Target date (usually today's date).
Usage :
  if (vrt.TradesToday (Date[0]) >= 02)
    then EntryOK = FALSE ;
or
  if (Condition1 and Condition2 and vrt.TradesToday (Date[0]) < 2)
  then begin
    { ... do something here ... }
  end ;

Easy Language interpretation provided by Samuel K. Tennis
  of VISTA Research and Trading, Inc. (c) April 1997, 1999
  Any unauthorized use of this material may constitute
  a violation of U.S. and International Copyright Laws.

EasyLanguage interpretation provided
   by  Samuel K. Tennis
   of  Vista Research (c) 1998, 1999
  Any unauthorized use of this material may constitute
  a violation of U.S. and International Copyright Laws.
}

Inputs: Date0 (NumericSimple) ;
Vars  : Loop              (00),
        Count             (00) ;

{ ------------------------------------------------ }

Count  =  00 ;

for  Loop  = 00 to 10  begin
  if  EntryDate (Loop)  = Date0  then  Count  = Count + 01 ;
end ; { next Loop }

vrt.TradesToday  = Count ;

{ ------------------------------------------------ }

{
Custom Programming Services provided by:
```

Section 7: Quizzes

Section One Workshop Questions

I. Match the word on the right to the phrase on the left that best describes it. Write the corresponding letter to the left of the number.

1. Variable	A. Has a specific meaning
2. Mathematical Operators	B. Used to document code
3. Reserved Word	C. Current bar being analyzed
4. Statement	D. Number of bars available for reference
5. Study Bar	E. Addition, subtraction, multiplication, division
6. Relational Operators	F. Storage location for temporary information
7. Comment Braces	G. Compare values to the left and right
8. MaxBarsBack	H. Order in which EasyLanguage evaluates expression
9. Expression	I. A complete instruction in *EasyLanguage*
10. Precedence of Operators	J. Programming statement fragment

II. Mark the following as either (E)xpression or (S)tatement :

1. Close > Open + (Range * 0.5)
2. Buy 300 Shares at Market
3. High + 14
4. + 2
5. Close of 5 Bars Ago
6. Open[3] * 1.004
7. Close > 6
8. Value1 = Close - Open
9. If (Close[00] > High[01]) then Condition1 = TRUE
10. Plot1 (MyPrice, “Line1”)

III. Put an "X" next to the words that are not acceptable variable names.

1. Value1
2. Condition 28
3. Does
4. MyHigh
5. myLOW
6. Days Low
7. Low-Down
8. Up3.2
9. Open*10
10. Buy_Lots
11. Low=Up
12. Up&Down
13. Op-1.3
14. Value14
15. Based
16. Market
17. Value103
18. Open
19. .MyPrice
20. Condition12

IV. What punctuation mark must appear at the end of each statement?

V. A Variable will always have (Circle all that apply):

1) name

2) time

3) data type

4) size

5) default value

VI. Number the following operations in their order of precedence.

OR

Multiplication and division

NOT

Parentheses

Addition and subtraction

Relational operators

AND

VII. If two or more operations are of the same level of precedence, operations are evaluated from:

1) right to left

2) left to right

3) top down

4) left to right

VIII. Mark the following either True or False.

1. You can change the order of evaluation by using parentheses.
2. Operations within parentheses are performed first.
3. The price element TIME refers to the beginning of the bar.
4. Nesting refers to that warm fuzzy feeling when you see "Excellent" in the screen.
5. Calculations begin on the first bar after the MaxBarsBack buffer is filled.
6. MaxBarsBack is a buffer which stores the number of bars that can be referenced in an analysis technique.
7. A number may contain up to 10 digits.
8. Relational operators usually describe the relationship between prices.
9. When EasyLanguage performs historical calculations, it moves an imaginary pointer through the data file.
10. SkipWords are Reserved Words.
11. The usual order of precedence is maintained within parentheses.
12. EasyLanguage pays particular attention to information contained within curly brackets.
13. Crosses over/above means greater on current bar but less than or equal to the previous bar.
14. True/false expressions are generally used in conditional statements where a subsequent action only happens if the preceding condition is either true or false.
15. All Reserved Words may be abbreviated.
16. A numeric variable may only be assigned to a condition that is true.
17. A statement always ends in a semicolon.
18. Many reserved words are taken from the daily jargon of traders.
19. Volume refers to daily data only.
20. In the phrase "Simple vs Series" the term "Series" refers to multiple data files.

IX. Mark the correct examples of numbers with an "X."

1. two	6. 69857684
2. 3.5	7. $240.55
3. 3,490	8. 500
4. + 4.2	9. Open
5. 7.8-	10. +5.6

X. Give 10 examples of reserved words:

1.	6.
2.	7.
3.	8.
4.	9.
5.	10.

XI. Give 4 examples of SkipWords:

1.

2.

3.

4.

XII. Write *EasyLanguage's* acceptable abbreviations to the right of the following price elements:

1. High
2. Low
3. Time
4. Open
5. OpenInt
6. Close
7. Volume
8. Date

XIII. Mark the following which are acceptable ways to write the high of today:

1. High of Today
2. H OF TODAY
3. high
4. High[0]
5. High
6. H

XIV. Pick the proper example of a nested comment.

1. [This is a{comment} within a comment]
2. <No this is a (comment) within a comment>
3. {Wait (a minute) this is it}
4. {No, no {I remember} this is a comment within a comment}
5. {It could be [just maybe] this one}

XV. Write the following as abbreviated expressions/statements acceptable to EasyLanguage:

1. Low of current bar minus the low of two bars ago

2. Close of today not equal to High of today

3. Open of today is greater than the Open of three bars ago

4. High of five bars ago divided by the High of today

5. Low of yesterday is less than or equal to the Low of today

6. Yesterday's high times 1.001

7. The average is greater than the close of the current bar but was less than or equal to the close of the previous bar.

8. If the open of today is greater than the close of two days ago make Condition1 true

9. Today's high divided by 1.001 is greater than or equal to the close of x (an input) bars ago.

10. The contents of the variable MySignal times 1.002 is less than yesterday's close

Section Two Workshop Questions

I. Match the word or term on the right to its best definition on the left. Write the corresponding letter to the left of the number.

Word or Term	Definition or Description
1. Plot statements	A. represent minimum interval move in a market
2. Nested If statements	B. single result is predicated on single or multiple condition; no action if false
3. Exit statements	C. used when an initial true condition(s) causes multiple actions to occur
4. Simple IF...THEN statements	D. used to create a visual study
5. Block IF...THEN...ELSE statements	E. used to initialize custom variables
6. Assignment statements	F. instruct EasyLanguage to place an order at a specified price
7. MinMove * 1 Point	G. used when multiple conditions must exist before a choice of actions is taken
8. Buy and sell statements	H. allow for action to be taken if initial condition is false
9. Variable declaration statements	I. used to give values to variables included in *EasyLanguage*

10. Block If statements (Begin...End) J. used to partially or completely liquidate a position

II. Mark the following statements with the letter corresponding to their type.

A.	Assignment statement	**E.**	Block IF...THEN...ELSE statement
B.	Variable declaration statement	**F.**	Nested If statement
C.	Simple IF...THEN statement	**G.**	Exit statement
D.	Block If statement (Begin...End)	**H.**	Plot statement.

```
1.  Value1 = 10;

2.  Plot1 (High - MyOffset, "MyTrend") ;

3.  If High > High[1]  Begin
       Condition1 = Low < Low[1] and Close < Close;
       Condition2 = MyPercent * Close[1] ;
    End ;

4.  If High > High[1] Then Buy 300 Shares at Market;

5.  if  Close  > Open  then begin
      Value1  = Close ;
      Value2  =  Open ;
    end
    else begin
      Value1 = Close[1] ;
      Value2 = Open[1] ;
    end ;

6.  Plot3 (((High - Close) / (High[1] - Close[1])),
"SecretFormula") ;

7.  Vars  : BuyaLOT (FALSE) ;
    BuyaLot = Close > Close[1] * 1.02 ;

8.  if  Open > Open[1]  then begin
      if  High[01]  > High[02]
        then Sell  5 Shares at Market ;
        else Sell 10 Shares at Close ;
    end ;

9.  Value7 = Value4 + Value5 ;

10. If  High <  High[01]  then  Sell 100 Shares at Market ;

11. Buy  ("le#1") 500 Contracts at Market ;
    ExitLong  ("lx#1") 200 Contracts at Close ;
```

```
12. if  High  > High[01] and High[01]  > High[02]  then  MySignal
=  True ;

13. if  Open  > High[01]  then begin
      if  High  > Close[01]
        then Buy 100 Shares at Market
        else Buy 10 Shares at Market;
    end ;

14. if  Close <  Close[01]  then begin
      Value1  = Close / Close[01] ;
      Condition1  =  TRUE ;
    end ;

15. Condition5 = High  > High[01]  ;

16. if  Open  > Open  then begin
      Condition1 = High  > High ;
      Condition2 =  Low  >  Low ;
      if Condition1 and Condition2  Then  Buy 100 Shares at Market
;
    end ;

17. if High[1] > High[2]  then begin
      Condition1  =  True ;
      Condition2  = False ;
    else begin
      Condition1  = False ;
      Condition2  =  True ;
    end ;

18. Condition1  = Value3  > Value2 ;

19. if  Close  > Close[1]  then begin
      if  Close  > Close[1] * 1.001
        then  Sell 10 Shares at Market
        else  Buy  5 Shares ON THE Close;
    end ;

20. if  Value25  > 50  then  Condition1  =  True ;

21. if Close <  Close[01] and Close[01] <  Close[02]
      then Sell 15 Shares at Market ;

22. If Condition1

      Then Sell ("MySell") 10 Contracts at Market
      ExitShort ("MySExit")  5 Contracts at Open + 5 Points Stop ;

23. Plot4 (Close / Close[01], "MyAverage") ;

24. Vars: OpenAbove (False), CloseAbove (False) ;
    OpenAbove  = Open  > Close[01] ;
    CloseAbove  = Close[01]  > High[01] ;

25. Value15  = Value4 - High[01] ;
```

III. Write the following statements in correct *EasyLanguage* syntax and note what type of statement you are using.

1. If the high of today is greater than the high of yesterday, you want to have the following choice: if the high of today is greater than the high of yesterday by 10 percent or more, you want to buy 100 shares of StockX at the market price. However, if the high of today is less than 10 percent higher than the high of yesterday, you want to buy 20 shares at the close.

2. You wish to buy 100 shares of XYZ at the open if MyCondition is true. If MyCondition is false, you don't wish to take any action.

3. You wish to buy 10 shares of SecurityY at market but you wish to partially liquidate that position by exiting long on 5 shares at today's closing price.

4. You wish to visually detrend the background data against a moving average of itself.. The first plot shall be the detrended open displayed as a 'left tick'. The High and Low will similarly be used as BarHigh and BarLow while the close will be represented as a 'right tick'.

5. Write a market order to buy 300 shares of ITT at today's close.

6. Write a stop order to buy 100 shares of XYZ at the open plus 3 points.

7. Write a market order to sell 100 shares of MS at the open.

8. Write a stop order to sell 300 shares of ABC at yesterday's high plus 2 points.

9. You want to write a limit order signal to sell 3 March pig belly contracts at 48.50.

10. If today's close is higher than yesterday's close and yesterday's close is higher than the close two days ago, you want to buy 100 shares of CBS at the open.

11. If today's high is higher than yesterday's high, you want to make the value of Value1 equal to 10 and the value of Condition1 equal to false.

12. If today's close for IBM is lower than today's high you want to make the following choice: If today's close is less than 3 percent lower than today's high you want to sell 10 shares of XYZ at the market price. However, if today's close is more than 3 percent lower than today's, you want to sell 20 shares of XYZ at today's close.

13. If today's open is less than yesterday's open, you want to make Value1 equal to yesterday's close minus the close two days ago and Condition1 equal to yesterday's high is greater than the high two days ago. If Value1 is greater than 30 and Condition1 is true, you want to buy 10 shares of StockX at market.

14. If today's high is greater than yesterday's high you want to make Value1 equal to today's close and Value2 equal to today's open. But, if today's high is not greater than yesterday's high you want to make Value1 equal to yesterday's close and Value2 equal to yesterday's open.

15. If today's high is greater than yesterday's high you want to buy 50 shares of XYZ at the market price. You then want to exit 10 shares at yesterday's high plus 2 points limit and the remainder at yesterday's high plus 3 points limit.

IV. Fill in the blanks in the following table

Market	1 Point Move = (fraction)	1 Point Move = (decimal)	X Point Move =	X Point Move = (fraction)	TradeStation Stores
Stocks	1/8	.125	5	5/8	.625
Grains	1/8	.125	8		
Bonds	1/32	.03125	4		
S&P	1/100	.01	3		
Pork Bellies	1/100	.01	10		

V. Mark the following either true or false.

1. Assignment statements are used when you declare custom variables.
2. Trading signals are always very complicated programs.
3. You should never put a semicolon after the Begin expression in block statements in *EasyLanguage™*.
4. When using a declared logical variable you must always use the words "= True" to indicate that you want the condition to be true before doing something.
5. In *EasyLanguage*, trading signals are logical sequences of statements.
6. Assignment statements are used to assign values and conditions to the numeric and logical variables included in *EasyLanguage™*.
7. You would use a variable declaration statement to assign a value to the numeric variable Value250.
8. You cannot assign values to variables conditionally on the values of other variables.

9. The variable Value1 is automatically initialized by *EasyLanguage* with a value of 0.
10. In variable declaration statement, you use "Var:" if you are declaring one variable, or "Vars" if you are declaring multiple variables.
11. You can use abbreviated forms of Value and Condition variables such as VAL1 or C1 and still not have to declare the variables.
12. To list multiple actions predicated on a proposition, you would use a block If statement (Begin...End).
13. The If expression in an IF...THEN statement always contains a comparison between two or more values that results in a logical condition of true or false.
14. You do not place a semicolon after the first End in an block IF...THEN...ELSE statement because the statement is not complete until you state the action to happen if the original condition is false.
15. Nested If statements are used when a single proposition must be satisfied before a choice of actions is taken.
16. Nesting allows you to imbed an IF...THEN...ELSE statement within an If statement.
17. Buy and sell statements are used to liquidate current positions.
18. Buy and sell orders can be hit many times, while exit orders can be hit only once per instance of an order.
19. Plot statements are used to chart or draw formulas.
20. Stop buy orders are filled if the market price moves to or below the stop price.
21. Systems can contain as many exit signals as you wish.
22. The purpose of limit orders is to insure a specific price or better.
23. If the market opens above a buy stop price, *EasyLanguage* assumes the order was filled at the open price.
24. You should always use the word points when referencing the result when one price is subtracted from another.
25. *EasyLanguage* stores the fraction equivalent of points for calculations.

Section One Workshop Answers

I. Matching words to their definitions.

1. Variable	F. Storage location for temporary information
2. Mathematical Operators	E. Addition, subtraction, multiplication, division
3. Reserved Word	A. Has a specific meaning
4. Statement	I. A complete instruction in *EasyLanguage*
5. Study Bar	C. Current bar being analyzed
6. Relational Operators	G. Compare values to the left and right

7. Comment Braces — B. Used to document code
8. MaxBarsBack — D. Number of bars available for reference
9. Expression — J. Programming statement fragment
10. Precedence of Operators — H. Order in which *EasyLanguage* evaluates expression

II. Expression (E) or statement (S)

1.	Close > Open + (Range * 0.5)	Expression
2.	Buy 300 Shares at Market ;	Statement
3.	High + 14	Expression
4.	+ 2	Expression
5.	Close of 5 Bars Ago	Expression
6.	Open[3] * 1.004	Expression
7.	Close > 6	Expression
8.	Value1 = Close - Open ;	Statement
9.	If (Close[00] > High[01]) then Condition1 = TRUE ;	Statement
10.	Plot1 (MyPrice, "Line1") ;	Statement

III. Acceptable variable names.

1.	Value1	Yes
2.	Condition 28	No, Space is not allowed
3.	Does	No, Reserved Word
4.	MyHigh	Yes
5.	myLOW	Yes
6.	Days Low	No, Space is not allowed
7.	Low-Down	No, Hyphen (minus sign) not allowed.
8.	Up3.2	Yes
9.	Open*10	No, Apostrophe (multiplication sign) not allowed.
10.	Buy_Lots	Yes
11.	Low=Up	No, Equal sign not allowed.
12.	Up&Down	No, Ampersand character not allowed.
13.	Op-1.3	No, Hyphen (minus sign) not allowed.
14.	Value14	Yes
15.	Based	No, Reserved Word
16.	Market	No, Reserved Word
17.	Value103	Yes, but Value103 is not predefined (00..99 only).
18.	Open	No, The Price "Open" is a reserved word.

19. .MyPrice — No, Variable can not start with a period.
20. Condition12 — Yes

IV. What punctuation mark must appear at the end of each statement?

A semicolon

V. A Variable will always have (Circle all that apply):

1) name

2) time

3) data type

4) size

5) default value1 (names) and 3 (data types), (default value)

VI. Order of precedence

1. Parentheses
2. Multiplication and division
3. Addition and subtraction
4. Relational operators
5. NOT
6. AND
7. OR

VII. If two or more operations are of the same level of precedence, operations are evaluated from:

~~1) right to left~~

2) left to right

~~3) top down~~

~~4) left to right~~

VIII. True or false

Result	Question
1. TRUE	You can change the order of evaluation by using parentheses.
2. TRUE	Operations within parentheses are performed first.
3. FALSE	The price element TIME refers to the beginning of the bar.
4. FALSE	Nesting refers to that warm fuzzy feeling when you see "Excellent" in the screen.
5. TRUE	Calculations begin on the first bar after the MaxBarsBack buffer is filled.
6. TRUE	MaxBarsBack is a buffer which stores the number of bars that can be referenced in an analysis technique.
7. FALSE	A number may contain up to 10 digits.
8. TRUE	Relational operators usually describe the relationship between prices.
9. TRUE	When *EasyLanguage* performs historical calculations, it moves an imaginary pointer through the data file.
10. TRUE	SkipWords are reserved words.
11. TRUE	The usual order of precedence is maintained within parentheses.
12. FALSE	*EasyLanguage* pays particular attention to information contained within curly brackets.
13. TRUE	Crosses over/above means greater on current bar but less than or equal on the previous bar.
14. TRUE	True/false expressions are generally used in conditional statements where a subsequent action only happens if the preceding condition is either true or false.
15. FALSE	All reserved words may be abbreviated.
16. FALSE	A numeric variable may only be assigned to a condition that is true.
17. TRUE	A statement always ends in a semicolon.
18. TRUE	Many reserved words are taken from the daily jargon of traders.
19. TRUE	VOLUME refers to daily data only.
20. FALSE	In the phrase "Simple vs Series" the term "Series" refers to multiple data files.

IX. Correct examples of numbers

1. ~~two~~	No, only numeric references
2. 3.5	Yes
3. ~~3,490~~	No, comma not allowed
4. ~~+ 4.2~~	No, spaces after the plus sign... Marginal
5. ~~7.8-~~	No, negation sign must precede number
6. 69857684	Yes, though loss of precision could possibly occur
7. ~~$240.55~~	No, dollar sign no allowed
8. 500	Yes
9. Open	Yes, price is actually a number
10. +5.6	Yes

X. Reserved words:

Any word(s) from the Reserved Word and/or SkipWords list are acceptable here.

XI. SkipWords:

Any word from the SkipWord list is acceptable here.

XII. Acceptable abbreviations of price elements:

Long Name	Abbreviation
1. High	H
2. Low	L
3. Time	T
4. Open	O
5. OpenInt	I
6. Close	C
7. Volume	V
8. Date	D

XIII. Mark the following which are acceptable ways to write the high of today:

1. High of Today
2. H OF TODAY
3. high
4. High[0]
5. High
6. H

Acceptable ways to write the high of today

1, 2, 3, 4, 5, 6 or "All of the above"

XIV. Pick the proper example of a nested comment.

1. ~~[This is a{comment} within a comment]~~

2. ~~<No this is a (comment) within a comment>~~
3. ~~{Wait (a minute) this is it}~~
4. {No, no {I remember} this is a comment within a comment}
5. ~~{It could be [just maybe] this one}~~

Proper example of a nested comment

4

XV. Abbreviations acceptable to *EasyLanguage™*. (May not include all correct variations. If you have an answer other than those listed below, check with your instructor to see if it is acceptable.)

1. Low of current bar minus the low of two bars ago

```
L- L[2] ; Low[0] - Low[2]
```

2. Close of today not equal to High of today

```
C <> H; Close <> High; Close[0] <> High[0]
```

3. Open of today is greater than the Open of three bars ago

```
O > O[3] ; Open[0] > Open[3] ; Open > Open[3]
```

4. High of five bars ago divided by the High of today

```
H[5] / H; High[5] / High[0]
```

5. Low of yesterday is less than or equal to the Low of today

```
L[1] <= L; Low[1] <= Low[0] ; Low[1] <= Low
```

6. Yesterday's high times 1.001

```
H[1] * 1.001; High[1] * 1.001
```

7. The average is greater than the close of the current bar but was less than or equal to the close of the previous bar.

```
Average Crosses over { or above } the Close
```

8. If the open of today is greater than the close of two days ago make Condition1 true

```
If O > C[2] Then Condition1 = True
```

9. Today's high divided by 1.001 is greater than or equal to the close of x (an input) bars ago.

```
H / 1.001 >= C[nBars], High[0] / 1.001 >= Close[nBars]
```

10. The contents of the variable MySignal times 1.002 is less than yesterday's close

```
MySignal * 1.002 < C[1] ; MySignal * 1.002 < Close[1]
```

Section Two Workshop Answers

I. Match the word to its best definition.

1-D, 2-G, 3-J, 4-B. 5-H, 6-I, 7-A, 8-F, 9-E, 10-C

Word or Term	Definition or Description
1. Plot statements	D. used to create a visual study
2. Nested If statements	G. used when multiple conditions must exist before a choice of actions is taken
3. Exit statements	J. used to partially or completely liquidate a position
4. Simple IF...THEN statements	B. single result is predicated on single or multiple condition; no action if false
5. Block IF...THEN...ELSE statements	H.allow for action to be taken if initial condition is false
6. Assignment statements	I. used to give values to variables included in *EasyLanguage*
7. MinMove * 1 Point	A. represent minimum interval move in a market
8. Buy and sell statements	F. instruct EasyLanguage to place an order at a speci fied price
9. Variable declaration statements	E. used to initialize custom variables
10. Block If statements (Begin...End)	C. used when an initial true condition(s) causes multiple actions to occur

II. Mark the statements with corresponding type.

A.	Assignment statement	**E.**	Block IF...THEN...ELSE statement
B.	Variable declaration statement	**F.**	Nested If statement
C.	Simple IF...THEN statement	**G.**	Exit statement
D.	Block If statement (Begin...End)	**H.**	Plot statement.

1. A. Assignment Statement
2. H. Plot Statement
3. D. Block If...Then Statement
4. C. Simple If...Then Statement
5. E. Block If...Then Else Statement
6. H. Plot Statement
7. B. Variable Declaration Statement, A. Assignment Statement
8. F. Nested If Statement
9. A. Assignment Statement
10. C. Simple If...Then Statement
11. G. Exit Statement
12. C. Simple If...Then Statement
13. F. Nested If Statement
14. D. Block If...Then Statement
15. A. Assignment Statement
16. D. Block If...Then Statement
17. E. Block If...Then Else Statement
18. A. Assignment Statement
19. F. Nested If Statement
20. C. Simple If...Then Statement, A. Assignment Statement
21. C. Simple If...Then Statement
22. C. Simple If...Then Statement G. Exit Statement
23. H. Plot Statement
24. B. Variable Declaration Statement A. Assignment Statement
25. A. Assignment Statement

III. Write the following statements in correct *EasyLanguage* syntax.

1. If the high of today is greater than the high of yesterday, you want to have the following choice: if the high of today is greater than the high of yesterday by 10 percent or more, you want to buy 100 shares of stock at the market price. However, if the high of today is less than 10 percent higher than the high of yesterday, you want to buy 20 shares at the close.

(Example of nested If statement)

```
If  High > High[1]  Then Begin
  If  High >= High[1] * 1.10
    Then Buy  ("le#1") 100 Shares at Market
    Else Buy  ("le#2") 20  Shares at Close ;
End ;
```

2. You wish to buy 100 shares of XYZ at the open if MyCondition is true. If MyCondition is false, you don't wish to take any action.

(Example of simple IF...THEN statement)

```
      If  MyCondition  Then  Buy  ("le.Main#1") 100 Shares
                                  { XYZ stock } at Market ;
(Note you don't need to say "If MyCondition = True."
```

3. You wish to buy 10 shares of SecurityY at market but you wish to partially liquidate that position by exiting long on 5 shares at today's closing price.

(Example of Exit statement -ExitLong)

```
Buy ("le#1") 10 Shares at Market ;
ExitLong ("lx#1") 5 Shares at the Close at the market ;
```

4. You wish to visually detrend the background data against a moving average of itself.. The first plot shall be the detrended open displayed as a 'left tick'. The High and Low will similarly be used as BarHigh and BarLow while the close will be represented as a 'right tick'.

(Example of plot statement)

```
Value1 = Average (Close, 14) ;

Plot1 (Open  - Value1, "Open ") ;

Plot2 (High  - Value1, "High ") ;

Plot3 (Low   - Value1, "Low  ") ;

Plot4 (Close - Value1, "Close") ;
```

5. Write a market order to buy 300 shares of ITT at today's close.

(Example of a buy order)

```
Buy ("le.main")300 Shares {ITT} at Close ;
```

6. Write a stop order to buy 100 shares of XYZ at the open plus 3 points.

(Example of stop buy order)

```
Buy ("le.main")100 Shares {XYZ} at Open + 3 Points Stop ;
```

7. Write a market order to sell 100 shares of MS at the open.

(Example of market sell order)

```
Sell ("se.#1") 100 Shares {XYZ} at Open
{note error checking glitch?}
Sell ("se.#2")100 Shares {XYZ} at Market ;
```

8. Write a stop order to sell 300 shares of ABC at yesterday's high plus 2 points.

(Example of stop sell order)

```
Sell 300 Shares {ABC} at High[1] + 2 Points Stop;
```

9. You want to write a limit order signal to sell 3 March pork bellies contracts at 48.50.

(Example of limit sell order)

```
Sell           3  MARCH PB at 48.50 Limit ; {Order ticket}
Sell ("se#1")3 Contracts at 48.50 Limit ; {EasyLanguage code}
```

10. If today's close is higher than yesterday's close and yesterday's close is higher than the close two days ago, you want to buy 100 shares of CBS at the open.

(Example of simple IF...THEN statement)

```
If Close[0] > Close[1] and Close[1] > Close[2]
  Then Buy ("le#1") 100 Shares {CBS} at Market ;
```

11. If today's high is higher than yesterday's high, you want to make the value of the VARIABLE Value1 equal to 10 and the value of Condition1 equal to false.

(Example of block If statement)

```
If High > High[1] Then Begin
  Value1 = 10;
  Condition1 = False;
End ;
```

12. If today's close for IBM is lower than today's high you want to make the following choice: If today's close is less than 3 percent lower than today's high you want to sell 10 shares of XYZ at the market price. However, if today's close is more than 3 percent lower than today's, you want to sell 20 shares of XYZ at today's close.

(Example of nested if statement)

```
if (Close < High) then begin

  if (Close < High * 1.03)

    then Sell ("se#1") 10 Shares {IBM} at Market

    else Buy ("le.#1") 20 Shares {IBM} at Close ;

end ;
```

13. If today's open is less than yesterday's open, you want to make Value1 equal to yesterday's close minus the close two days ago and Condition1 equal to yesterday's high is greater than the high two days ago. If Value1 is greater than 30 and Condition1 is true, you want to buy 10 shares of StockX at market.

(Example of block If statement (Begin...End))

```
if (Open < Open[1]) then begin
  Value1 = Close[1] - Close[2] ;
  Condition1 = High[1] > High[2] ;
  if Value1 > 30 and Condition1
    then Buy ("le.#1) 10 Shares { STOCKX } at Market ;
end ;
```

14. If today's high is greater than yesterday's high you want to make Value1 equal to today's close and Value2 equal to today's open. But, if today's high is not greater than yesterday's high you want to make Value1 equal to yesterday's close and Value2 equal to yesterday's open.

(Example of block IF...THEN...ELSE statement)

```
if High > High[1] then begin

  Value1 = Close ;

  Value2 = Open ;

end
else  begin

  Value1 = Close[1] ;

  Value2 = Open [1] ;

end ;
```

15. If today's high is greater than yesterday's high you want to buy 50 shares of XYZ at the market price. You then want to exit 10 shares at yesterday's high plus 2 points limit and the remainder at yesterday's high plus 3 points limit.

(Example of Entry and Exit Signals)

```
If (High > High[1])then Buy 50 Shares {of XYZ} at Market ;

ExitLong ("lx.Target#1") 10 Shares AT$ High[1] + 4 Points Limit ;

ExitLong ("lx.Target#2") 40 Shares AT$ High[1] + 8 Points Limit ;
```

Market	1 Point Move = (fraction)	1 point move = (decimal)	X Point Move =	X Point Move = (fraction)	TradeStation stores
Stocks	1/8	.125	5	5/8	.625
Grains	1/8	.125	8	**8/8ths or 1**	**1**
Bonds	1/32	.03125	4	**4/32nds**	**.125**
S&P	1/100	.01	3	**3/100**	**.03**
Pork Bellies	1/100	.01	10	**10/100ths**	**.1**

V. Mark the following either True or False.

1. **FALSE** - Assignment statements are used when you declare custom variables.

2. **FALSE** - Trading signals are always very complicated programs.

3. **TRUE** - You should never put a semicolon after the Begin expression in block statements in EasyLanguage.

4. **FALSE** - When using a declared logical variable you must always use the words "= True" to indicate that you want the condition to be true before doing something.

5. **TRUE** - In EasyLanguage, trading signals are logical sequences of statements.

6. **TRUE** - Assignment statements are used to assign values and conditions to the numeric and logical variables included in EasyLanguage.

7. **TRUE** - You would use a variable declaration statement to assign a value to the numeric variable Value250.

8. **FALSE** - You cannot assign values to variables conditionally on the values of other variables.

9. **TRUE** - The variable Value1 is automatically initialized by EasyLanguage with a value of 0.

10. **FALSE** - In variable declaration statement, you use "Var:" if you are declaring one variable, or "Vars" if you are declaring multiple variables.

11. **FALSE** - You can use abbreviated forms of Value and Condition variables such as VAL1 or C1 and still not have to declare the variables.

12. **TRUE** - To list multiple actions predicated on a proposition, you would use a block If statement (Begin...End).

13. **TRUE** - The If expression in an IF...THEN statement always contains a comparison between two or more values that results in a logical condition of true or false.

14. **TRUE** - You do not place a semicolon after the first End in an block IF...THEN...ELSE statement because the statement is not complete until you state the action to happen if the

original condition is false.

15. **FALSE** - Nested If statements are used when a single proposition must be satisfied before a choice of actions is taken.

16. **TRUE** - Nesting allows you to imbed an IF...THEN...ELSE statement within an If statement.

17. **FALSE** - Buy and sell statements are used to liquidate current positions.

18. **TRUE** - Buy and sell orders can be hit many times, while exit orders can be hit only once per instance of an order.

19. **TRUE** - Plot statements are used to chart or draw formulas.

20. **FALSE** - Stop buy orders are filled if the market price moves to or below the stop price.

21. **TRUE** - Systems can contain as many exit signals as you wish.

22. **TRUE** - The purpose of limit orders is to insure a specific price or better.

23. **TRUE** - If the market opens above a buy stop price, EasyLanguage assumes the order was filled at the open price.

24. **FALSE** - You should always use the word points when referencing the result when one price is subtracted from another.

25. **FALSE** - EasyLanguage stores the fraction equivalent of points for calculations.

25. **FALSE**

Appendix #A - Reserved Word List

The TradeStation 4.00 *EasyLanguage* User's Manual contains a Reserved Words list (page 127). That list is incomplete. I have also included terms unique to Version 5.0 of **TradeStation**. Please replace the list in the manual with the following list:

Word or Symbol	*Definition*
-	Subtraction sign (Numerical Operator)
" "	Quotation marks (double quote) surround a string constant
(	Open parenthesis, used in formulas
)	Close parenthesis, used in formulas
*	Multiplication sign (Numerical Operator)
,	Comma, used as separator in formulas and lists
.	Period - numeric decimal point
/	Division sign (Numerical Operator)
:	Colon - formatting separator
;	Semi-colon Statement terminator
@	Called the "at sign", this symbol is an anachronism left over from System Writer Version 1.0 where it was used to denote a function.
[	Called the left square bracket, this symbol is used in bar offsets. For example, [3] is equivalent to three bars ago. Also used to identify array elements. For example, MyArray[4] is element number four in the array called MyArray.
]	Called the right square bracket, see " left square bracket" above for usage.
{	Called the open comment brace, or left comment brace, this symbol marks the beginning of a comment area. Users may write personal notes inside the comment area. The information inside the comment brace is ignored by TradeStation. Must be accompanied by a close comment brace to be successful.
}	Called the close comment brace, this symbol marks the end of a comment area. Must be accompanied by an open comment brace to be successful.
+	Addition sign (Numerical Operator, String Operator)
<	Less than sign (Relational Operator)
<=	Less than or equal to sign (Relational Operator)
<>	Not equal to sign (Relational Operator)
=	Equal to sign (Relational Operator) and Assignment
>	Greater than sign (Relational Operator)
>=	Greater than or equal to sign (Relational Operator)
#BeginAlert	ezl40 Initiates alert procedure when true.
#BeginCmtry	ezl40 Initiates commentary procedure when true.
#BeginCmtryOrAlert	ezl40 Initiates commentary or alert procedure when true.
#End	ezl40 Closes the alert or commentary procedure.
A	SkipWord - used to clarify statements.
Above	Works together with the KeyWord "Crosses." Used to detect when one value exceeds another. For example: RSI crosses above 80.
ActivityData	ezl50
AddToMovieChain	ezl40 Assigns a movie file to a reference number.
Ago	Refers to the bar number being referenced. For example: Open of 3 bars ago.

Alert	Triggers an audible alert on the close of the bar, except if Update every tick is turned ON. For example: If C > O then Alert = true;
AlertEnabled	Checks to see if Enable Alert check box is checked
All	Used in exit orders (systems only) to control # of contracts.
An	SkipWord - used to clarify statements.
And	Use to link multiple conditions. For example: If Condition 1 and RSI(C,14) < 80...Both conditions must be true in order for the entire statement to be true.
Array(s)	Allows a user to save values as they are received. Each array has a certain number of elements associated with it.
ArraySize**	**
ArrayStartAddr**	**
Ask	ezl50
Ask (Num)	ezl50
Asset	ezl50
AssetType	ezl50
At	SkipWord - used to clarify statements.
At$	Used in exit signals (systems only) to anchor the prices on the bar of entry. For example: AT$ Low refers to the low of the bar on which the order was generated.
AtCommentaryBar	See CheckCommentary.
Bar(s)	Used to refer to specific bars, synonymous with DAYS(S). For example: Low of 1 bar ago.
Based	SkipWord - used to clarify statements.
Begin	Creates a Block or Compound Statement. Must have a matching End. Frequently used with Decision Statements. Required with all Iterative (Loop) Statements.
Below	Works together with the KeyWord "Crosses." Used to detect when one value moves beneath another. For example: RSI crosses below 20.
Bid	ezl50
Bid (Num)	ezl50
Bool**	**
Buy	Enter a long position (systems only) in the market.
BuyAlert*	* (Obsolete, removed in ezl50)
By	SkipWord - used to clarify statements.
Byte**	**
C	Short for Close.
Call	ezl50
Cancel	ezl50
Char**	**
CheckAlert	Checks the status of an alert condition on a bar-by-bar basis for real-time data, and on the last bar of historical data.
CheckCommentary	Checks the status of the Expert Commentary Tool on a bar-by-bar basis. Returns True if the user clicked the mouse on this bar of data.
Close	Refers to closing price of a bar.
Commentary	Sends text to the commentary window.
CommentaryCL	Sends text terminated with a Carriage-return Line-feed to commentary window.
CommentaryEnabled	Checks to see if Enable Commentary check box is checked.
Condition0...99	True/False variables. Used to store the return of a true/false

	statement. For example: Condition1 = C > O....
CONTRACT(S)	Used with other KeyWords such as BUY, EXITLONG, EXITSHORT, and SELL (systems only). Refers to the number of future contracts or stock shares purchased. For example: Buy ("le.Main") 2 contracts at market ;
CONTRACTMONTH	ezl50
CONTRACTYEAR	ezl50
COST	ezl50
CREATELEG (NUM)	ezl50
CROSS(ES)	Used together with one of the KeyWords ABOVE, BELOW, OVER and UNDER.
D	Short for Date
DATA1...50	The data series a System, Study, or Function is referencing. For example: Open of Data2
DATE	Format: YYMMDD. Refers to a stamp place on all bars of data. For example: If Date = 930705 then ......
DAY(S)	Used to refer to specific bars. For example: Low of 1 day ago. In the previous example, if daily data were being loaded, the word day would be interpreted in the traditional way. However, if intraday data were being loaded, it would mean 1 bar ago.
DEFAULT	ezl50
DEFINECUSTFIELD	ezl50
DEFINEDLLFUNC**	**
DELTA	ezl50
DELTA (NUM)	ezl50
DOES	SkipWord - used to clarify statements.
DOUBLE**	**
DOWNTICKS	Sum of ticks within a bar that have a lower value than the previous tick or have a value equal to the previous tick.
DOWNTO	One of the KeyWords in an Iterative Statement (For Loop). If the initial value in the loop is less than the final value, use DOWNTO. Example : FOR LOOP = HI.VAL DOWNTO LO.VAL BEGIN...END ;
DWORD**	**
ELSE	The ELSE clause of a Decision Statement allows users to specify what should be done if the condition in the IF statement is false.
END	Must match BEGIN...Defines termination of a complex statement.
ENTRY	Used in exit order (systems only) to control scope of this order.
EXITLONG	Used to partially or completely liquidate a long position (systems only).
EXITSHORT	Used to partially or completely liquidate a short position (systems only).
EXPIRATIONDATE	ezl50
EXPIRATIONSTYLE	ezl50
FALSE	Used to set a condition variable to false or to check the status of the condition variable.
FILE	Used in a print statement to send the contents to a specified disk file.
FIRSTNOTICEDATE	ezl50
FLOAT**	** Data Type used with a DLL. Floating Point (Real) Number
FOR	An element of the Loop statement. The FOR statement instructs that a set of operations will be executed repeatedly while a progression of values is assigned to a the Loop Counter.

FROM	SkipWord - used to clarify statements.
FUTURE	ezl50
FUTURE (NUM)	ezl50
FUTURETYPE	ezl50
GAMMA	ezl50
GAMMA (NUM)	ezl50
GETPLOTBGCOLOR	ezl50
GETPLOTCOLOR (NUM)	ezl50
GETPLOTWIDTH (NUM)	ezl50
H	Short for High.
HIGH	The highest tick of the bar.
HIGHER	ezl50
I	Short for OPENINT.
IF	Used in a Decision Statement to check the status of a condition or set of conditions.
INCLUDE	ezl50
INCLUDESYSTEM	Allows the user to include one system within another (systems only). Makes it possible to write larger systems.
INPUT(S)	Used as a substitute for Numeric, Boolean or String values. Allows greater flexibility by enabling input values to be changed on the fly from within the Charting Application.
INT**	**
IS	SkipWord - used to clarify statements.
L	Short for Low.
LASTTRADINGDATE	ezl50
LEFTSIDE	ezl50
LEG (NUM)	ezl50
LEGTYPE	ezl50
LIMIT	Type of Buy/Sell order (systems only)...this price or better.
LONG**	**
LOW	Lowest tick of the bar.
LOWER	ezl50
LPBOOL	** Data Type used with a DLL. "LP" means "Long Pointer".
LPBYTE**	**
LPCHAR**	** ??
LPDOUBLE**	**
LPDWORD**	**
LPFLOAT**	**
LPINT**	**
LPLONG**	**
LPSTR**	**
LPWORD**	**
MAKENEWMOVIEREF	ezl40 Used to obtain or allocate a new movie reference to which to assign a movie file in order to play it.
MARKET	Refers to the OPEN of the next bar (systems only). Type of order.
MIVONASK	ezl50
MIVONBID	ezl50
MIVONCLOSE	ezl50
MIVONRAWASK	ezl50
MIVONRAWBID	ezl50
MOC*	* Market On Close order (Obsolete, SWP)

ModelPosition	ezl50
ModelPrice	ezl50
ModelVolatility	ezl50
ModelVolatility (Num)	ezl50
Multiple**	**
NewLine	Contains a Carriage-Return Line-Feed used when sending output to Printers, Disk Files and the Expert Commentary Window
Next	Used with Bar to refer to one bar in future (Next Bar). Preferable to "Today" and "Tomorrow".
NoPlot (Num)	ezl50
Not*	*
Numeric	Define input to function as a number.
NumericRef	ezl50
NumericSeries	Define input to function as a number with MaxBarsBack history.
NumericSimple	Define input to function as a number without history.
NumFutures	ezl50
NumLegs	ezl50
NumOptions	ezl50
O	Short for Open. Do not confuse with 0 (the number zero).
Of	SkipWord - used to clarify statements.
On	SkipWord - used to clarify statements.
Only	Used in exit orders (systems only) to control # of contracts.
Open	The first tick of the bar. Can also be used as a type of order, synonymous with MARKET (this usage systems only).
OpenInt	Number of contracts/shares outstanding at the close of a bar (daily data only).
Option	ezl50
OptionType	ezl50
Or	Used to link multiple conditions. For example: If Condition1 or RSI (C,14) < 80..... Either one of the conditions must be true in order for the entire statement to be true. Boolean logical operator.
Over	Used with Crosses, same as Above. Example : RSI crosses over 50
Pause*	* (Obsolete, SWP)
Place	SkipWord - used to clarify statement.
PlayMovieChain	ezl40 Plays the movie identified with the reference number and file assigned to movie chain.
PlaySound	ezl40 Plays a .WAV file.
Plot	Followed by 1..4. Display value of study on chart (study only).
Plot1...4	Used in indicators to plot whatever is desired (study only).
Pob*	* (Obsolete, I can not even recall what this was)
Point(s)	Minimum interval by which trades in that commodity are measured.
Pointer**	**
Position	ezl50
PositionStatus	ezl50
Print	Designed to provide the opportunity to print information to a variety of places.
Printer	Used with a Print Statement to direct output to the printer.
Profit*	* (Obsolete, SWP)
Protective*	* (Obsolete, SWP)
Put	ezl50

RawAsk	ezl50
RawBid	ezl50
Repeat*	* Part of the Iterative Statement Repeat Until (Obsolete, SWP)
Rho	ezl50
Rho (Num)	ezl50
RightSide	ezl50
SCO*	* Stop-Close-Only, a type of order. (Obsolete, SWP)
Screen*	* (Obsolete, SWP)
Sell	Takes the user into a short position (systems only).
SellAlert*	* (Obsolete, removed in ezl50)
SetPlotBGColor (N1, N2)	ezl50
SetPlotColor (N1, N2)	ezl50
SetPlotWidth (N1, N2)	ezl50
Share(s)	Used in Buy and Sell statements (systems only) to specify the quantity of shares desired. Synonymous with Contract(s)
Skip*	* (Obsolete, SWP)
StartDate	ezl50
Stop	Type of order (systems only) - "Get me in at this price or worse"
Strike	ezl50
String	Type of string used for function inputs.
StringRef	ezl50
StringSeries	Type of string with MaxBarsBack buffer used for function inputs.
StringSimple	Type of string with out MaxBarsBack buffer used for function inputs.
T	Short for Time.
Target*	* (Obsolete, SWP)
TargetType	ezl50
Text	Undocumented function returns a formatted character string.
Than	SkipWord - used to clarify statements.
The	SkipWord - used to clarify statements.
Then	The second KeyWord of a Decision (If...Then) Statement. The "If" checks the condition, whereas "Then" gives the action to be executed if true.
TheoreticalGrossIn	ezl50
TheoreticalGrossOut	ezl50
TheoreticalValue	ezl50
TheoreticalValue (Num)	ezl50
Theta	ezl50
Theta (Num)	ezl50
This	SkipWord - used to clarify statements.
Ticks	Sum of UpTicks and DownTicks.
Time	The ENDING time of the bar in HHMM format (1315 is 1:15pm).
To	One of the keywords in a FOR Loop statement. If the initial value in the loop is greater than the final value, use "TO."
Today	Refers to the current bar <u>regardless</u> of DataCompression for the chart.
Tomorrow	Refers to the next bar <u>regardless</u> of DataCompression for the chart.
Tool_Black	ezl40 Numerical constant used to assign a color to a drawing object.
Tool_Blue	ezl40 Numerical constant used to assign a color to a drawing object.
Tool_Cyan	ezl40 Numerical constant used to assign a color to a drawing object.
Tool_DarkBlue	ezl40 Numerical constant used to assign a color to a drawing object.
Tool_DarkCyan	ezl40 Numerical constant used to assign a color to a drawing object.
Tool_DarkGray	ezl40 Numerical constant used to assign a color to a drawing object.

Tool_DarkGreen	ezl40 Numerical constant used to assign a color to a drawing object.
Tool_DarkMagenta	ezl40 Numerical constant used to assign a color to a drawing object.
Tool_DarkRed	ezl40 Numerical constant used to assign a color to a drawing object.
Tool_DarkYellow	ezl40 Numerical constant used to assign a color to a drawing object.
Tool_Dashed	ezl40 Numerical constant used to assign a line style to a drawing object.
Tool_Dashed2	ezl40 Numerical constant used to assign a line style to a drawing object.
Tool_Dashed3	ezl40 Numerical constant used to assign a line style to a drawing object.
Tool_Dotted	ezl40 Numerical constant used to assign a color to a drawing object.
Tool_Green	ezl40 Numerical constant used to assign a color to a drawing object.
Tool_Magenta	ezl40 Numerical constant used to assign a color to a drawing object.
Tool_Red	ezl40 Numerical constant used to assign a color to a drawing object.
Tool_Solid	ezl40 Numerical constant used to assign a line style to a drawing object.
Tool_White	ezl40 Numerical constant used to assign a color to a drawing object.
Tool_Yellow	ezl40 Numerical constant used to assign a color to a drawing object.
Total	Exits the amount specified on all open positions (systems only). For example, if the user goes long twice and each time acquires three contracts, and if he or she has an exit signal that reads If C > C[1] then ExitLong 5 contracts TOTAL on the close, the following would take place: The system would buy three contracts, then another three contracts. Once the IF condition was met, the user would be exited from the first three contracts, and then from two of the three contracts from the second buy.
True	Used to set a condition variable to true or to check the status of the condition variable or Boolean expression.
TrueFalse	Defines variable or input to a function as a Boolean value.
TrueFalseRef	ezl50
TrueFalseSeries	Boolean input to function with MaxBarsBack history.
TrueFalseSimple	Boolean input to function with no history.
Under	Works together with the KeyWord Crosses, same as Below Used to detect when one value moves beneath another. For example: RSI crosses under 30.
Units	ezl50
Unsigned**	**
Until*	* Part of Iterative Repeat Until Statement (Obsolete, SWP)
UpTicks	Number of ticks greater than or equal to the previous tick during a bar.
V	Short for Volume.
Value0...99	Pre-declared numeric variables.
Var(s)	Short for Variable(s). Declaration statement.
Variable(s)	Used to declare a user's own variables.
VarSize**	**
VarStartAddr**	**
Vega	ezl50
Vega (Num)	ezl50
Void	**
Volume	Number of trades that occurred during the bar (daily, weekly, monthly data only)
Was	SkipWord - used to clarify statements.

WHILE	KeyWord of an ITERATIVE (LOOP) STATEMENT; While <expression> begin....end;
WITH	ezl50
WORD**	**
YESTERDAY	Refers to the previous bar, regardless of the DataCompression of chart (not necessarily a day).

* Indicates that words are reserved for compatibility. They are not functional in **TradeStation** at this time.

** Indicates that these are DYNAMIC LINK LIBRARY (DLL) KEYWORDS used in conjunction with the DEFINEDLLFUNC DECLARATION STATEMENT. See file called USERDLLS.WRI stored in the C:\OMEGA\PROG\ directory for further explanation.

ezl40 Indicates that this word is only valid in *EasyLanguage* 4.xx or later.

ezl50 Indicates that this word is only valid in *EasyLanguage* 5.xx or later.

Note: In *EasyLanguage*, words may be typed using uppercase, lowercase or any combination. For example, HIGH, High, hiGH and high mean the same thing.

Appendix #B - Resources

A very short list of a few available resources.

Windows Magazine

Technical Analysis of Stocks and Commodities (TASC) **Magazine**

Futures Magazine

John Hill, ***Futures Truth***

David Green, ***Commoditiy Traders Club News***

Nelson Freeburg, *Formula Research*

The Disciplined Trader by Mark Douglas

Tricks of the Floor Trader by Neal T. Weintraub

Neal T. Weintraub

Neal Weintraub is floor trader, CTA, an instructor at the Chicago Mercantile Exchange and teaches Futures at Keller Graduate School. He received a direct appointment from the President of the United States for a direct commission in the United States Naval Reserve.

As a member of the NFA, Neal teaches a no nonsense approach to trading without hype. Students may reach him at 1-800-753-7085

TradeCenter Inc.

Trade Center, Inc.

Joe Tapias / President

105 Crescent Bay Drive, Suite B

Laguna Beach CA. 92651

800 894 8194 / 949 376 2800 Int'l

949 376 2812 Fax

http://www.tradecenterinc.com

joe.tapias@tradecenterinc.com

Genesis Financial Data Services

All historical data used during the development of this book was courtesy of *Glen Larson* and **Genesis Financial Data Services**.

Physical Address	**Genesis Financial Data Services**
	425 E. Woodmen Road
	Colorado Springs, CO 80919
or :	**Genesis Financial Data Services**
	P.O. Box 49578
	Colorado SPrings, CO 80949

E-Mail Addresses

Billing Department:	*billing@gfds.com*
Web Development:	*webmaster@gfds.com*
Sales Department:	*sales@gfds.com*
Technical Support:	*support@gfds.com*
Web Development:	*webmaster@gfds.com*

Fax Numbers::

General Fax Number	1(719) 260-6113

Phone Numbers

Sales Department :	1(800) 808-DATA
Billing Department :	1(719) 260-6119
Sales Department :	1(719) 260-8145
Technical Support :	1(719) 260-6111

Hours of Operation

Sales Department :	8:30am to 5:30pm Mountain Std	Mon Thru Fri
Technical Support :	7:00am to 8:00pm Mountain Std	Mon thru Fri
	9:00am to 1:00pm Mountain Std	Sat

Crash Proof Advisors Inc.

Crash Proof Advisors is a real time OEX Option Timing service providing trading signals generated with our proprietary trading system and Omega's **TradeStation**. Signals are delivered to subscribers Through E-mail, Pager, Abbott Chat, and our interactive Trading Room.

We want to take this chance to thank Samuel K. Tennis for all his help In turning our ideas into a highly profitable trading system using *EasyLanguage*.

From Doug Patrick, President

Crash Proof Advisors Inc.

5820 North Federal Hwy. Suite D-4

Boca Raton, Fl 33487

URL: www.CrashProofAdvisors.com

E-mail: mailto:webmaster@crashproofadvisors.com

Index